ROUTLEDGE LIBRARY EDITIONS: EDUCATION

EDUCATION

EDUCATION
In Search of a Future

Edited by
HUGH LAUDER AND PHILLIP BROWN

Volume 184

LONDON AND NEW YORK

First published in 1988

This edition first published in 2012
by Routledge
2 Park Square, Milton Park, Abingdon, Oxfordshire OX14 4RN

Simultaneously published in the USA and Canada
by Routledge
711 Third Avenue, New York, NY 10017

First issued in paperback 2014

Routledge is an imprint of the Taylor and Francis Group, an informa company

© 1988 Selection and editorial material copyright H. Lauder and P. Brown

All rights reserved. No part of this book may be reprinted or reproduced or utilised in any form or by any electronic, mechanical, or other means, now known or hereafter invented, including photocopying and recording, or in any information storage or retrieval system, without permission in writing from the publishers.

Trademark notice: Product or corporate names may be trademarks or registered trademarks, and are used only for identification and explanation without intent to infringe.

British Library Cataloguing in Publication Data
A catalogue record for this book is available from the British Library

ISBN 13: 978-0-415-50091-3 (Volume 184)
ISBN 13: 978-0-415-75280-0 (pbk)

Publisher's Note
The publisher has gone to great lengths to ensure the quality of this reprint but points out that some imperfections in the original copies may be apparent.

Disclaimer
The publisher has made every effort to trace copyright holders and would welcome correspondence from those they have been unable to trace.

Education:
In Search of a Future

Edited by
Hugh Lauder and Phillip Brown

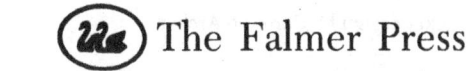 The Falmer Press

(A member of the Taylor & Francis Group)

London • New York • Philadelphia

UK	The Falmer Press, Falmer House, Barcombe, Lewes, East Sussex, BN8 5DL
USA	The Falmer Press, Taylor & Francis Inc., 242 Cherry Street, Philadelphia, PA 19106-1906

©Selection and editorial material copyright H. Lauder and P. Brown 1988

All rights reserved. No part of this publication may be reproduced, stored in a retrieval system, or transmitted in any form or by any means, electronic, mechanical, photocopying, recording or otherwise, without permission in writing from the Publisher.

First published 1988

British Library Cataloguing in Publication Data

Education: in search of a future.
  1. Great Britain. Education
  I. Lauder, Hugh II. Brown, Philip, 1957–
370'.941

ISBN 1-85000-406-4
ISBN 1-85000-407-2 Pbk

Library of Congress Cataloguing in Publication Data is available on request

Jacket design by Caroline Archer

Typeset in California by
Chapterhouse, The Cloisters, Formby L37 3PX
Printed and bound in Great Britain by
Redwood Burn Limited, Trowbridge, Wiltshire

Contents

Acknowledgements vii
Introduction viii

1 Education and the Working Class: A Cause for Concern 1
  Phillip Brown
2 Traditions of Socialism and Educational Policy 20
  Hugh Lauder
3 Democracy and Fraternity: Towards a New Paradigm for the Comprehensive School 50
  Michael Fielding
4 Costing Democracy: Schooling, Equality and Democracy in Sweden 75
  Stephen J. Ball
5 The Idea of a Socialist Education 91
  Colin Lacey
6 Education, Production and Reform 99
  Robert Moore
7 A Socialist Education for Girls 131
  Ann Marie Wolpe
8 Towards a Democratic Science Education 150
  Alison Kelly
9 Body Matters: Towards a Socialist Physical Education 174
  John Evans
10 The Playground Project: A Democratic Learning Experience 192
   Patricia White
11 Democratic Renewal in Schools: A Place for Socio-Technical Change 207
   Martin Lawn
12 Youth Training and the Manpower Services Commission: Possibilities and Limitations 221
   Shane J. Blackman

Notes on Contributors 244
Index 247

Acknowledgements

This volume is the result of a seminar on Democracy and Education held at Homerton College, Cambridge, in June, 1987. We would therefore like to thank Alan Bamford and David Bridges for enabling us to hold the seminar at Homerton College. We would also like to express our thanks to Malcolm Clarkson of Falmer Press for his encouragement and efficiency, and to all the contributors for their cooperation and willingness to meet tight deadlines.

Introduction

Since the media launch of Callaghan's Great Debate at Ruskin College in 1976, education has been in search of a future. Until then there had been a post-war consensus about the benefits education could confer both on individuals and society as a whole. In particular, it was believed that increased expenditure on education could help to promote the life-chances of the working class through the alleviation of poverty and upward social mobility. It was also assumed that there was a clear connection between educational expansion and economic growth. The merits of education seemed unequivocal.

Callaghan's speech registered a mounting discontent with the assumptions on which the post-war educational consensus had been founded, but did little to quell the chorus of criticism from the political Right, employers and the media who asserted that the comprehensive school was failing to maintain educational standards and failing to meet the needs of industry as Britain slumped into recession. In the wake of Mrs. Thatcher's third election victory the Right has mapped out a future for the educational system in Baker's Education Reform Bill (1987), which demonstrates its commitment to centralized control, 'market solutions', and the extension of educational and social inequalities.

To date, the Left has failed to respond to the Right's initiatives in education, particularly in terms of offering an alternative educational agenda. The result has been little debate about policy options on the Left, and this is reflected within the Labour party, which has entered the last two elections with poorly-focused and unimaginative educational programmes. One of the reasons for the Left's failure or unwillingness to defend the educational system has been its own disenchantment with the promises held out by the liberal consensus on schooling. Many of those on the Left now believe that education can not make major improvements in the life-chances of the working class. Moreover, increasingly influential neo-Marxist critiques of capitalist education have claimed that far from being a force for liberation, education reproduces existing class, gender, and racial divisions.

Another problem confronting the Left is that the new Right has challenged the foundations of the Welfare State. The Left has always been

Introduction

ambiguous about the Welfare State. On the one hand, as part of the post-war generation, it has taken it for granted. To explain and justify why secondary education should be universal, why it should not be organized on a system of early selection, and why it should not be treated like any other commodity which can be bought and sold in the market place, is analagous to being asked how it is that we are capable of walking or running without falling over. In other words, such questions challenge 'common sense' understanding about the nature of the post-war social world.

On the other hand, under the influence of Marxist theories in the 1970s, the Left has been extremely critical of the Welfare State. In the sociology of education the idea that social theories about education could influence policy in any significant sense has given way to a preoccupation with theories of localized resistance (Willis, 1977; Apple, 1982; Arnot and Whitty, 1982), as the only hope for achieving significant educational and social change. Frustrated by the failure of the Welfare State to significantly improve the lot of the working class, such responses are understandable but misguided, because they fail to recognize some of the strengths of the Welfare State and the benefits it offers to disadvantaged people. It is also misguided because the attack on the Welfare State is premised on the assumption that it is here to stay; indeed it was seen by many on the radical Left as an essential feature of late-capitalist development. However, the unthinkable — the dismantling of the Welfare State — is now firmly on the agenda of the new Right. The Left, although now alarmed by such proposals, are also alarmingly disarmed in the current battle for education and the Welfare State.

Those of us who are concerned about the social, economic and moral consequences of Thatcherism confront two tasks: to develop a critique of the philosophy and policies of the new Right, and to develop credible alternative policies. This book is devoted to the latter project in the educational sphere because an adequate assault on Thatcherism can not only be won on an appeal to social justice, and an alternative philosophy of education. It must also be based on alternative policy initiatives which at present are sadly lacking. It seemed important, therefore, that we concentrate on generating, in a modest way, some much-needed debate among those who believe that education can have an alternative and better future to that currently on offer under Thatcherism. In this endeavour our initial task, paradoxically, is to persuade theorists of the Left that educational policy-making does matter. By abdicating responsibility for educational policy, social theorists concerned with education have allowed the new Right to define and dominate the educational agenda. It is part of the purpose of this book to show why educational policy-making is important for the Left, and in doing so, to sketch an alternative educational strategy. This enterprise does not involve a nostalgic re-statement of the need to recapture a glorious past or engage in sentimentalizing about a Utopian future. What is required is the development of a theoretical and practical structure which builds

Introduction

upon the advances that have been made, shows how new Right initiatives can be turned to good socialist account, and which recognizes the limitations and unintended consequences of liberal democratic reforms. The aim is to develop feasible socialist policies in education. This challenge should not make us despondent or unnecessarily pessimistic, for as Brian Simon (1986) has noted:

> The historical record clearly shows that there is nothing inevitable about educational advance. Far from progress being linear, advances are more often met by setbacks, by new crises, by ideological and political struggles of all kinds. Our present age is no exception. The chances of success will be greater ... the more clearly we recognize the obstacles that must be overcome if we are to turn existing potentialities into realities.

Clearly a book of this kind cannot cover all the issues relevant to policy-making in education. Rather, the intent underlying this volume is to signal the importance of an area of theoretical and practical concern which has been neglected for far too long. The hope is that these papers will stimulate debate and further practical policy proposals in our search for alternatives to the Education Reform Bill.

In the first paper Phillip Brown argues that the educational system is standing on the verge of a 'third wave' in its socio-historical development. This 'third wave' represents the rise of the *parentocracy*, where a child's education is dependent upon the wealth and wishes of parents, rather than the efforts and abilities of pupils. Recent research conducted into working-class schooling leads him to argue that 'third wave' policies will do little to overcome Britain's social and economic problems. In conclusion it is suggested that there are compelling reasons why the Left must get involved in policy issues, in order to develop an alternative politics of education.

Hugh Lauder examines the relationship between the Left and post-war educational policy in detail. He argues that the development of educational policy has not been well served by the dominant socialist traditions in education. On the one hand, he locates the current debacle facing the comprehensive system in terms of the liberal assumptions which had a major impact on comprehensive reorganization in the 1960s. On the other, he suggests that socialists have in the past decade abdicated a concern with policy-making because of the influence of the 'correspondence' paradigm and its more sophisticated variants. In place of these theories he sketches an alternative view of the relationship of education to the economy, based on Gramsci and, more recently, the work of Rob Moore (in this volume). On the basis of this alternative view of the school–society relationship, Lauder argues for the development of the comprehensive system of education based on a participatory democratic framework.

Michael Fielding continues the exploration for socialist foundations to State education by showing how the key concepts of liberty, equality and

Introduction

fraternity are related. He then goes on to discuss the way the principles derived from these concepts can have practical expression within a comprehensive school. The theme of democracy in practice is given a comparative perspective by Stephen Ball who describes how Sweden has been able to create a democratic system of education within the context of a capitalist economic system. Ball is not suggesting that British socialist policy either could or should follow the Swedish example. Rather, the importance of his paper lies in demonstrating that it is possible for a democratic education system to exist under capitalism and that it is worth struggling for. Part of the struggle involves challenging the new Right platform which is based on a particular discourse about 'standards' and 'economic efficiency'. The Swedish education system represents a practical refutation of the imperatives of 'standards' and 'efficiency' as these terms are interpreted by the new Right.

The paper by Colin Lacey also considers the kind of socialist education which can 'swim in a "sea of capitalism".' He suggests that the task of a socialist education is to inform students about the problems and issues confronting Britain and the rest of the world. Students must be empowered with the knowledge and skills to make their own judgement about the future. Lacey argues that the redefinition of the educational enterprise must be built on the concept of 'collective intelligence' which he defines as a measure of our ability to face up to the problems that confront us collectively and to develop collective solutions. He convincingly shows that some of what currently passes for 'education' in our schools renders children 'less intelligent' than they need be.

Robert Moore examines the relationship between the educational system and the labour market. Sociologists have focused on the 'correspondence' between education and the social relations of production, and, Moore argues, they have as a result tended to ignore labour market processes which perpetuate inequalities of future life-chances, irrespective of attempts to generate greater equality of opportunity within the school. Moore suggests that if significant improvements in the life-chances of working-class pupils are to be achieved, far greater attention will need to be directed at reforming the labour market. The chapter by AnnMarie Wolpe considers the question of a socialist education for girls. She argues that much of the existing feminist literature on education has worked within a social democratic framework which has centred on the problem of generating equal opportunities for girls and women in a capitalist/patriarchal society. Wolpe questions the wisdom of this approach. She also suggests that if a socialist education for girls is to be achieved we must consider the relationship between education, family roles and sexuality.

In one of a number of chapters in this volume which examine how the principles of democratic education can be translated into practice, Alison Kelly considers the prospects for a democratic, non-sexist science education. She points out that science is something which all political

Introduction

parties believe to be a 'good thing', because it is assumed to have a direct bearing on technical development and economic growth. In recent years there have been a number of significant curriculum innovations in science which have espoused egalitarian and democratic aims. Kelly critically evaluates these in order to reveal their strengths and weaknesses when measured in terms of achieving a democratic science education. The possibilities for the implementation of such a curriculum are then considered in the light of current government policy; she finds that we remain some distance from developing a 'Science for All'. If science education has assumed a central place in the curriculum, the same thing cannot be said for the arts and PE. In the past the arts and PE have been the 'Cinderella' subjects of the curriculum because they appeared to have little relation to the economic imperatives placed on education. However, a democratic-socialist education would emphasize the necessity for a balanced curriculum and as such PE would be considered important. John Evans argues that PE is rooted in politics for at least two reasons; firstly, it helps to mark and perpetuate class divisions, and secondly, the struggle over the kinds of people education should be 'producing' has shifted into the sporting arena. Evans' chapter describes how pressure is being applied to the PE curriculum in order to encourage the development of Thatcherite qualities of individual competitiveness by the Right-minded media. In the light of these observations Evans asks what a socialist PE curriculum would be like and he critically examines recent curriculum initiatives to see how far they go in achieving a democratic and egalitarian physical education. Pat White describes an attempt to introduce democratic decision-making into rules about the use of a playground in a London primary school. In a sense, the attempt to introduce democracy in this way is a crucial test case for the possibilities of democratizing education. After all, if democratic decision-making cannot be brought to bear on how a playground is to be used, the prospects for its more general application are grim. While White argues that there is still some way to go with the project, the prospects look good. Perhaps even more importantly the processes involved in attempting to introduce democracy in this way have illuminated the practical problems and possibilities that others wishing to follow a similar route will encounter.

The chapters by Lawn and Blackman conclude the volume with an examination of education, training and industry. Martin Lawn considers the imposition of capitalist management strategies in education, and argues that some of these strategies are consistent with democratic educational principles, especially those associated with 'socio-technical theory'. Central to this theory is the concept of the Quality Circle (QC) which has been applied in industry, for example by Volvo. Underlying this concept is the assumption that the quality of production will be enhanced if there is room for worker autonomy, initiative and participation in decision-making. Lawn argues that Thatcherite initiatives in the management of education are following an outdated and inefficient model in which workers are given little autonomy. As such, teachers should not accept a model which does not reflect the most advanced thinking in industry. By this argument Lawn is able to show that the new managerialism favoured by the Thatcher government in order to achieve managerial efficiency in the educational service, is based on forms of bureaucratic control which have proved to be counterproductive to the needs of modern industrial corporations, and will have equally negative and stultifying consequences for our schools.

In the last chapter, Shane Blackman argues that, historically, market-led strategies for training youth have failed, and that this failure is being perpetuated by the Manpower Services Commission (MSC) precisely because it is reliant on market-led initiatives in training. Moreover, the hierarchies that have in the past been associated with skill-training are being perpetuated by the MSC even though fundamental changes in the economy have caused the definition of 'skill' to be changed. However, Blackman argues that there is evidence that the policies of the MSC could be turned in a progressive direction if the State rather than the market takes responsibility for youth training.

Finally, we should emphasize that the chapters in this book do not express a single theoretical or political orientation, although a number of contributors would consider themselves as writing from a democratic-socialist perspective. What unites the contributors is an opposition to Thatcherite policies in education. In our view this secular approach to policy debate is in keeping with the reality of the age: the fact is that Thatcherism remains because of the divisions within the centre and Left. It seems imperative, therefore, that a dialogue is opened up among those who oppose the regressive nature of Thatcherite policies in order that common ground for a new educational settlement can be found. To the extent that there is agreement amongst contributors it rests upon the need for the development of democracy in education.

References

APPLE, M.W. (1982) *Education and Power*, London: Routledge and Kegan Paul.
ARNOT, M. and WHITTY, G. (1982) 'From reproduction to transformation: recent radical perspectives on curriculum from the USA', *British Journal of Sociology of Education*, 3 pp. 93–103.
DEPARTMENT OF EDUCATION AND SCIENCE (1987) *Education Reform Bill*, London: HMSO.
SIMON, B(1986) *Does Education Matter?* London: Lawrence and Whishart.
WILLIS, P. (1977) *Learning to Labour*, Farnborough: Saxon House.

Chapter 1

Education and the Working Class: A Cause for Concern

Phillip Brown

Introduction

The provision of equal educational opportunities for all children was a central plank of post-war liberal democratic reform. It was also a major cause for concern among sociologists who sought to show the extent of the untapped 'pool of ability', and the continuation of 'restrictive' practices which prevented working-class children benefiting from 'secondary education for all'. Education and the working class nevertheless remained a major cause for concern and the success of the educational system was frequently measured in terms of its ability to promote educational and social mobility among the working class. However, by the mid-1970s it was 'only the daring or the self-interested who were willing to call for more educational growth as a certain way to economic and social salvation' (Kogan, 1978, p. 4). Educational reforms had not only failed to produce a more equitable society, but it was also believed (according to a growing number of politicians and industrialists) to have failed to improve Britain's economic competitiveness. Moreover, the economic recession of the early 1980s was accompanied by a significant political shift to the Right. Therefore, whereas in the 1960s Britain's economic prosperity was seen to depend upon the school's ability to tap the 'pool of ability' such efforts are now identified as a social and economic liability. Issues about equality of opportunity have been translated into issues about raising educational and moral standards, and making the education of the working class more vocationally relevant.

As a consequence, the educational system in Britain is standing on the verge of the 'third wave' in its socio-historical development. This 'third wave' represents the rise of the *parentocracy*, where a child's education is dependent upon the wealth and wishes of parents, rather than the efforts and abilities of pupils' (Brown, forthcoming). To use the 'wave' analogy popularized by Toffler (1981) it can be argued that the 'first wave' involved the development of elementary state education for the 'lower orders'. The education of the working class was primarily concerned with the inculcation of basic information and knowledge seen to be appropriate for their *predetermined* (ascribed) place in society. Floud and Halsey (1958) note that:

> in caste and estate societies education serves a differentiating function, maintaining the styles of life of different strata and the supply of appropriately socialised recruits to them (p. 177).

The 'second wave' can be characterized as one involving a shift from an education determined by an accident of birth to one based upon one's age, aptitude and ability. In other words, far greater emphasis is placed on the selective aspects of the educational process. The importance attached to individual achievement as a determinant of one's educational and occupational career was particularly evident in the writings of Parsons (1961), and informed much of the debate about education in the post-war period 1944–1976. Parsons argued that in advanced industrial societies the school confronts a dual problem of selecting the most able individuals and facilitating their educational and social advancement irrespective of social class, gender or race, as well as the problem of internalizing the commitment and capacities necessary for the successful performance of their future adult roles.

We all know that the characterization of advanced industrial societies as one involving a shift from 'particularistic' to 'universalistic' modes of social organization, including the shift from ascription to achievement, has not been fulfilled (Goldthorpe *et al.*, 1980; Harris, 1983). The unequivocal conclusion of research evidence is that despite the liberal democratic reforms since 1944, the working classes have not significantly improved their educational or life chances. Nevertheless, ideological support for the 'third wave' in education is based on the argument that post-war experiments in social engineering, which include the scrapping of the tripartite system in most of England and Wales, are largely responsible for what the Right believe to be a significant decline in educational and moral standards, and the reason why school leavers are poorly prepared for the world of work (Social Affairs Unit, 1982).

The 'third wave' involves a major programme of educational privatization under the slogans of 'parental choice', 'educational standards', and the 'free market'. We have already witnessed a sizeable expansion of independent (private) fee-paying schools and the expansion of the Assisted Places Scheme. The introduction of a voucher scheme also seems to be increasingly likely as middle-class schools 'opt out' of local authority control and find it impossible to cope with the demand for places, and Local Education Authorities (LEAs) are starved of resources, and working-class schools sink into a deepening crisis. Early selection is also on the way with national testing at the ages of 7, 11, 14, and 16. Obviously, Kenneth Baker, the Conservative Minister for Education, has been heavily influenced by the Jesuit dictum 'give me a child until he is seven and I will give you the man'

Education and the Working Class

(*sic*). Moreover, the basis for selection can no longer rely on arguments about three different types of intelligence which informed the thinking behind the 1944 Education Act. Arguments for selective organization of this sort, which exclude the vast majority of working-class pupils from acquiring the credentials necessary for educational and social advancement are now stripped of their scientific veneer given the exposé on Burt's work on IQ, to reveal the utilitarian and social bases for such divisions. What we are seeing is the restoration of *social* rather than educational authority and discipline *through* the classroom (Hall, 1983, p. 3) and in the organization of English education.

Education and the working class is however, not only a matter for concern because of the likely consequences of the 'third wave', but also because the Left have failed to mobilize support for an alternative *popular* politics of education. One of the causes of this failure has been the problem of finding a credible way of supporting institutions and practices which critical theorists and the radical Left have condemned in the recent past. Previous criticisms of the educational system were premised on the assumption that the Welfare State was here to stay, therefore much of the criticism made of liberal democratic policies was a venting of frustration due to the fact that the educational system had failed to live up to its expectation as a source of progressive social change. These criticisms were accompanied by a decisive swing to the Left as Marxist accounts of schooling the working class gained increasing attention and support from the mid-1970s. The educational system was increasingly seen to be organized in order to reproduce existing inequalities rather than to eradicate them. This focus on the reproduction function of schooling in capitalist societies meant that there was little point tinkering around with minor educational reforms because they would have little impact. This focus also meant that the incorporation of working-class pupils within the school was defined in terms of the effectiveness of the system in reproducing and legitimating their inevitable failure. As a result, considerable political significance has been attached to working-class *resistance* to school, rather than their educational achievement, as the only hope for fundamental social change.

The direction of critical and radical theory in the sociology of education has had two unfortunate consequences, which has made it difficult to launch a popular politics of education. Firstly, it has led to an evacuation of policy debates about education, and has left teachers and educationalists defenceless in the political battle with the new Right. Secondly, the aetiology of working-class educational behaviour and performance has been abandoned as a source of knowledge which may help us to develop progressive policies for educational change. The purpose of this chapter is to challenge the way schooling the working class has been understood by sociologists in general, and Marxists in particular. I will argue that the focus on working-class resistance to school has led to a self-imposed impasse due to a failure to adequately theorise the relationship between social class and educational performance. I will then argue that a return to research into the causes of working-class educational performance is required in order to develop policies which are desperately needed to challenge the ideological basis, and practical consequences of the 'third wave'. In the final section I will briefly outline some of the features of a popular politics of education, in the hope that the cause this chapter addresses does not become a lost one.

Explaining Working-Class Educational Behaviour

My remarks in this section will be limited to those theories which have had a major impact on the way sociologists have understood working-class educational behaviour and performance. The usual distinction is between structural functionalist accounts which underscore the liberal democratic approaches of the 1950s and 1960s and critical theories, particularly the Marxist approaches which have dominated proceedings since the mid-1970s. The sociology of education in Britain (as we have already noted) grew out of a liberal democratic commitment to establish equal educational opportunities for all children. As a consequence sociologists were more concerned with the demonstration rather than explanation of institutional sources of inequality in education (Bernstein, 1975; Murphy, 1981). In a review of the sociology of education in 1958, Floud and Halsey outlined a new agenda for enquiry. They suggested that sociologists must become concerned with more subtle aspects of social inequality than the social and material deprivation which had traditionally provided the focus of their attentions. The problem was increasingly seen to be one of working-class 'educability' (Flude and Ahier, 1974), which had somehow to be remedied before pupils from a working-class background could take advantage of increasing levels of educational provision:

> The educability of an individual, given his [or her] personal endowment and unique life-history, represents his [or her] socially determined *capacity to respond* to the demands of the particular educational arrangements to which he [or she] is exposed (Floud and Halsey, 1958, p. 183 emphasis added).

The focus on working-class educability led to an examination of the cultural, emotional and psychological consequences of material and social disadvantage (DES, 1967), the enduring features of which were believed to be manifest in class inequalities in educational attainment. This way of understanding the education of the working class not only had a significant impact on liberal attempts to explain the persistence of educational disadvantage despite greater equality of opportunity, but also had important consequences for educational policy.

Inequalities in educational attainment were not seen to be the manifestation of an unequal and unjust social structure which require a transformation of the whole society, but as *technical* problems which the educational system has the potential to overcome. Therefore, those areas which inhibit the free movement of talent (family background; selective schools) and the creation of talent (early selection; streaming) (Bernbaum, 1977) were all believed to be surmountable given appropriate policies and injection of resources. However, by the time of the 1973 oil crisis the optimistic belief that the educational system could generate equal educational opportunities and contribute to Britain's economic efficiency were regarded with growing scepticism, for it had become apparent that the introduction of comprehensive schooling and programmes of compensatory education had not significantly improved the academic performance of working-class pupils. Marxist writers rejected any idea of the school as a liberating force, offering the 'royal road' to social mobility:

> It is probably cultural inertia which still makes us see education in terms of the ideology of the school as a liberating force ... and as a means of increasing social mobility, even when the indications tend to be that it is in fact one of the most effective means of perpetuating the existing social pattern ... (Bourdieu, 1974, p. 32).

Rather than attempt to explain the educational failure of working-class pupils in terms of individual and collective class attributes which handicap them in their capacity to respond to educational opportunities, the concern among Marxist writers has been to show the unequal nature of capitalist societies and to demonstrate the inevitability of working-class educational failure. From this standpoint the school is primarily seen as a means of reproducing the existing structure of social and economic inequalities:

> The educational system, basically, neither adds to nor subtracts from the degree of inequality and repression originating in the economic sphere. Rather, it reproduces and legitimates a pre-existing pattern in the process of training and stratifying the workforce (Bowles and Gintis, 1976, p. 265).

There are important differences within Marxist accounts of schooling in capitalist societies, particularly in the degree of 'relative autonomy' assigned to the educational system from the demands of capitalist production. The idea of a direct correspondence between school and industry which is offered by Bowles and Gintis has been rejected by those Marxists who prefer to emphasize the relative autonomy of the school from the factory, and to focus on the way the educational system successfully legitimates its selection process, so that those it fails see their failure as the result of a 'fair' rather than a 'fixed' contest (Bourdieu and Passeron, 1977). Despite such differences, the Marxist attack on liberal democratic approaches derives less from a judgement concerning the inadequacy of previous understandings of the attributes and ambitions of working-class youth or the schools' selection processes, than from a different theory of the nature of the society in which we live, and a different understanding, therefore, of the structural location of the educational system.

Despite the important differences between liberal democratic and Marxist *structural* explanations, they share important similarities when it comes to explaining the *process* of schooling. Both liberal and Marxist structural explanations interpret the process of schooling in terms of the functions of the education system, which are premised upon their different theories of British society. It may also be argued that both assume the existence of a common or dominant culture, when attempting to explain working-class educational experiences. Marxist accounts, although they make a clear distinction between the values, attitudes and interests of the working and middle classes, nonetheless see both classes as sharing bourgeois ways of thinking and acting as a result of the inculcation of a dominant ideology (Abercrombie *et al.*, 1980). An attendant feature of approaches which rely on the notion of a common or dominant culture is (as previously noted), that they assume a universal demand for education across all classes and also that all pupils share similar educational and occupational aspirations. This has led to a failure to take seriously the possibility of class differences in pupil aspirations. This is because explanations of social class differences in educational performance are understood in terms of differential class access to socially agreed goals, rather than as representing cultural differences in the very *definition* of desirable goals. Explanations of this type therefore focus on the school as the site of what I have called the process of *educational* differentiation (Brown, 1987a). The school is a sifting and sorting mechanism which, given existing inequalities in the selection process, ensures that pupils from middle- and working-class backgrounds arrive at educational and occupational destinations appropriate to their class membership. When it comes to explaining working-class educational behaviour therefore, differences are to be found not so much in terms of whether the perspective adopted is liberal or Marxist, but whether it is *structural* and based on the process of *educational* differentiation or *cultural* based on the process of *cultural* differentiation.

In class-cultural explanations of working-class educational underachievement it is not so much the class bias in the school's selection process which is emphasized but the process of cultural differentiation. Such accounts recognize that working-class pupils may be unwilling rather than unable to respond to what is on offer in the school. Hence, if you want to understand the pattern of working-class underachievement it is not the school's but the pupils' selection processes which hold the key. It is the relative novelty of attempting to explain working-class educational underachievement in class-cultural terms which helps to explain the attention which Willis' book *Learning to Labour* has received since its publication in 1977. The basic contention of Willis' approach is that the development of a counter-school culture is not a consequence of education failure as explained by Hargreaves (1967) and Lacey (1970), but a cause. The detail of

Willis' account is well known and need not detain us, nor need criticisms of his argument which are also dealt with elsewhere (Lauder *et al.*, 1986; Brown, 1987a). Indeed, the reason for highlighting the distinction between the process of educational and cultural differentiation is not to jettison what has gone before in favour of yet another 'new' sociology of education, but to suggest that the attempt to explain working-class educational experiences needs to be redefined in terms of the inter-relationship between educational and cultural processes as I will attempt to explain below. This redefining of the issue also highlights the importance of engaging in policy debates if we are truly interested in generating a better and more equitable education system.

In the late 1970s *Learning to Labour* came as a relief to many of those who had committed themselves to increasing educational opportunities for the working class, but who saw their efforts fail to translate into a more equitable society. The argument developed in *Learning to Labour* lifted the responsibility for working-class failure from the shoulders of the teacher. They were no longer portrayed as the controllers in the state machine (Althusser, 1972; Bowles and Gintis, 1976), but as those unfortunates at the sharp end, forced to survive in a blackboard jungle inhabited by working-class youth, resistant to any attempt by teachers to get them to make an effort in school because they knew it was a rigged contest which they could never win. The account of working-class underachievement offered by Willis dignified the actions of the academic failures, as well as the teachers. The Lads' (an anti-school subcultural group who were the main focus of his study) rejection of school was not portrayed as yet another depressing case of working-class 'failure' but as a class-cultural victory which repelled all attempts by the state to incorporate the working class into middle-class institutions such as the school, although Willis recognized that in the longer-term this rejection decisively secured the reproduction of their disadvantage in the search for jobs. Willis' theory of working-class educational resistance has also influenced the direction of radical theory in recent years. Freed of its earlier deterministic and over-socialised propensities, there has been a growing number of sociologists on both sides of the Atlantic, who have identified working-class resistance to school as a potent force for social transformation (Arnot and Witty, 1982; Aronowitz and Giroux, 1986). The lack of such a potential in previous Marxist explanations of education and the working class had always been an embarrassing absence, particularly as it was Marx who stated that the important thing is not to understand society but to change it!

There are, however, important theoretical and empirical weaknesses concerning the transformative potential attached to theories of resistance. These include the unjustifiable claim, given the absence of empirical data, that the anti-school subculture when adopted by working-class males, manifests a radical potential for the transformation of society. This potential is premised on the belief that the rejection of schooling by working-class pupils is an expression of a class-cultural resistance to the state. Therefore any resistance to school is 'read' as a resistance to capitalism *per se* (see Cohen, 1980), despite the fact that there is little to suggest from the transcripts offered by Willis and others, that those who are rejecting school also reject the principles of capitalism. The Lads' resistance does pose problems for the day-to-day operation of the school, but not to the wider social order, unless they reject the moral basis of the society in which they live — the work ethic, the distribution of goods and services, individualism — which they do not appear to do. Problems with the way the notion of resistance have been used in radical theory, have been recognized by Aronowitz and Giroux (1986):

> the current use of the concept of resistance by radical educators suggests a lack of intellectual rigor and an overdose of theoretical sloppiness. It is imperative that educators be more precise about what resistance actually is and what it is not, and be more specific about how the concept can be used to develop a critical pedagogy (p. 104).

Given that Aronowitz and Giroux are interested in the development of a critical pedagogy it is surprising that they continue to advocate a theory of resistance as a major conceptual tool for the radical theorist. They suggest that resistance must be situated in a perspective that takes the notion of emancipation as its guiding interest (p. 105). Yet how are we to understand this in terms of the educational process? The acquisition of school knowledge (albeit in a more progressive form) and the development of intellectual skills is a necessary prerequisite for the development and articulation of critical ideas and for participation in the democratic process. Therefore, what would appear to be modes of working-class 'conformity' rather than resistance to school, may offer the best opportunity for personal and collective emancipation from bourgeois ideology, and for the personal empowerment required to battle against the more repressive and unjust forms of social organization. Indeed it is in circumstances of raised educational and occupational expectations which remain unmet which sociologists have shown to offer the greatest destabilizing potential, not the classroom resistance of the male anti-school subculture. The resistance of the male anti-school subculture, has to date, shown nothing to challenge the sexism and racism which operates in the school and working-class neighbourhoods, indeed their resistance reinforces such beliefs and practices. Therefore, I rather doubt whether the concept of resistance does 'represent more than a new heuristic catchword in the language of radical pedagogy' (p. 104).[1]

Another problem with theories of resistance is, they have little that is constructive to offer to the classroom teacher, and are so far removed from policy debates that the new Right has seized the ideological initiative, and has been allowed to define the educational crisis in its own terms and for its own ideological purposes virtually unopposed. Moreover, the concentration

Education and the Working Class

on pupil resistance has diverted attention away from the empirical and theoretical study of working-class educational behaviour. Such an endeavour is essential if a popular politics of education is to be achieved, and provide the resources for educationalists, teachers, parents and pupils to challenge the educational reforms proposed by the new Right. The remainder of this section will be used to show why a reconsideration of the way we have understood the educational behaviour of working-class pupils is necessary, and why education really matters to the working class (Simon, 1986).

On the basis of a recent study I conducted of 'ordinary kids' in industrial South Wales, it was immediately apparent that the educational system does not simply 'fail' pupils from a working-class background, nor do these pupils simply 'fail themselves' either individually or collectively. It is therefore necessary to reject as one-sided, any account which is based on either the process of educational or cultural differentiation.[2] Working-class educational behaviour and attainment is best understood as an interplay between class-culture understood as a set of resources which give rise to different ways of being in school and becoming adult among working-class youth on the one hand, and the organization and selection processes of the school on the other. It is this inter-relationship which holds the key to explaining variations in working-class responses to school.

In the South Wales town of Middleport pupils identify three different ways of being a working-class pupil — 'Rems', 'Swots' and 'Ordinary Kids'. The term 'Rem' is taken from the word 'remedial'. However, it is important to note that although the term 'remedial' is used with reference to non-examination pupils, it has important moral connotations. It is not that the Rems are believed to be 'thick', but rather that they are unwilling to 'make an effort'. It was the members of the conspicuous male anti-school subculture who were most likely to be referred to as Rems. The 'Swots' are alternatively those pupils located in the upper bands of the school and who were identified as spending all their time working and never having a laugh or getting into trouble with teachers. In the two working-class schools included in the research, to be studying for 'O' levels was almost by definition to be a Swot. The 'Ordinary Kids' stand somewhere between the Rems and Swots. They are defined with reference to what they are not (Rems or Swots), rather than for what they are, 'ordinary' or 'average'. These different ways of being in school and the orientations to school life which this involved,[3] are explicable in terms of the way these pupils made sense of their educational experiences when related to the cultural-defined ways in which it was possible to become a working-class adult. These working-class 'frames of reference' (FORs) — which can be characterized in terms of Getting In, Getting On or Getting Out of the working class — are the historical product of the shared social and educational experiences of working-class people, which are imbued with social significance and convey varying degrees of social status. At the heart of these social experiences are the economic activities of adults living in the locality. It is therefore hardly surprising that occupational identity has had an important impact on the demand for education, and that this demand has been limited as a consequence of class inequalities.[4]

The Rems' rejection of the school as boring, irrelevant and frequently repressive, is based upon a FOR which can be characterized in terms of 'get into' the culture proper: away from a world of school kids and into the world of working-class adults and employment at the earliest possible opportunity. The Swots are more willing to accept the demands of school life and 'swot' for examinations. Their FOR is characterized in terms of a belief that by arming themselves with enough qualifications to compete for middle-class jobs they can 'get out' of their class of origin. Yet the majority of working-class pupils neither simply accept nor reject the school, but comply with it despite the fact that much of the academic curriculum is irrelevant to their present and future lives, as Mark put it: 'Say somebody wants to be a motor mechanic, I can't see where history comes into it. I can't really see what History has got to do with it 'cos it just deals with the past'. Nevertheless, Mark like the other male and female Ordinary Kids made an effort in school because they could see instrumental reasons for 'doing a bit' and for achieving modest levels of attainment (usually leading to CSEs). At the heart of the Ordinary Kids' response to school is a FOR which can be characterized in terms of 'Getting on' within the working class, although this FOR has been seriously affected by the collapse of job opportunities for school leavers in the early 1980s. In Middleport, 'getting on' usually meant boys being able to enter craft apprenticeships and girls entering clerical and personal service jobs.

If these findings can be replicated in other parts of England and Wales, it could help us to explain one of the reasons why working-class pupils have not pursued an academic career and why so many of them have deserted full-time education at the first hurdle. Given the social and historical context of the postwar period, within working-class neighbourhoods such as those found in Middleport, academic achievement was never necessary for the vast majority of working-class pupils to realize their childhood ambitions and maintain a sense of personal dignity and respect. However, this has not, and does not, preclude some working-class pupils developing a FOR in terms of 'getting out', which places a premium on school success. It neither rules out the contention that the school has an important impact on which pupils develop which FOR. The FORs exhibited by particular pupils are not simply the result of early childhood socialization. The educational system does play a part in reinforcing or transforming pupil FORs. There is a loose fit between family background and pupil 'frames of reference' because of the interaction between the 'institutional context and the processes of class cultural production' (Hogan, 1982, p. 61). A recognition of the school's role in framing the life-chances of working-class youth is important because it avoids the tendency for 'cultural' accounts to drift into forms of voluntaristic explanations, which underplay the significance of the school's ability to determine the life-chances of pupils, whether or not large numbers of working-class children were to be convinced of the value of academic success. It ignores the way in which the school is structured and organized and the differential power relations which pupils from a disadvantaged background confront. It is in terms of the school's selection processes that we can understand why the school has the potential to transform the FORs of particular pupils, and why it has failed to offer much of a challenge to the educational and social identities of working-class children in general. The Middleport study supports the view that in order to win pupil compliance teachers do try to convince all pupils that 'swotting' is worth while, and that if they work hard they can achieve a better future than that which confronts their school friends. However, 'swotting' has a social and moral significance which means that it incurs social costs, such as social stigma and isolation from childhood friends. Swotting is not therefore a viable option for the majority of working-class pupils (given its irrelevance to their present and future lives), unless opportunities are seen to exist for educational and social advancement (and even then they may be rejected).

It is this inter-relationship between class-culture and school structure which provides the key to understanding intra-class variations in the demand for education. It also helps us to understand why the structure of educational opportunities and content of schooling has an important impact on working-class educational behaviour and why youth unemployment and the process of deindustrialization in working-class neighbourhoods is likely to have a major impact on working-class FORs. The conclusion to be drawn from this discussion is that if education and the working class mattered in the past, it matters even more as we reach the end of the Twentieth Century. It may not only become more important as a route out of the growing underclass of long-term unemployed, but it will also be crucial in order to empower people, individually and collectively, to cope with, and struggle for, change. In what remains of this paper it is impossible to do more than note some of the main ideas upon which a popular politics of education needs to be built.

Towards a Popular Politics of Education

A popular politics of education must recognize that education does matter, although its potential for overcoming Britain's social and economic problems are obviously limited. Nevertheless, in a society which will remain capitalist for the foreseeable future, there are important political and ideological battles over the structure, organization and content of education which need to be fought, won and re-won in order to secure the ground we have gained, let alone advance towards a more democratic and equitable society. Within capitalist societies there are important differences in the degree of inequalities and degree of repression. There are also important differences in the structure, organization and content of the educational system, which offer varying degrees of opportunity to different social classes, genders and racial groups. What the Right's political assault on the educational system has surely taught us is that, if liberal educational reforms are difficult to implement, and if it is difficult to demonstrate that they have conferred a positive advantage on the working class (however see McPherson and Willms, 1987), it is easy to restructure schooling to the disadvantage of those who are already disadvantaged. The shift towards comprehensive forms of school organization is an important advance, despite its many limitations. It does provide the basis for new forms of curricula innovation and pupil assessment. If the idea of equality of opportunity is to be more than an ideological justification for explaining why some (usually from a middle-class background) make it, and others (usually from a working-class background) do not, the comprehensive school is fundamental (Hargreaves, 1982).

A popular politics of education must recognize that the educational system is in crisis. There may well be a decline in educational and moral standards in schools but its nature, causes and the way we need to respond are very different from those advocated by the Right. The contemporary educational crisis cannot simply be overcome by extending provision, such as by abolishing private schools (although I believe this to be essential because we should never allow education to be a free market commodity like the purchase of a car, so that if you have the money you can buy a better and faster model). The fact is that education in England and Wales has succeeded in alienating a large proportion of working-class pupils who leave at sixteen and never return to any kind of formal education. Moreover, as a result of the declining exchange value of qualifications for jobs in parts of England and Wales the situation in many schools is getting worse. Growing numbers of ordinary working-class pupils now feel that they have less of a stake in school and society. They are being stripped of a sense of dignity and respect because the occupations which form an element to social identity and to becoming adult in a respectable fashion have disappeared, and so has one of the major reasons for bothering to make an effort in school. The increase in working-class alienation from school is associated with a sense of fatalism and powerlessness, which is likely to result in a growing sense of entrapment and social disorganization within working-class neighbourhoods, rather than to their emancipation.

I have already argued that the view expressed by some radical intellectuals that 'education' should be rejected by the working classes because it is provided by a capitalist state must itself be rejected as condescending. It is also idealist because it is premised on the assertion that the male anti-school subculture involves a rejection of capitalist forms of social organization. It has been argued that there is no evidence to support this view. The different forms of resistance and incorporation exhibited by working-class pupils, for example the ordinary kids' unwillingness to swot for academic subjects and qualifications which they perceived to be irrelevant, not only ensures that they will not win the 'badges of ability' (Sennett and Cobb, 1977) which can be traded in the labour market and institutions of higher education, but it also prevents them from acquiring the intellectual and conceptual skills necessary for the development of a critical literacy. They know how to add-up and subtract. They know how to read a newspaper or write a letter to a friend, yet the confidence and ability to articulate ideas and to defend them is unnecessarily limited by existing school practices and processes. They are rendered less intelligent than they need to be (see Lacey in this volume). The way the ordinary kids understand their personal troubles are often parochial and individualistic, and unrelated to issues of social structure. The preservation of a sense of dignity and respect is premised on the damnation of others sharing a similar social background and life-chances. This form of resistance to the academic curriculum should not be 'celebrated' or 'castigated' but it should form a major starting point for curriculum innovation and educational change.

A popular politics of education must begin from where people are, not from where we feel they ought to be. The challenge confronting the comprehensive school is to make school knowledge and the learning process more intrinsically meaningful and interesting. Lacey's paper argues that the role of a socialist education is to inform young people of the problems and issues, and encourage them to develop the skills and knowledge with which to make their own judgements about the future. Although this form of education is critical and constructive it is not a blue-print for indoctrination, but the basis for a collective intelligence. However, educational initiative, to date, from Newsom to the Technical and Vocational Education Initiative (TVEI), fail to meet the requirements of a popular politics of education.

Anchoring curricula innovation onto the concrete experiences of daily life does not mean the celebration of that (or any) particular life style (GAOC, 1987). On the contrary, it should highlight the social, geographical and historical limits of our own experiences. Therefore, a popular education should not be restricted to the immediate concerns and experiences of pupils. Yet we know that a large proportion of working-class girls and boys have rejected much of the 'academic' curriculum which is the dominant definition of 'education', not (I would want to argue), always because it deals with abstract ideas, but because they are disconnected both due to artificial subject boundaries and because they are remote and disconnected from their present and future lives. However, the basis for a comprehensive education must take into account the concerns and interests of the majority of pupils, not only the minority who have benefited disproportionately from a narrow academic curriculum in order to enter institutions of higher education. A broad integrated curriculum is required for *all* pupils which includes technical and practical subjects which help to anchor and give academic study more relevance and importance beyond its acquisition for school certificates.

A popular politics of education must be founded upon the development of personal and collective 'empowerment'. An education for citizenship will need to offer the conceptual armoury necessary to participate fully in a liberal capitalist democracy. Therefore a critical literacy will need to be based on democratic principles which facilitate considered choices on the bases of adequate information as part of the development of a collective intelligence (see Lacey op. cit.). Education therefore should not be an instrument for perpetuating the status quo, but must empower people to make considered judgements and to work for change. For example, in a discussion of vocational education Dewey (1916) noted that:

> an education which acknowledges the full intellectual and social meaning of a vocation would include instruction in the historic background of present conditions, training in science to give intelligence and initiative in dealing with material and agencies of production; and study of economics, civics, and politics, to bring the future workers into touch with the problems of the day and the various methods proposed for its improvement. Above all, it would train power of readaptation to changing conditions so that future workers would not become blindly subject to a fate imposed upon them (p. 372).

But Dewey recognized that this ideal has to contend with the inertia of existing educational traditions and opposition from those who have a 'vested interested in preserving an educational system which does not threaten their ability to use others for their own ends' (p. 372-3). The point here is that all pupils can benefit both individually and collectively from receiving an education which empowers them with the capacity for critical thought, and to articulate their feelings in a way that allows them to go beyond the confinements of their immediate experiences and contribute to a process of social and economic change. Indeed, the development of a popular education is not a flight of fancy but a concrete necessity if the educational system is to play its part in serving the social and economic needs of British society in the late Twentieth Century (see Brown, 1987a).

A popular politics of education must be organized so as to expand the educational and occupational opportunities of the working class, not to restrict them. This is crucial not only because some working-class parents and pupils may view the school as the only way out of the de-industrial rut, poverty, and a life on the dole, but because the motivational patterns of working-class pupils are based on the inter-relationship between identities and institutions. As we have seen, pupil understandings of being in school are closely connected to class-cultural understandings of becoming a working-class adult (Blackman, 1987). It is only when the school offers an 'out' both subjectively and objectively that the costs and benefits of being defined as a 'swot' and 'getting out' of the working class are truly posed for the majority of these pupils. They will not therefore, easily give up an understanding which serves to define who they are, and to maintain a sense of social dignity unless there are genuine opportunities to make a new future.

A popular politics of education must return the aetiology of educational behaviour and performance to the centre stage of sociological debate, because the policies which will be needed to inform a popular politics of education must be based on grounded theory and empirical evidence in order to gain popular appeal among teachers, parents, administrators and pupils, and avoid unintended consequences.

A popular politics of education must recognize the limitations of the past, but build upon the advances which have been made (Simon, 1986). This has proved particularly difficult because the Right have challenged the principles of the Welfare State which many of us have previously taken for granted. This does not mean accepting things as they are, demanding a return to how things were, or starting from where we think things should be. We must however, overcome the problem of opting for short-term gains which may impede or lose sight of longer-term aims. We must also make sure that educational theory and its policy implications are sufficiently grounded to prevent it from being 'defined out' as irrelevant (Matiesen, 1980). Matiesen has noted that there are considerable pressures in liberal capitalist democracies to 'neutralize' social movements by defining the demands for reform into existing social (or educational) arrangements without changing very much. If the demand for change cannot be 'defined in' there will be a tendency for them to be 'defined out' of legitimate consideration as irrelevant, 'cranky' or the ideas of the 'loony left'. The way these processes work are complex and cannot simply be put down to a capitalist conspiracy. Nevertheless, a recognition of these tendencies clearly creates difficulties for those who wish to engage in social and educational policy debates in the hope of pushing towards significant and progressive change. The problems associated with this endeavour at the present time are particularly acute given the current climate of opinion and because the Left is on the defensive.

Matiesen has argued that the task is not to solve or resolve the major dilemma between short-term reforms and social transformation but to dissolve it (Downes, 1980, p. 72). The dilemma of reform versus social transformation is dissolved by insisting that both goals must be pursued. As Downes has noted, to make this more than sheer word magic a certain strategy must be followed. This strategy involves distinguishing between reforms which do not extend educational and social inequalities and which therefore can be pursued without detriment to long-term aims, and those which may extend inequalities, such as the privatization of schooling, which must be resisted (see Downes, 1980, p. 72). What is therefore required is an 'action theory' which 'avoids both immaculate theoretical conception on the one hand, and token administrative "practical" changes on the other' (p. 72).

At the moment we seem to have the worst of both worlds. We have both 'immaculate theoretical conception' which has led to an abandonment of any hope of generating social change so long as we remain in a capitalist society, and therefore socialist intellectuals have contributed little to the ideological and policy debates which are required to challenge the new Right. We also have evidence of 'token administrative practical change', exhibited by the 'effective schools movement' (Reynolds, 1985; Reid, 1987) and the applaudable efforts of some teachers to make 'progressive' use of new resources made available through such programmes as TVEI. Although such efforts are to be welcomed their impact will always remain limited because they fail to challenge the political agenda upon which, for example, the 'new vocationalism' is based (Brown, 1987b; Grace, 1987). Progressive social and educational change cannot be reaped solely within the confines of the school. A popular politics of education has to be set for education, not just in education (Hall, 1983), and as Hargreaves (1982) has noted, one of the major challenges confronting the teaching profession is to win broad appeal among parents and politicans which cannot be achieved within the confines of the classroom and staffroom. Theory and practice, therefore, need to work in conjunction so that theory does not become 'defined out' as irrelevant, and challenging practices become neutralized. Moreover, the aetiology of working-class educational performance which is based on a specification of the inter-relationship between identities and institutions may help us to develop such an action theory. It is hopefully clear from what has already been said, that every attempt must be made to defend post-war educational reforms which benefit all pupils (i.e., the shift to the comprehensive school), as well as engaging in affirmative action.

A popular politics of education must begin with concrete issues such as the consequences of the Right's Education Reform Bill and attempt to increase awareness and broaden the range of concern beyond that which is going on inside the educational system. The initial focus of a campaign for a popular politics of education must obviously be the school, but the growing level of concern being expressed by parents about Baker's Education Bill suggests that there is considerable potential for broadening the campaign to show how Thatcherism is affecting the quality of education in ways that cannot be tackled within the confines of the educational system. Therefore, it is necessary to challenge other institutional structures and practices which inhibit the full potential for individual and collective intelligence, for example, due to the vested interests which preserve an overly-narrow academic curriculum; the limited opportunities for higher education; sexism and racism which confront school leavers in the labour market; and the opportunity for middle-class parents to 'opt out' of the state system and buy a privileged education. This challenge, as Tawney (1982) has noted, must be premised on an appeal to the principles of social justice:

An appeal to principles is the condition of any considerable reconstruction of society, because social institutions are the visible expression of the scale of moral values which rules the minds of individuals, and it is impossible to alter institutions without altering that valuation (p. 10).

Summary

In this chapter it has been argued that we stand on the verge of a 'third wave' in the socio-historical development of the English educational system. This development offers little comfort to those who want to see an extension of social justice and democracy in our schools. However, before a major offensive can be effectively launched against the ideological foundations of the Right's programme for educational reform, critical and radical intellectuals need to be convinced of the importance of entering the fray; after all, education is too important to be left to the new Right! We must re-arm ourselves with concrete policies for a truly popular politics of education. Some of the ammunition is readily available, but to give it fire power depends upon the development of a new realism in the sociology of education, which must rediscover its original concerns about education and the working class. The alternative is the 'third wave' of major educational reforms which will inevitably extend and deepen the hereditary curse upon English education which remains its organization upon lines of social class (Tawney, 1982; Brown, forthcoming).

However, if we begin to meet the challenge confronting the comprehensive school there does seem to be considerable potential given the problems and concerns of teachers, parents, pupils and educationalists, for a powerful and broad-based popular politics of education. It is a popular politics which can do much to challenge the foundations of Thatcherism, and offer some hope to those who have most to lose. We do have a choice.

Acknowledgements

I would like to thank Shane Blackman, Liz Brown and Chris Harris for their comments on an earlier draft of this paper.

Notes

1   A further problem, of course, is that it is unclear how the school resisters are going to generate the level of social unrest which would be required to lead to significant social change. The most likely consequences are an extension and concentration of social control and repression of the young working class in particular and working-class neighbourhoods in general.

2. For a more detailed discussion of this argument see Brown (1987a).
3. The evidence collected in this study revealed that amongst those groups who 'made an effort' in school — 'ordinary kids' and 'swots' — the response to school was dominated by 'instrumental' concerns. It was also evident, however, that the two groups had different kinds of instrumental orientations. Amongst the academic pupils (the 'swots'), the instrumentalism was 'normative'. In other words, despite the predominance of the pursuit of qualifications, there was also a degree of intrinsic interest in some of the academic elements of the school curriculum. For them what was learnt at school, even if it did not directly relate to their occupational interests, was viewed as a necessary prelude to the acquisition of knowledge which was both 'required' and 'desired'. These pupils were more attuned to the formal culture of the school than the 'ordinary kids'. The latter adopted a form of 'alienated instrumentalism'. This can be regarded as 'alienated' because their involvement in school was fairly limited. They did not identify with its perceived aims, nor what teachers 'stand for', nor the academic curriculum. Those elements of interest and perceived 'relevance' that did exist for them were in the 'practical' rather than the academic side of the curriculum.
4. Such a belief is supported by the conclusions drawn by Goldthorpe *et al.* (1980) from their study of social mobility in contemporary Britain:

> Where inequalities in class chances of this magnitude can be displayed, the presumption must be . . . that to a substantial extent they do reflect inequalities of opportunity that are rooted in the class structure, and are not simply the outcome of the differential 'take-up' of opportunities by individuals with differing genetic, moral or other endowments that do not derive from their class position (p. 252).

References

ABERCROMBIE, N., HILL, S. and TURNER, B.S. (1980) *The Dominant Ideology Thesis*, London: Allen and Unwin.
ALTHUSSER, L. (1972) 'Ideology and ideological state apparatuses', in Cosin, B.R. (Ed.) *Education: Structure and Society*, Milton Keynes: Open University.
ARNOT, M. and WHITTY, G. (1982) 'From reproduction to transformation: recent radical perspectives on curriculum from the USA', *British Journal of Sociology of Education*, 3 pp. 93–103.
ARONOWITZ, S. and GIROUX, H. (1986) *Education Under Siege*, London: Routledge and Kegan Paul.
BERNBAUM, G. (1977) *Knowledge and Ideology in the Sociology of Education*, London: Macmillan.
BERNSTEIN, B. (1975) *Class, Codes and Control, Vol. 3*, London: Routledge and Kegan Paul.
BLACKMAN, S. (1981) 'The labour market in school' in Brown, P. and Ashton D. (Eds) *Education, Unemployment and Labour Markets*, Lewes: Falmer Press.
BOURDIEU, P. (1974) 'The school as a conservative force: Scholastic and cultural inequalities', in Eggleston, J. (Ed.) *Contemporary Research in the Sociology of Education*, London: Methuen.
BOURDIEU, P. and PASSERON, J.C. (1977) *Reproduction: In Education, Society and Culture*, London: Sage.
BOWLES, S. and GINTIS, H. (1976) *Schooling in Capitalist America*, London: Routledge and Kegan Paul.
BROWN, P. (1987a) *Schooling Ordinary Kids: Inequality, Unemployment and the New Vocationalism*, London: Tavistock.
BROWN, P. (1987b) 'Schooling for inequality? Ordinary kids in school and the labour market', in Brown, P. and Ashton, D. (Eds) *Education, Unemployment and Labour Markets*, Lewes: Falmer Press.

BROWN, P. (forthcoming) 'Education', in Brown, P. and Sparks, R. (Eds) *Beyond Thatcherism*, Milton Keynes: Open University Press.
COHEN, S. (1980) *Folk Devils and Moral Panics* (2nd edition), Oxford: Martin Robinson.
DEPARTMENT OF EDUCATION AND SCIENCE (1967) *Children and their Primary Schools (Plowden Report)*, London: HMSO.
DEWEY, J. (1916) *Democracy and Education*, New York: Macmillan.
DOWNES, D. (1980) 'Abolition: possibilities and pitfalls', in Bottoms, A.E. and Preston, R.H. (Eds) *The Coming Penal Crisis*, Scottish Academic Press.
FLOUD, J. and HALSEY, A.H. (1958) 'The sociology of education: A trend report and bibliography', *Current Sociology*, 3,3 pp. 165-93.
FLUDE, M. and AHIER, J. (1974) *Educability, Schools and Ideology*, London: Croom Helm.
GAOC (1987) *Hidden Messages*, Oxford: Blackwell.
GOLDTHORPE, J.H. et al. (1980) *Social Mobility and Class Structure in Modern Britain*, Oxford: Clarendon Press.
GRACE, G. (1987) 'Teachers and the State in Britain: a changing relationship', in Lawn, M. and Grace, G. (Eds) *Teachers: The Culture and Politics of Work*, Lewes: Falmer Press.
HALL, S. (1983) 'Education in Crisis', in Wolpe, A.M. and Donald, J. (Eds) *Is There Anyone Here From Education*, London: Pluto Press.
HARGREAVES, D. (1967) *Social Relations in a Secondary School*, London: Routledge and Kegan Paul.
HARGREAVES, D. (1982) *The Challenge for the Comprehensive School*, London: Routledge and Kegan Paul.
HARRIS, C.C. (1983) *The Family and Industrial Society*, London: George Allen and Unwin.
HOGAN, D. (1982) 'Education and class formation: the peculiarities of the Americans', in Apple, M.W. (Ed) *Culture and Economic Reproduction in Education*, London: Routledge and Kegan Paul.
KOGAN, M. (1978) *The Politics of Educational Change*, Manchester: Manchester University Press.
LACEY, C. (1970) *Hightown Grammar*, Manchester: Manchester University Press.
LAUDER, H., FREEMAN-MOIR, J. and SCOTT, A. (1986) 'What is to be done with radical academic practice?', *Capital and Class* 29, pp. 83-110.
MATIESEN, T. (1980) *Law, Society and Political Action: Towards a Strategy Under Late Capitalism*, London: Academic Press.
MCPHERSON, A. and WILLMS, J.D. (1987) 'Equalisation and improvement: Some effects of comprehensive reorganization in Scotland', *Sociology*, 21, 4, pp. 509-39.
MURPHY, J. (1981) 'Class inequality in education: Two justifications, one evaluation but no hard evidence', *British Journal of Sociology*, 32 pp. 182-201.
PARSONS, T. (1961) 'The school class as a social system: Some of its functions in American society', in Halsey, A.L. et al. (Eds) *Education, Economy and Society*, New York: Free Press.
REID, K., HOPKINS, D. and HOLLY, P. (1987) *Towards the Effective School*, Oxford: Blackwell.
REYNOLDS, D. (Ed) (1985) *Studying School Effectiveness*, Lewes: Falmer Press.
SENNETT, R. and COBB, J. (1977) *The Hidden Injuries of Class*, Cambridge: Cambridge University Press.
SIMON, B. (1986) *Does Education Matter?*, London: Lawrence and Wishart.
SOCIAL AFFAIRS UNIT (1982) *Educated for Employment?* London: Social Affairs Unit.
TAWNEY, R.H. (1982) *The Acquisitive Society*, Brighton: Wheatsheaf.
TOFFLER, A. (1981) *The Third Wave*, London: Pan Books.
WILLIS, P. (1977) *Learning to Labour*, Farnborough: Saxon House.

Chapter 2

Traditions of Socialism and Educational Policy

Hugh Lauder

In the wake of Mrs Thatcher's third electoral victory, and with the possibility of a return to a fully selective education system now on the cards, there is a pressing need for the left to reassess its theories and policies. In some areas, economics and social philosophy[1] for example, a new tradition of socialist thought appears to be emerging; one which characterizes itself by a hard-nosed realism prepared to examine the practical limits and possibilities for socialist change — in the light of current fundamental shifts in social formation and political alignment. In education, that type of debate has still to emerge, although a number of writers have clearly articulated a dissatisfaction with the current state of socialist thought (Ahier, 1983; Aronowitz and Giroux, 1986; Simon, 1986) from varying positions on the Left. To my mind it is Ahier who has identified the most significant absence in the literature, namely policy.

In this chapter I focus on policies designed to democratize education because there are sound social, political and educational reasons why the development of democracy in education should be seen as central to the development of human freedom. But to argue for democracy in education *and* for policies designed to achieve this aim is to run, immediately, into difficulties. For a start, neither major strands of Labour party thought nor theories of the Welfare State in Britain have entertained the democratization of state and social life seriously (Baron *et al.*, 1981). Then again, while educational thought has often gestured toward the necessity for democracy in education precious little has been done to think through the implications of such a necesssity.[2] What is more, the espousal of the influential 'correspondence' paradigm in the sociology of education has meant that the questions of educational policy have been eschewed precisely because, according to this paradigm, significant educational change cannot take place until capitalism has been replaced by socialism.

If, as I shall argue, we ought to take the construction of democratic policy in education seriously then we must engage in an uncertain and risky venture. We need to ensure, *pace* the correspondence paradigm, that the reforms advocated are meaningful — that they will affect people's lives by increasing their freedom. But the problem, always, in arguing for democratic–socialist reforms in a capitalist society is that they have the potential to become double agents — the very context in which they are applied may mean that they end up working for the powerful and the privileged rather than empowering those for whom they are designed, the working class, women and ethnic minorities.

Clearly, arguing for policies designed to democratize education involves a series of complex issues: we need to come to terms with the reasons for the Labour Party's failure to introduce a significant measure of democracy in education, if now, we are to press for a new partnership between parents, teachers, and students in schools. We also need to rethink the school/society relationship at the theoretical level if we are to make any sense of the idea that policies for the democratization of schools can be pursued effectively under capitalism. The practical benefits of democratizing education need to the restated, showing how they can lead to increased personal freedom and improve equality of life chances for those who are exploited by the present anti-democratic system. But it also has to be shown how these democratic policies can be grounded in the changed social circumstances which now confront us.

To provide such an analysis is to attempt to introduce a strong dose of the new realism[3] into democratic–socialist thought in education. However, it is equally important that in concentrating on the immediate and practical we don't accept too little,[4] thereby failing to push at the boundaries of change enough and so falling into a kind of theoretical purgatory. In this context we need to advocate practical and sometimes local changes cognisant of the economic boundaries capitalism imposes while not losing a wider vision of an alternative socialist future. Hall (1984) articulates the dilemma succinctly when he asks:

> Can they (the electors) be won to a vision, not simply a programme of the future? Here there is somethimg to learn from Thatcherism, after all. Paradoxically she does raise hearts and minds an inch or two because, vile, corrupt, awful as her vision of the future is, we know what it is... It is an 'alternative future'.
> It is a philosophy of life.
> The one thing nobody knows is what Labour conceives to be an 'alternative' way of life... In its profound empiricism, it has mistaken adaption to the present as progess toward the future (p. 35).

One way of attempting to steer a course around the problem of a visionless realism while avoiding the dilemma of double agent policies is to think of policies in terms of non-reformist reforms. These are reforms which would be necessary in any socialist transformation of society, rather than reforms designed to co-opt or ameliorate those exploited by capitalism. Such policies will clearly have a limited effect within capitalism, yet they are reforms necessary to a socialist transformation and as such can be both realistic and inspirational. Of course, the concept of non-reformist reforms brings its own set of problems but I shall argue that in an uncertain world it does at least provide some guide for democratic-socialists. These issues, then, create an agenda for thinking through some of the difficulties involved in the aim of fostering policies to democratize education in a hostile environment.

Labour Party socialism has spawned a theory of schooling resting on the twin pillars of citizenship and equality of opportunity. Citizenship, in the context of education can take on a number of meanings but they have in common the idea that schools should be used as a forum for creating social harmony. However this latter concept has always been overshadowed by the idea of equality of opportunity which has spearheaded Labour's educational theory and policy since the 1920s. While the concept has undergone change it retains a core set of ideas which were forged at a particular historical moment; that period between 1880 and 1930 which saw the Labour Party's ascendancy to Parliamentary power and which has been called by Hall and Schwarz (1985) a passive revolution. Equality of opportunity therefore carries with it a network of related concepts which take us to the core of Labour Party thinking about the state and welfare provision. Looking at how this concept came to occupy such a key role in parliamentary socialist politics will help us to grasp the nature of the problems now confronting Labour. For arguably, the current crisis in Labour Party thought, triggered by Thatcherism, has its origins in the passive revolution. To understand the influences which forged Labour policy at that time is at once to grasp the major reconceptualization of Parliamentary socialist policy which is necessary and to see the possibilities for its implementation.

Equality of Opportunity and the Passive Revolution

In a recent book Jones (1983) made the following observations about the notion of equality of opportunity and its relationship to Labour Party educational policy:

> Equal opportunity has been the motivating slogan of Labour's programme, without significant challenge, for fifty years. As a precise set of demands, it has gone through many mutations but its core meaning remains: equal access for all social classes to education, so as to equalize the occupational chances of the individuals who comprise those classes... (It) is conventionally presented as *the* expression of working class educational aims, as if it summed up the wisdom and experience of the class. In fact like most other political ideologies, it achieved its dominance only after successfully contesting other objectives and strategies. It became the decisive — almost the sole — influence on Labour Party policy in the 1920s (p. 52).

Jones' general point about the effect of this victory for the concept of equality of opportunity is that it blunted radical working-class educational aspirations and replaced them with individual educational aspirations which proved divisive:

> It not only discourages any attempt to define educational purpose in terms of the advancement of the class as a whole, but also fosters a positive hostility between individual educational betterment and collective advance (p. 52).

Now the claim of equality of opportunity centred on its ability to promote justice, harmony and efficiency. As such, the crucial issue on which its legitimacy turned revolved around working-class access to middle-class education. The class structure would remain and so would the structure of knowledge which helped to keep it in place but individuals would have the opportunity to move from one class location to another. In contrast, the claims of a working-class education centred on the issue of popular control and the content of education.[5] There was a belief that working-class education should be fundamentally different from that of other classes since it should be directed toward the development of a socialist consciousness, and thereby the eradication of the class structure.

Although the struggle between these competing conceptions of socialist education left 'equality of opportunity' triumphant, the inherent contradiction between this concept and the maintenance of the class structure did not escape socialist contemporaries at the time[6] nor did the potential divisiveness of policies centred on equality of opportunity. The question, then, that needs to be asked is how an essentially individualistic liberal notion, that was inherently contradictory, came to be adopted by the Labour Party. To answer it we need to look more closely at the nature of the passive revolution and the influence of 'new' liberal thought upon it.

Hall and Schwarz characterize the period between 1880 and 1930 as a passive revolution, taking the term from Gramsci (1971). For the latter, a passive revolution was one 'installed from above in order to forestall a threat from below'.[7] Such revolutions mark an important re-ordering of the state and civil society as a means of re-establishing the social relations of production on a more secure base. British capitalism, during this period, was undergoing a crisis due to a reluctance to change to modern forms of production, and to exploit new markets. The net result was that capital investment flowed out of the domestic economy into foreign investments, causing a decline in profitability. Socially this crisis was marked by increasing unrest with pressure for democratic representation mounting from women and the working class.

In ideological terms this intense pressure for change, and in particular democratic representation, was answered by a thorough revamping of liberal thought. Its *laissez-faire* variety which emphasized the need to minimize state intervention and thereby maximize individual freedom gave way to a more social understanding of the relationship of the individual to society. In Freeden's words:

> Liberalism was still concerned with the optimal expression and development of the individual, but this was obtainable by reflecting the scientific and ethical truth that man could only realise himself in a community, rather than through a human organisation tending towards theoretical anarchy. A new trust emerged in social action via the state — not as a necessary evil but as the just and right way of attaining human ends (1978, p. 257).

In all the 'new' liberalism aimed for a delicate balance between production and consumption, wealth and welfare, quantity and quality. The intention was to promote equality of opportunity and dignity but it was given little practical systematic expression. State intervention was based on a utilitarian 'numerical approach to happiness'[8] which produced piecemeal reforms which had no coherent underlying rationale except that of the empirical identification of 'need'.

In part this untheorized approach was a function of the concept of citizenship that the 'new' liberals adopted. In general, their aim was to enable citizens to participate in society at the level required to maintain human dignity. They assumed that a common culture would develop on this basis resulting in increased fraternity or respect for persons. In practice this created a weak concept of citizenship because 'participation in society' was judged against an abstracted notion of dignity. This meant that the state's responsibility for welfare support did not extend far beyond protection from absolute poverty. In turn this prompted a piecemeal approach to welfare provision based on the identification of needy groups and individuals who had slipped through the net.

However, this concept of citizenship was further vitiated by some 'old' liberal assumptions which sat uneasily alongside the optimism of the 'new' liberal doctrines. The conflict between self-interested pragmatism and the hope of social solidarity was nowhere more apparent than in the assumption that a common culture could be generated in spite of massive disparities in wealth and status[9]. By the same token, the social and ethical justification for state intervention had to be leavened with the argument that welfare provisions would create a healthier and more productive workforce. Freeden notes that:

> The age was, however, also one in which efficiency had a magic ring... Even for liberals who perceived the dangerous undertones of this doctrine, it was convenient to demonstrate that their social philosophy could also... score on this account and meet the test of 'business' considerations (pp. 240).

As a result of these weaknesses inherent in the concept of citizenship, the 'new' liberal theory of social provision amounted to an attempt to use the state to mediate between a near anarchic individualism and the social discord it threatened.

In contrast, in some Western societies, notably Sweden and France, the role of the state in welfare provision was seen quite differently. In these societies as, Ashford (1986) notes:

> Social policies were not simply governmental functions, but efforts to enhance the participatory vitality of ... politics, to create new associational links, and to enable the less privileged to become fully active, responsible members of society (p. 309).

Implicit in Sweden's welfare policy, for example, were two additional links between the individual and society which created a far stronger concept of citizenship. Firstly, welfare provision was tied directly to the notion of democracy; the aim was not so much to enable human dignity *per se* but to allow its expression in democratic participation. Secondly, it was appreciated that social solidarity depended on more than the hope of a common culture; in particular, it rested on wage solidarity. Central to this idea was the concept of the social wage which provided security and sustenance for wage labourers as a guarantee against the risks of being unemployed in a market economy.

Similarly, the social wage was considered essential to the labour movement as a whole since the unity of the movement could be threatened by the unemployed if they didn't receive an adequate social wage to compensate for their loss of income. The concept of wage solidarity, then, represented the essence of a socialist welfare state because it decommodified wage labour, and provided universal entitlements on the basis of the redistribution of wealth.[10]

In other words, citizenship on this model implied far more than providing minimal support in the hope that this would realize a common culture and respect for persons; it involved a set of conceptual and policy links which attempted to come to terms with the problems capitalism posed for wage earners. For it was assumed that it was only with the security of a social wage, access to universal benefits and the redistribution of wealth that genuine democratic participation would be possible. The difference between this model of citizenship and that developed in Britain is summed up by Ashford when he says that in the cases of Sweden and France the development of a comprehensive social policy was based on the assumptions of social radicalism whereas in the British case social policy was predicated on the 'old' liberal assumption of radical individualism.

One reason why welfare provision in Britain was not directly related to the demands of democracy was that both the new liberals and dominant Labour Party theorists were pragmatic and anti-democratic. Halevy wrote of the disinterested Machiavellianism of British social policy,[11] while Milliband (1961) has remarked of the early Labour parliamentarians:

> whether orthodox or otherwise (they) had little need to engage in

what was in any case for most of them the highly uncongenial task of theoretical debate (p. 33).

Given the gap created by the lack of distinctive socialist theoretical work done within the Labour Party the damage-limitation exercise of the 'new' liberalism was simply continued by Labour.[12] Indeed the dominant Fabian thinking which emerged within the Labour Party was both statist and elitist (Ashford, 1986)

The achievements of the passive revolution should not be underestimated: the franchize was extended, widespread welfare provisions were initiated and in education, the slogan of equal opportunities helped to establish secondary schooling for the working class. However, the price of these reforms was capitalism's continuing dominance and as a result class still determined opportunities and decision-making remained elitist. Labour had played its part in the passive revolution to make important gains but they carried the seeds of their own destruction.

The Legacy of the Passive Revolution in the Comprehensive Reforms of the 1960s

The destructive legacy of the passive revolution on the Labour Party is nowhere more apparent than in the comprehensive educational reforms of the 1960s and early 1970s. For some in the Labour Party the shift from the tripartite system to comprehensivization signalled the beginning of the end of the class structure which had persisted despite the formal opportunities afforded by the extension of secondary schooling. Moreover, the promise held out by comprehensive reorganization was endorsed by the massive expansion of the tertiary sector. Now working-class students would have genuine opportunities to work their way up the educational ladder and into professional and managerial occupations. However, it seems clear that comprehensive reorganization was at best a partial success.[13] In the first place, not all local authorities abolished the tripartite system and, more significantly, private schooling remained. This meant that not all children had access to the same resources and hence opportunities.

The second way in which comprehensivization can be seen as a partial reform takes us to the heart of socialist debate about education because insofar as a vision of schooling was implemented it represented a particular strand of socialism: one which had its roots in the passive revolution and which owed as much to the 'new liberalism' of that period as it did to anything distinctively socialist.

Central to this 'socialist' vision of comprehensive schooling, which has been most closely associated with Tony Crosland, were two aims: the use of schools to promote equality of opportunity and the promotion of citizenship. Within this vision equality of opportunity assumed double significance; on the one hand it worked as a social principle of fairness, on the other it operated as an efficiency principle. The 1960s were the time of Wilson's 'white hot technological revolution' in which Britain was to be dragged kicking and screaming into the twentieth century. This was to be done by creating a meritocracy which would abolish the privileges of class.

Underlying this view was the notion that Britain's relatively poor economic performance was, at least in part, a function of class: that class prohibited the most talented people from reaching the positions of leadership necessary to promote adequate levels of economic growth. Associated with this idea were three others; the first was the assumption that in a technologically-driven meritocracy all jobs would be upgraded, requiring a higher level of skilled performance and hence education. This led directly to the second assumption — that education, particularly at the tertiary level, required expanding so that the work force could be better trained to meet the demands of the new technological society. The third assumption concerned the nature of class which was quite clearly described by Crosland (1964) in the following:

> The second distinctive socialist ideal is social equality and, the classless society. The socialist seeks a distribution of rewards, status and privileges egalitarian enough to minimize social resentment, to secure justice between individuals, and to equalize opportunities; and he seeks to weaken the existing deep-seated class stratification, with its concomitant feelings of envy and inferiority, and its barriers to uninhibited minglings between the classes (p. 77).

The assumption here is that 'the classless society' is in fact an unequal society resting on a vertical continuum or ladder which people can freely ascend or descend depending on merit, which in turn is determined by individual ability and effort. Class in this view comprises a set of mental attitudes and a way of life which can be weakened by 'minglings between the classes'.

In this view education has a central role to play: it is effectively the motor of economic growth because it produces an increasingly educated work force, necessary to the demands of a technologically-oriented economy and it distributes individuals into the appropriate positions within the economy according to the most rational criterion — merit. Given this view, what does socialist schooling amount to? Essentially it involves equal access to the same opportunities; it does not mean that all students should have access to the same curriculum as such, but that they should have equal rights of access to the curriculum relevant to their ability levels. Indeed, Crosland thought that streaming was necessary if schools were to achieve the aims consistent with his wider view of society. Accordingly, the goals of citizenship and of promoting a common culture were reduced, as the quote above suggests, to softening the social resentment caused by selection and streaming. It was, perhaps, Harold Wilson who best encapsulated the aims of the comprehensive reforms when he said that with comprehensivization every child would have access to a grammar school education.

But the problem with Crosland's social-democratic view of the school–society relationship is that experience and research suggest it is mistaken on almost every count. There has certainly been a technological revolution but it has not meant that all jobs have been upgraded. While it is true that blue-collar jobs are diminishing there are many white-collar jobs that have been de-skilled as a result of the new technology (Wood, 1982). It has also proved naive to believe that economic performance rests on individuals' abilities and skills (Berner, 1974; Bowles and Gintis, 1975). The plain fact is that the current economic crisis is a function of the major changes occurring in the capitalist world economy (Armstrong et al., 1984) and the root cause of the crisis has to be located at a systems not an individual level. When we come to the role of education it is now clear that the social-democratic view of class which locates class in the attitudes and aspirations of individuals is untenable. Schools have not been able to boost the life-chances of working-class students in the numbers consistent with a near meritocracy (Halsey et al., 1980).[14] While there is some evidence that comprehensive reorganization has boosted the life-chances of some working-class students (McPherson and Willms, 1987), contrary to the claims of the popular press, it now seems clear that class needs to be understood as a systematic structure generated by the power relations of production and the labour market (Giddens and McKenzie, 1982): a structure which implicates schooling in the inequalities it produces. Perhaps the period of reform and experimentation which characterized the 1960s and early 1970s and which failed to live up to expectations was best characterized by Halsey (1972) when he said:

> In summary... liberal policies failed basically on an inadequate theory of learning. They failed to notice that the major determinants of educational attainment were not schoolmasters but social situations, not curriculum but motivation, not formal access to the school, but support in the family and the community (p. 8)[15]

When we look behind the relative failure of comprehensive reform we find the ghost of the 'new' liberalism lurking. The aim of equality of opportunity was quintessentially liberal in its emphasis on the promotion of individuals' life-chances; particularly since the latter could be calculated by studies of origins and destinations which exemplified the 'numerical approach to happiness'.[16] Similarly, the aims of citizenship and social solidarity could only be interpreted in a weak liberal sense because they were embedded in an elitist and hierarchical view of society: one which was reflected in the internal organization of comprehensive schools. Consistent with the school organization was a liberal humanist curriculum governed by the demands of the universities.[17] Finally, the developing professional ideology of teachers considered them 'experts' which legitimized their exclusive control over the curriculum and pedagogy.[18]

In what sense were the liberal assumptions underlying this model of comprehensive schooling so flawed that they sabotaged it? The question can best be answered in the light of the Thatcherite attack on education because it has so ruthlessly exposed the weakness of these assumptions. There are three prongs to this attack. Comprehensives have failed to increase equality of opportunity; they have failed to maintain standards; and they have been unresponsive to popular aspirations regarding education. From a socialist perspective comprehensives were vulnerable to these charges because they accepted liberal aims — equality of opportunity, 'academic' excellence — and methods, rather than developing their own.

An alternative socialist education would have stressed the aim of education for democratic citizenship with quite different, although equally high, standards. Such an aim would have involved democratic participation by parents and students and, the notion of equality of opportunity would have been understood quite differently: as the eradication of educational privilege through the abolition of private schools and a commitment to positive discrimination for the working class, ethnic minorities and women. Arguably an education based on these radical democratic foundations would have commanded greater support amongst parents and students, particularly during the past five years when teachers have attempted to defend state education from the worst excesses of Thatcherism.

This section began by examining the roots of the comprehensive education crisis in the passive revolution. But if the news for state education, to date, has been nearly all bad then it is appropriate to end this section with an observation which carries some hope. If we began this century with the economic restructuring which triggered the passive revolution then it is clear we are now in the midst of another economic restructuring and an accompanying social revolution. It is a time of crisis for the Left but out of it can come a radical rethinking of socialist aims and policies with respect to democracy, welfare provision and education. This would involve jettisoning the legacy of 'new' liberal thought and developing an alternative radical democratic agenda.

Before sketching out what this would mean for education we need to examine the plausibility of such a programme in the light of some recent neo-Marxist theories of education. These theories have issued a fundamental challenge to the idea that socialist policy-making is worthwhile in a capitalist society and, in part, can be held responsible for the failure of social theorists of education to inform left-wing policy-making. What such a critical examination will allow us to do is to appraise the limits and possibilities of a radical democratic education which must exist in a capitalist world while pointing in the direction of socialism.

In 1976 Bowles and Gintis published *Schooling in Capitalist America*, the first sustained Marxist treatize on education. It comprized a systematic 'refutation' of the liberal view and argued that it is the capitalist mode of production which determines the nature and outcomes of schooling. At the time it provided an alternative theory of education to that espoused by

Crosland, which explained the failure of the comprehensive reforms to equalize life chances. The centre piece of their argument is the notion of correspondence between education and work under capitalism. As they put it:

> The educational system helps integrate youth into the economic system... through a structural correspondence between its social relations and those of production. The structure of social relations in education not only inures the student to the discipline of the work place, but develops the types of personal demeanour, modes of self presentation, self image, and social class identifications which are the crucial ingredients of job adequacy (1976, p. 131).

What, in effect, they are doing here is applying the classical Marxist base/superstructure metaphor to education. As a consequence they argue that education cannot be changed and cannot act as a force for change until the social relations of capitalist production have been overthrown.

Since 1976 this version of Marxist theory has been influential in sociology of education, although it has undergone change and refinement. Working within the original model Harris (1979) and Sharp (1980) have tried to locate knowledge, ideology and language as responses to the needs of capital, while Gintis and Bowles (1980) and Carnoy and Levin (1985) have sought to theorize change in terms of contradictions between education and the economic base and the resistance they produce. An example of this latter thinking is provided by Carnoy and Levin when they argue:

> Schools must produce workers who meet the needs of capitalist production. This means developing workers with appropriate cognitive and vocational skills... with behaviours, habits and values predisposing them to the organization of capitalist production...

> However, at the same time the schools are charged with producing citizens who know and care about democratic rights and equal opportunity... The result is that schools generate a range of functions that contradict the efficient reproduction of capitalist workers (1985, p. 147-8).

A more sophisticated analysis which sees culture as a crucial intervening variable within this functionalist approach was initiated by Willis (1977) and developed by Apple (1982a) and Giroux (1983). Apple's (1982a) chapter 'Curricular form and the logic of technical control: building the possessive individual' is important because it provides a good example of the way cultural analysis can be used within the correspondence paradigm to provide a sophisticated explanation of the role of schooling in the creation of subjects necessary for corporate capitalist production *and* consumption. Here he argues that the increasing technical control of the curriculum in American schools has the effect of producing the 'possessive individual' of corporate capitalism: one who is isolated from social interaction with others and who acquires thereby the necessary traits and orientations for the current processes of production and consumption.[19]

Although the lineage of cultural analysts from Willis through Apple to Giroux eschew the simple base/superstructure model espoused by Bowles and Gintis and stress the creative capacity for resistance that oppositional cultures can provide, they accept a central tenet of the problematic generated by the original correspondence theory: namely that schools purvey the dominant culture, Apple's analysis being but one example of this. The overall tenor of the theory is captured by Giroux when he says:

> dominant ideologies are not simply transmitted in schools, nor are they practised in a void. On the contrary, they are often met with resistance by teachers, students, or parents, and must therefore, to be successful, repress the production of counter-ideologies. Moreover, schools are not simply static institutions that reproduce the dominant ideology, they are active agents in their construction as well (1983, p. 91).

In one way this statement takes us a considerable distance from Bowles and Gintis' original formulation because it captures the dynamics of what is taught, suppressed and resisted; in another it takes us no further because it is assumed both that schools exist to reproduce the dominant ideology and that the dominant ideology corresponds to the needs of capital. Consequently the theoretical space for relative autonomy in education is confined to the localized resistance that students are teachers may put up.

Yet there are a number of reasons why we should consider rejecting such a model. At the general level it ignores important differences between various types of schooling under capitalism. For example, Sweden has a system for schooling which appears quite consistent with socialist aspirations, as Ball has shown (in this volume). Moreover, it is also clear that economic crisis and restructuring have impacted differently in different societies depending on the place of education within specific political cultures.

What these differences in the relationship of education to the economy suggest is that education as a system should be seen as more autonomous than radical sociologists have claimed. In this context Moore (1988) has argued that Bowles and Gintis' analysis confuses social relations of production with social relationships within production. Consequently they fail to take into account the fact that the formal education system is fundamentally concerned with *knowledge production* with its own assumptions, rules and aims. Looked at in this way the mode of knowledge production is, as Bourdieu (1977) has suggested, an historical and arbitrary product in relation to the interests of capital. As such, interests and alliances have to be created with respect to the nature and aims of knowledge production and the classes it comes to serve: there is no automatic connection between schooling and the capitalist mode of production nor are the dominant ideologies of knowledge production necessarily consistent with the dominant ideologies of capital. Hence Moore glosses recent Thatcherite initiatives in education as part of an '*ideology of production regulating education* rather than an *educational ideology servicing production*'.[20]

The differences between the assumptions underlying commodity and knowledge production can be seen if we look at the view of knowledge and human nature presupposed by the two forms of production. Capitalist production uses knowledge to enhance the development of technology; it is therefore primarily interested in an epistemology which helps to predict observable outcomes (i.e., empiricism). Its psychology is behaviourist in that it is concerned to measure and price skilled human performances for the labour market; and it regards human nature as fundamentally directed toward the pursuit of self-interest which means the pursuit of the extrinsic rewards of wealth, status and power — the possessive individual.

In contrast, it is typically only in some sectors of tertiary education that empiricism reigns as a theory of knowledge, albeit powerfully in the natural and social sciences. Within secondary education and parts of tertiary education the guiding epistemological assumptions are those of a rationalist-objectivism of the kind advanced in the forms of knowledge thesis by Paul Hirst and other members of the 'London School' of philosophers of education.[21] In this view knowledge is divided into distinct forms such as mathematics, the natural sciences, history etc., and it assumes that individuals are cultural initiates into these forms: the argument being that one could only become a 'rational man' (*sic*) by learning to see the world through the unique perspective the various forms of knowledge provide.

In the primary school the dominant epistemology and view of human nature is again different. Here, there is a genetic epistemology, often associated with Piaget, which adopts as its central educational metaphor the notion of 'growth'.[22] This translates into a view of the curriculum as a seamless web of knowledge in which childrens' intellectual growth occurs through the pursuit of cognitive interests.

These varying assumptions about knowledge and the way humans learn produces different pedagogies: it is not difficult to see how the forms of knowledge thesis leads to strong subject boundaries and teacher-initiated learning, while in contrast, the idea of growth and the associated notion of a seamless web of knowledge create a curriculum with weak subject boundaries and pupil-initiated learning. What is difficult from a correspondence theorist's point of view is to explain either the intention or the practice of these diverse pedagogies as corresponding to the needs of capital.

In fact, they don't try. Rather, they employ a general strategy of dismissing the founding assumptions of educational practice and the pedagogies they generate by arguing that they have little causal impact on the minds and life-chances of individuals. Hence they argue for one or both of the following positions. The content of schooling is irrelevant and it is the form which helps in shaping student's destinies. For example, Bowles and

Gintis (1976) and Carnoy and Levin (1985) argue that it is the hierarchical and authoritarian structures of schooling that determine the dispositions and attitudes of students. While more subtly Willis (1977) argues that it is the commodified form credentials take which determine students' response to schooling. Alternatively it is argued that content is important but it is that of the hidden curriculum which is decisive in shaping perceptions (Apple, 1979; Giroux, 1983). However, it can be argued that what, in fact, is most decisive is the formal or overt curriculum because it creates the divisions by which middle-class students gain and working-class students lose.[23] What, then, needs to be explained is how arbitrary knowledge structures come to be related to specific class interests. It is, surely, a major omission in the sociology of education that we have no plausible theory of the relationship of knowledge production and pedagogy to class interest: a lacuna created, in part, by the influence of the correspondence paradigm.

All we have at the present time is Bourdieu's (1977) theory which shows how what he calls fractions of the middle class, have used the culturally arbitrary nature of the academic curriculum to exert symbolic violence in the pursuit of class interests, and Bernstein's (1977) more speculative but highly suggestive paper, where he attempts to make the connection between the development of the progressive primary curriculum and the interests of elements of the middle class.[24] Yet neither theorist really elaborates the question of how a particular form of knowledge production comes to be related to the professional self-interest of educators nor how that self interest comes to be generalized to a particular class or class fraction.[25] But when we consider the nature of the assumptions underlying knowledge production and pedagogy one point stands out clearly: the aims of education are largely intrinsic to the interests of the educational process itself and the privileges it has constructed rather than servicing capitalist production.

This becomes most apparent when we look at credentials as the linkage between education and the labour market. The fact is that the traditional certificates of CSEs, O-levels, A-levels and degrees make far more sense as internal screening devices by which academics and teachers are chosen than they do as sources of information for employers about specific skills. It is surely for this reason that the MSC has adopted behaviourist-oriented skills programmes by which its clients can be more accurately assessed by employers.[26]

In sum, the aim of primary and secondary schools has been to produce personal growth or provide an initiation into rationality rather than create the possessive individual. Consequently much of education's power and autonomy has centred on the liberal ideology of personal development. It is precisely for this reason that the main thrust of the Thatcherite assault on education has been concerned to wrench it into line with what are perceived to be the demands of capital. However, an unintended consequence of the pedagogy designed to meet these liberal aims is that education has systematically discriminated against working-class students, women and racial minorities.

Underlying the difference between the correspondence theorists and the alternative view being advanced here is a fundamentally different conception of the relationship of education to the economic base. In the correspondence theory it is assumed that there is a necessary connection between the economic base and education. In terms of the present economic crisis, then, a reduction in educational expenditure, the proletarianization of teachers and greater control of the curriculum are all seen as necessary, hence inevitable, political responses to the needs of the emerging phase of capitalism.

In the alternative Gramscian view I am arguing for, the 'correspondence' between economic base, civil society and state is always contingent and a matter of political and ideological struggle. For Gramsci (1971), 'correspondence' is created by the political formation of historic blocs,[27] of which Thatcherism's present dominance is an example. In this view whether there is a reduction in educational expenditure and teachers are proletarianized is a matter of political struggle (Grace, 1987; Lauder and Yee, 1987). The outcome is not a foregone conclusion. Similarly, because there is no direct connection between the assumptions underlying knowledge production and the economic base, the nature of the curriculum will not be predetermined by economic interests but will be the result of class conflict and compromise. In this respect it is worth pointing out that correspondence theorists will find it difficult to theorize the changes in content to the curriculum that are currently being made through the Technical and Vocational Education Initiative (TVEI), City Technology Colleges (CTC) and the Manpower Services Commission (MSC) initiatives precisely because they regard the content of the overt curriculum as epiphenomenal. However, in the Gramscian view being defended here, such changes are explicable in terms of class conflict over the autonomy and privilege that a liberal education accords the middle class and, in so far as this implies a return to selectivity, an attack on working-class opportunities.

There is a further important difference between the correspondence and Gramscian views. For the former, change in education is meaningless independent of change in the economic base. Consequently, the practical imperative of the correspondence theory is for revolutionary change to capitalist social relations of production. In the writing of correspondence theorists this has boiled down to a set of abstract appeals for resistance on the flimsy basis of the resistance to schooling shown by some working-class youths (Lauder et al., 1986).[28] In the alternative democratic-socialist view, the fact that changes between the economic base and the wider society are seen as contingent, the outcome of political struggle, implies that political and indeed policy interventions are worthwhile.[29] The task, therefore, is to develop policies which can create an alternative historic bloc to Thatcherism. In education this means the creation of policies for a new settlement which will overcome the divisive agenda now being enacted.

So far, this paper has been concerned with a ground-clearing exercise, looking at the problems socialist traditions have created for themselves in education and the general ways in which we can learn from their mistakes. In what follows, I want to sketch a framework for the democratization of education according to the participatory principle that anyone affected by a decision should have a say in its making. It has been part of the argument of this paper that the liberal influence on socialist policy-making has blinded socialists to the connection between equality and participatory democracy.[30] In a phrase, democracy is the antidote to inequality because it has the potential for creating a way of life which breaks down the dominance structure and the psycho-social attributes associated with class, gender and racial exploitation.

Towards Democracy in Education

One of the consequences of the correspondence theory has been that the critique of capitalist schooling has failed to show how schools — especially working-class schools — may be improved in ways consistent with socialist principles. For too long radical sociologists of education have ignored the experience of working-class students (Brown, 1987) concentrating on their objective potential as revolutionary agents rather than considering how their aspirations for good quality schooling can be satisfied. From a democratic-socialist perspective this has proved damaging on two counts. Firstly, withdrawal from policy-making has, as we now know to our cost, left the field open for the new Right to advance virtually unopposed. Secondly, the way socialist gains are made in a capitalist world is by examples of good socialist practice: the imperative is to develop socialism by starting from the aspirations and concerns of working-class people and showing how socialist practices can speak to their aspirations.[31] In education this means addressing the question of good working-class schooling because it is now generally recognized that the comprehensive restructuring of the 1960s failed to address this issue in an adequate way. The arguments and proposals for democratic education that I want to advance have as their initial focus a curriculum for working-class schools. However, for reasons, which will become apparent, I also think these proposals should be applicable to all secondary schooling.

In thinking about developing a democratic curriculum the essential imperative of the new realism is to turn the spaces and tendencies generated by the economic crisis and Thatcherite policies to good purpose. There are two recent developments that are particularly relevant in this context: the removal of the hegemony of the academic curriculum from the upper school and the emphasis on the importance of work experience to education.[32] These changes allow for the possibility of a curriculum which is the antithesis of the academic curriculum — integrated rather than subject-bound, democratic instead of hierarchical, work-related rather than patrician in outlook, yet intellectually rigorous. The aim is to equip individuals with the relevant technical and political understandings to become fully participating citizens in a democracy. But as we shall see the concept of citizenship used here is far stronger than that implied by Crosland's theory.

Such a curriculum should be based on the following foundations: democracy, solidarity or fraternity, critical self-understanding, equality of necessary skills and an integrated curriculum relevant to working-class experiences. (For a complimentary but different treatment of some of these concepts see the chapter by Fielding). Since democracy is the most important aspect of these foundations, it is this with which I shall begin.

Democracy

Citizenship, underwritten by the principle of participatory democracy is clearly a stronger concept of citizenship than that which informed comprehensive reorganization in the 1960s because, here, equal power rather than a faith in inter-class 'mingling' provides the basis for social solidarity *and* equality. We can grasp the significance of the importance of democracy to equality and social solidarity in a concrete way if we reflect on a major aspect of the 'problem' of working-class schooling — the difficulty working-class pupils have in coming to terms with the middle-class ethos of the school. As Brown pointed out in the preceding chapter, working-class pupils make a series of tenuous accommodations with a situation in which they can feel foreign and alienated.

A solution to this problem is to provide working-class pupils with the power to act on the school according to the principles of participatory democracy. This would enable them to have a genuine say in what happens to them in school, thereby reducing their alienation and, correspondingly, creating a commitment to education. In turn, the commitment to education would generate an important element in the equalizing of working-class life-chances.[33]

There is a distinction, drawn by White (1986), between self-esteem and self-respect which I think is salient here. The former concept refers to a psychological state in which one has a good opinion of oneself and is confident about one's abilities, while the latter concept is tied into the social and institutional structures which order our lives:

> The democratic conception of self-respect ... is based on a conception of oneself as a moral person with certain moral rights, one of which is to be treated as an equal, and moral duties, with responsibilities for one's actions ... if an authority structure is to be morally acceptable, it must foster people's self-respect, not diminish it or worse (p. 97).

To bring this distinction alive and to show how vitally important it is in educational terms let us consider that, by now infamous group, Willis' lads. They have considerable self-esteem created by their use of others as objects for their self-aggrandizement and their street-wise knowledge of the way the world 'really' works. But equally they don't have self-respect in White's terms because they don't treat themselves or others as moral persons with equal rights. They have power which has been conferred by the breakdown of social solidarity, in part created by the authoritarian school structure in which they refuse to acknowledge their 'place' because it is meaningless to them. To accept 'their place' in an alien and authoritarian school structure would be, precisely, to render themselves impotent — and so they resist what they see as the oppressive demands of the school to preserve their self-esteem.

What the lads represent is a breakdown of social order based on hierarchical authority structures which fail to promote self-respect, since they provide neither the power nor the responsibility which would enable the lads to exercise some say in how their lives are ordered. What White's democratic conception of self-respect points to is a new form of social solidarity, both within schools and the wider society, based on genuine democracy and equality. In the educational context this implies a participatory democratic form of school organization (White, 1983) and a curriculum which is negotiated.

Solidarity

In using the term 'solidarity' I mean what has previously been referred to in the philosophical literature as 'fraternity'. However, as a number of commentators have pointed out, the latter has sexist connotations and following Halsey (1986) I prefer to use the term solidarity.

Enough has already been said about the necessity of basing solidarity — the attitudes necessary for civilized living such as tolerance, fairness and the ability to see another's point of view — on the principles of participatory democracy. However, in the educational context the connection between solidarity and democracy assumes a specific importance in relation to learning. This is because there is evidence to suggest that the dominance structures of class, race and patriarchy create a micro-politics of learning which works through the peer group determining learning outcomes (Lauder and Khan, 1988). There is also evidence that students learn better in groups rather than individually.[34] As such there are good arguments for organizing learning in terms of democratic group practices. But, of course, democratic arrangements for learning are not sufficient; the virtues associated with solidarity are necessary if groups are to work effectively. Arguably, it is also through group interaction that such virtues can be learnt.

Hugh Lauder

Critical Self-understanding

If democracy and solidarity refer to the organization of power, the principles of interaction and the qualities needed to make them work, then critical self-understanding refers to an important aspect of *content* in the formal and hidden curriculum. In particular, the concern here is to expose students to theories which enable them to see the world as *socially* constructed rather than natural and therefore immutable. The aim is to get them to think critically about their own circumstances and the ways in which their situation can be changed. This means exposing them to theories of class, race and gender inequalities and the effects they have on people's lives.

'Critical reflection' has become one of the most over used phrases in the radical lexicon and something needs to be said about the context in which it is being employed here. In an interesting article, Bowers (1984) has argued that neo-Marxist educators have espoused a form of radical individualism in connection with the concept of critical reflection. More specifically, he shows how the advocacy of critical reflection as a basis for political practice, in the work of Friere, Giroux and Harris, trades on the assumption of liberal individualism, for these authors take it as read that the locus of authority for action resides in the authenticity of the individual who is opposed to a culture which is seen as oppressive. In noting this point Bowers raises some important issues that have yet to be adequately examined by neo-Marxist educationists. As he puts it:

> It is possible to view the dichotomous thinking that pits the individual (always a source of virtue) against the authority of culture (generally viewed as dehumanising and oppressive) as growing out of the necessity not to equivocate about social justice issues ... (but) the advocates of consciousness-raising fail to consider how the authority of the individual must be limited if community is to exist. It is this silence that raises the question of cultural nihilism (p. 387).

Bowers' observations raise more issues than can be addressed in this chapter; however, there are some points worth making here. The solidarity created by traditional working-class ways of living has been 'deconstructed' by gender, ethnic and regional divisions thereby presenting capital with greater opportunities for exploitation. Given the differences which now exist in cultural outlook and expectations between various working-class groups it is, conceivably, only through participatory democratic mechanisms that the shared interests of workers can be expressed.[35] As such, 'critical reflection' needs to be taken out of the institutional and cultural vacuum it is so often situated in, by correspondence theorists, and placed in a democratic participatory context — be it within the trade union movement or the schools.[36] In this way critical reflection would be confronted by the demands of diverse cultural perspectives and the practical imperatives set by specific contexts. Moreover, the constraints imposed by the rules of participatory democracy would provide the authority and discipline necessary to promote *social* rather than individual change. In this sense, democratic mechanisms would be used to recreate social solidarity out of the fragmenting forces of radical individualism and pluralism giving critical reflection a practical context in which to operate.

An Integrated Curriculum

The fundamental concern of the curriculum being outlined is to impart basic skills and critical understandings which are relevant to working-class experience. This begs the question of pluralism raised above. However, one way in which critical self-understanding must involve a common set of concerns is in relation to fundamental human problems such as poverty, the exploitation of the eco-system, peace and various forms of oppression (see Lacey in this volume). One aim of this curriculum is to show how the individual, as a member of a group, is implicated in these human problems. In the liberal–rationalist subject-oriented curriculum many of the conceptual connections that need to be made so that students can gain an holistic understanding of themselves in relation to fundamental human problems, are either not made or taught haphazardly. But the justification for teaching subjects rather than in an interdisciplinary way rests on epistemological assumptions like those articulated in the forms of knowledge thesis (see Hirst, 1965, 1974). That thesis has now been strongly challenged[37] and it is generally recognized that we come to understand the world through global theories or paradigms which frequently cut across subject boundaries.[38] One implication of this latter position is that conventional academic subjects are just that — historical creations rather than 'mirrors of nature'.[39]

Once we accept there are no epistemological considerations against an integrated curriculum there are two further arguments we can mount in its favour with respect to working-class education. Firstly, it obviates the social labelling which transforms a strongly subject-bound curriculum into a hierarchy in which 'academic' male-tagged subjects are at the top and 'non-academic' female-tagged subjects at the bottom. Secondly, an integrated curriculum reflects thought processes which more often than not cross subject boundaries. To remove the latter is, therefore, to remove artificial barriers, which middle-class students may have been socialized into understanding but working-class pupils have not.[40]

In addition, it seems important that the integrated curriculum is approached through project work. There are two reasons for this: if the curriculum is broken down into modules or projects this would enable working-class students, who have not been socialized into the rules of the academic 'game', to see the *point* of what they are doing. Furthermore, many of the understandings and skills necessary for good quality reasoning are not explicitly taught within the traditional curriculum; encouraging project work would help working-class students to utilize resources like libraries, museums and other sources of information and evidence. In turn, the development of their own projects would allow students to consider how knowledge fits together to create a theory or 'story' which has explanatory power. At the same time they would learn that the reasoning methods taught in school can be applied to the world outside; in short, they would learn how to connect their everyday world to wider social and political movements, particularly if their project work was related, in a critical sense, to work experience.

Equality of Skills

Clearly there are competencies that must be taught if students are to become citizens in a democratic society. These include: literacy, numeracy, computer awareness and the few techniques that can be taught to aid effective negotiation. The fact is that unless these skills are learned, working-class students will be under a severe handicap in relation to their middle-class counterparts — both in terms of access to work and in their ability to organize socially and politically. It is, perhaps, a mark of the new realism of the 1980s that such a list and the rationale for it seems unexceptionable and requires no futher comment.

Conclusion

The curriculum foundation outlined above is designed to achieve what liberal theories of schooling have not been able to do successfully, to link democracy and equality to create a new form of solidarity, based on principles of social justice. In arguing for a curriculum of this kind, I am aware of the immense difficulties involved in attempting to implement it, particularly in working-class schools, where pupils know they are likely to be confronted by unemployment and where, consequently, democracy is likely to be seen as irrelevant in a harsh world. But the problems of unemployment and alienation merely give point to the need to develop a systematic approach to welfare provision based on the strong concept of citizenship argued for in this paper: education cannot provide answers on its own. The curriculum I propose above must not be treated as an isolated initiative — a band-aid for working-class schools — because it courts the danger of becoming a deeply conservative, rather than radical initiative.

If we see this curriculum as solely for working-class schools, we are once again confronted with the same dilemma that faced socialists at the turn of the century: either to continue with the present subject-bound credential-led curriculum in order to promote a few working-class students out of their class at the expense of the many, or to reject the individualist ethic of this curriculum and develop an alternative working-class education along the lines of the integrated curriculum suggested above. The socialist response then, as Jones (1983) points out, was in favour of a working-class education and there are grounds for arguing the same case now. After all, it seems far more defensible to provide an alternative education which creates a sense of community solidarity and an understanding that knowledge is indispensable to power than continuing with a system which is being designed to foreclose on the life-chances of working-class youth (see Brown in this volume). To advocate an alternative working-class education is to translate the new Right's sloganizing about self-reliance into socialist terms, for a policy of this kind would rely heavily on the resources of working-class communities.

However, there are at least two problems with this course of action: it may be rejected by working-class communities because if there is anything we have learnt from the Thatcher years it is that the working class is far from homogeneous. Clearly some working-class groups see themselves, rightly or wrongly, as having greater opportunity than others, within the present education system. They may, therefore, reject a curriculum which prevents their children participating in the credential race. Equally disturbing is the possibility that an alternative curriculum of this kind could ghettoize working-class people, creating a second-class citizenry through a process Conservatives like Bantock would approve of. The crucial role in this rests with teachers and their communities and what together they consider valid *curriculum* knowledge. Unless they are prepared to teach the theory and practice of democratic politics a curriculum of this kind will lose its bite and end up merely as pacifying working-class frustrations.

The choices here are unenviable. To advocate a policy of implementing such a curriculum throughout working-class schools courts the risk of creating resentment among some working class people. However, failure to implement it means that many working-class students will leave school rejecting the valuable sources of knowledge schools have to offer. It seems to me that in an era of radical individualism and pluralism these choices have to be determined by communities themselves: indeed in terms of a democratic-socialist politics this seems to be the only solution. In practical political terms this means reversing the Thatcher government's drive to centralize control of education and to give greater power to the communities schools serve. It also means that some communities may pursue extremely Conservative educational policies. That is a risk democratic-socialists would have to take.

Clearly the attempt to reform working-class education in isolation from reform in the wider educational and social system would pose some acute dilemmas. However, there is a further alternative. To take the Swedish route (see the chapter by Ball) by making a democratic curriculum of this kind *the* curriculum for the secondary system — that is, to have a genuinely comprehensive system of education, in which schools are organized as participatory democracies with a negotiated curriculum. In such a system both selection and specialization would be left as late as possible and the career choices students made would not be on a class, gender or racial basis as they are now.

Such a transformation of education would need to be accompanied by related changes within the Welfare State and the economy which is why I have argued that a change to a democratic education would require a profound change in our political culture. Such changes would include a reduction in pay differentials so that the material basis to the 'mystique' surrounding high-credential jobs would be removed. This would allow working-class students to 'see' that higher education is something they could achieve.[41] Moreover, the currently segmented nature of the labour market would need to be reformed so that people in the working-class secondary sector could have the same opportunities regarding career structures and further education as those in the primary sector. In other words, socialists need to pay far closer attention to labour market reform (as some of the contributors to this volume make clear) precisely because it impacts so significantly on freedom and inequality in education.

If parents are to be drawn more closely into educational decision-making they need time and education to be made aware of the issues involved. Most working-class parents are under great stress and what teachers often take for apathy when parents do not appear to take as much interest in education as they might is due to a combination of lack of time and apprehension created by teachers' ideology of professionalism.[42] Therefore what is required is time for the process of parental education and involvement and that can be gained by various provisions, such as those created by the 150-Hours project in Italy,[43] and more directly by a statutory reduction in the working week. Moreover, if we are to avoid the creation of a permanent underclass, the increase in employment created by a reduction in the working week needs to be coupled with the decommodification of labour by the development of adequate and comprehensive unemployment benefits.

There are, no doubt, other provisions that are necessary[44] but I think the general point has been made — that changes to democratize education cannot be achieved in isolation. If the Labour Party is serious about improving freedom and equality in education, then the days of the British numerical approach to happiness are over.[45] What is required is an integrated approach to the democratization of the Welfare State and the labour market which enables all citizens to participate equally within democratic society. These reforms would be significant in increasing life-chances and freedom. But they would only constitute a first step because we know that a major source of class inequalities lies in the authoritarian nature of capitalist work relations[46] and it is only with their democratization that a major breakthrough in the decomposition of class inequalities can be expected. The issue before us now is whether we are to endure an aggressive revolution of the Right which will return us to the social policies of the mid-nineteenth century or progress toward a participatory democratic society.

Acknowledgements

My thanks to Gerald Grace and Anne Dupuis who helpfully commented on earlier drafts of this paper. Thanks are also due to Peter Cuttance and George Risborough who responded to my urgent pleas for information and papers from the other side of the world. Any errors or omissions in the paper are mine.

Notes

1 See for example Nolan and Paine (1986) and Nove (1983) in the field of economics. See also the social and philosophical debate in the New Statesman, 6/3/87. In economics a fruitful debate also has developed between Mandel (1986) and Nove (1987).
2 White (1983) has made the only sustained attempt to think through the practical implications of democratizing schools.
3 The new realism is an attempt to rethink socialist policies in the light of the social changes underlying the Thatcherite revolution. See the references cited in note 1. for examples of the debate being initiated by new realists.
4 It seems to me that some of the new realist work does not go far enough. This is particularly so of those contributing to the issue devoted by the New Statesman (cited above) to the new realism. The brand of socialism being advocated in that issue does indeed appear visionless.
5 See Jones (1983, p. 54).
6 While the victory of 'equality of opportunity' signalled a more general victory for a Labour Party representing an amalgam of liberal and labourist views, socialist education was never entirely stricken from the political agenda. See Jones (1983), Baron et al. (1981) and Grace (1987).
7 Hall and Schwarz (1985, p. 25).
8 Freeden (1978, p. 15).
9 The liberal view that respect for persons can be achieved within a hierarchical system with disparities in wealth and status remains. See for example Peters (1966) for a philosophical treatment that makes this assumption. It was Arnold (1869) who articulated most clearly the idea of a common culture as a means of creating social solidarity. Johnson (1979) argues that Arnold and Peters are part of the same tradition of conservative cultural critics of capitalism.
10 This discussion of the differences between socialist and liberal welfare states is taken from Esping-Andersen (1985). For a fuller discussion of the issues involved here for education in relation to the new Right see Lauder (1987).
11 Quoted in Ashford (1986, p. 304).
12 In fact the liberal ideas of the Labour Party were sutured to the economism of the trade union movement to produce the dominant ideology of 'labourism'. See Foote (1985).
13 See Baron et al. (1981) and Ball (1984) for discussions of the partial nature of comprehensive reforms. It should be noted, however, that there were some important experiments in democratic comprehensive education in the 1960s and 1970s. Equally significant were the establishment attacks on them. For a discussion of these see Fletcher et al. (1985).

14 When it was realized that liberal reforms were not producing the desired increase in equality of opportunity, various kinds of compensatory or complimentary education projects were implemented. The most sophisticated examples of these, in theory, were the Educational Priority Areas (EPAs) developed by Halsey, because they took into account the environment within which schools were situated. They also emphasized the importance of parental involvement. See Banting (1985).

15 As one of the most influential academics in postwar secondary education, a study of the changes in Halsey's thought from a liberal to a workplace democratic conception of education, especially with respect to solidarity would pay dividends. Compare, for example, his earlier (1961) and more recent writings (1983, 1986).

16 There are two sides to the political arithmetic tradition of origins and destinations. On the one hand, it exemplifies the utilitarian approach to social science; on the other hand its demonstration of the persistence of inequalities over time suggests that class is a structural rather than attitudinal property. It therefore harbours a radical potential, as Goldthorpe et al. (1980) have argued.

17 See the following section for an explanation of why the liberal humanist curriculum reflected the elitist and hierarchical structure of schools. See Johnson (1979) who locates the roots of the liberal humanist curriculum in a critical conservative response to industrialization.

18 See Grace (1987) for an analysis of the 'professionalization' of teachers. He argues that the ideology of professionalism as interpreted by teachers involved the idea of political neutrality. As a result teachers historically distanced themselves from the political links which became necessary to defend education against Thatcherism at a later date. In other words, 'professionalization' has cost teachers dear.

19 Apple's ideas appear to have been in the process of transition when writing this paper. For example, his *Education and Power* (1982b) suggests a shift from the dominant ideology view.

20 Moore (1987, p. 241).

21 See Hirst (1965, 1974), and Hirst and Peters (1970).

22 See also the work of Dewey (1938).

23 In one sense the emphasis on the hidden curriculum is understandable from a 'correspondence' theory perspective. If the concern is with a revolutionary transformation of society, then understanding the influences which inure people to capitalism is important. By the same token it may be argued that if the concern is with life-chances within capitalism then changes to the overt curriculum which give working-class students greater access to knowledge and credentials is more important. However from a democratic-socialist perspective this is a false distinction since we need to know in what ways particular curricula favour various class interests if we are to develop the basis for a socialist curriculum within capitalism. But we also need to understand the nature of the hidden curriculum so that the curriculum we develop is genuinely democratic.

24 See Bourdieu and Passeron (1977) and Bernstein (1977) for elaborations of their respective theories. It is worth noting that both these theorists have either been rejected by more orthodox Marxist educationists (see Sharp, 1980) or have been appropriated to suit the correspondence paradigm. For example, Bourdieu's theory of cultural capital is often cited but his analysis of education as relatively autonomous because of the culturally arbitrary nature of knowledge has not been pursued. However, perhaps the clearest example of the way the correspondence theory has deflected analysis away from the social production of knowledge is Harris' *Education and Knowledge* (1979). Harris was trained as a philosopher of education and was therefore well placed to make the connections between, the liberal-rationalism of the London School and class interests; instead he chose to ground his critique in the informal curriculum, leaving any analysis of the relationship between the formal curriculum and class interests untouched.

25 For discussions of some of the issues involved in developing such a theory see Whitty and Young (1976) and Livingstone (1983).
26 A good example of the argument that, historically, the curriculum has served the ruling class rather than the needs of capital is Weiner's (1982). Grace (1985) also argues that the ruling class' contempt of industrialization even permeated the elementary school curriculum.
27 For Gramsci an intellectual and moral bloc is formed by an intellectual-mass dialectic in which a particular moral and social vision is created. This becomes an historic bloc when it takes on the capacity for making history.
28 Willis (1977) for example argues that the lads in his study are potential revolutionary agents. However, a close analysis of his theory suggests that they are more likely to be agents in an extreme right-wing sense than potential socialists.
29 This view would reject the revolutionary Marxist claim that the bourgeois state needs 'smashing' since these are aspects of the bourgeois state that would indeed carry over into a socialist state; the principle of universal benefits would be one example. In education, the thesis being argued here assumes that a substantial move towards socialist education can be made within capitalist societies.
30 Peters' (1966) worthy classic provides a clear example of the failure of liberal philosophers to make the connection between democracy and equality.
31 Once a teleological view of history is rejected then working-class political behaviour has to be explained as much by rational calculation as by ideology. As such, examples of good socialist practice assume far greater importance. Indeed, given the new Right's attempts to get rid of socialist practices that appear to work, we can assume they consider them a major threat. The abolition of the Greater London Council is a case in point.
32 See Castles and Wustenberg (1979) for an elaboration of the historical importance socialists have attributed to the connection between education and work.
33 This point extends to the general decomposition of the class structure. Kohn (1977) claims that the conditions of working life determine people's perceptions of themselves and others and, that those who have no say in determining their work conditions have a circumscribed view of self in relation to society. Insofar as this is correct, then it is by democratic participation that a positive valuation of self as an agent who can act upon society develops. At the level of agency rather than structure, belief in oneself as an agent is a necessary condition for an egalitarian and democratic society.
34 The major work on this has been undertaken in the United States by Johnson and Johnson (1975).
35 Even so, different cultural groups have different theories and practices relating to democracy and it would not be easy to reconcile these varying practices since they relate to groups' self-identity. The danger is that unless these differences in participatory practices are recognized new forms of domination may arise.
36 Presumably any workplace democratic school organization which considered, say, racism in the school, would inevitably also look outward to the racism in society. In other words, the consideration of the particular in schools would lead to a more general political education.
37 See Walker (1981) and Evers and Walker (1983).
38 See Hooker (1975).
39 The phrase is Rorty's from the title of his (1980) book. In case this seems to be raking over old coals in terms of the dispute between the London School of philosophers of education and the new sociologists which flared in the early 1970s, it isn't. I take it that dispute has been settled by the present consensus in epistemology and social theory that foundational relativism exists, thereby allowing for the social production of knowledge but that rational judgements can be made between competing theories. See Hesse (1980).

40 A pilot project of a curriculum based on these principles is currently being developed in three working-class schools in Christchurch, New Zealand. For a preliminary discussion of this curriculum see Lauder and Khan (1988). I understand a similar curriculum is being developed in Sheffield. It should be said that there are 'fissures' within the curriculum principles being articulated here. For example, there is a clear hiatus between on the one hand having a negotiated curriculum and on the other insisting that certain skills be taught; and between a negotiated curriculum and the attempt to relate the interests of students to the wider issues concerning fundamental human problems. Resolving these 'fissures' involves a process of negotiation whereby students' immediate interests are related to their social interests.

41 The claim that wage differentials need to be reduced in order to promote increased participation in tertiary education by working-class students runs counter to the new Right view that it is by widening pay differentials that an incentive is created for working-class students to enter tertiary education. New Right thought eschews any analysis of the influence of class, racist and patriarchal structures on human motivation. From research we are currently conducting on working-class school leavers it seems clear that 'able' working-class youths do not consider tertiary and particularly university education, quite simply because it is beyond their world. One way of bringing the world of the university closer is therefore to bring those with a university education closer by reducing pay differentials. Details of this research can be obtained by writing to the author.

42 A consequence of making the theoretical assumption that education is relatively autonomous in the sense outlined in this chapter is that the internal politics of education assumes importance for policy-making. For example, the present concept of professionalism and the privileges it has created would need to be changed to allow greater say in decision-making from parents. Moreover, the implementation of an integrated curriculum would challenge the present power structure in schools, centred on subject-based departments and hierarchies.

43 The 150-Hours project does not create provision for parental involvement in their children's education but it does provide an example of how time can be extracted from employers for workers' education. I see no reason why such provision should not be extended to workers' involvement in their children's education. For more on the 150-Hour project see Taliani (1979) and Yarnit (1980).

44 I have not, for example, analysed the relation of welfare arrangements to education from a woman's perspective. In this respect feminist literature is far in advance of this chapter. See for example David (1980).

45 In these days of the 'great moving right show' no party other than Labour has the remotest possibility of developing democratic-socialist practices. For a debate as to whether Labour can go beyond its labourist/liberal ideology to develop a genuinely democratic-socialist politics see Foote (1985) and Samual and Stedman Jones (1983). The argument in Wainwright (1987) seems to me particularly relevant to the general thrust of this paper.

46 See Kohn (1977) for research which relates the authoritarian nature of the workplace to class inequalities. See also Lane (1979) for an interesting discussion of the difficulties in breaking down psycho-social class attributes. Finally it should be acknowledged since the work of Bourdieu and Foucault, amongst others, that the possession of knowledge can constitute a form of stratification and exclusion. It is not only the workplace that needs to be democratized, knowledge also does. The reduction of inequalities therefore looks to be a long and complex business.

References

AHIER, J. (1983) 'History and sociology of educational policy', in Ahier, J. and Flude, M. (Eds) *Contemporary Education Policy*, London: Croom Helm.
APPLE, M. (1979) *Ideology and Curriculum*, Boston: Routledge and Kegan Paul.
APPLE, M. (1982a) 'Curricular form and the logic of technical control: Building the possessive individual'. in Apple, M. (Ed.) *Cultural and Economic Reproduction in Education*, London: Routledge and Kegan Paul.
APPLE, M. (1982b) *Education and Power*, Boston: Routledge & Kegan Paul.
ARMSTRONG, P., GLYNN, A. and HARRISON, J. (1984) *Capitalism Since World War II*, London: Fontana.
ARNOLD, M. (1869) *Culture and Anarchy*, London: Smith-Elder.
ARONOWITZ, S. and GIROUX, H. (1986) *Education Under Seige*, London: Routledge and Kegan Paul.
ASHFORD, D. (1986) *The Emergence of the Welfare States*, Oxford: Blackwell.
BALL, S. (1984) 'Comprehensives in crisis?', in Ball, S. (Ed.) *Comprehensive Schooling*, Lewes: Falmer Press.
BANTING, K. (1985) 'Poverty and Educational Priority', in McNay, I. and Ozga, J. (Eds) *Policy-Making in Education*, Oxford: Pergamon Press.
BARON, S., FINN, D., GRANT, N., GREEN, M. and JOHNSON, R. (1981) *Unpopular Education*, London: Hutchinson.
BERNER, B. (1974) 'Human capital, manpower planning and economic theory: some critical remarks', *Acta Sociologica*, 17, pp. 236-55.
BERNSTEIN, B. (1977) *Class, Codes and Control*, Vol. 3. 2nd ed, London: Routledge and Kegan Paul.
BOURDIEU, P. and PASSERON, J. (1977) *Reproduction: In Education, Society and Culture*, London: Sage.
BOWERS, C. (1984) 'The problem of individualism and community in neo-Marxist educational thought', *Teachers College Record*, 85, pp. 365-90.
BOWLES, S. and GINTIS, H. (1975) 'The problem with human capital — A Marxian critique', *American Economic Review*, 65, pp. 74-82.
BOWLES, S. and GINTIS, H. (1976) *Schooling in Capitalist America*, London: Routledge and Kegan Paul.
BROWN, P. (1987) *Schooling Ordinary Kids*, London: Tavistock.
CARNOY, M. and LEVIN, H. (1985) *Schooling and Work in the Democratic State*, Stanford: Stanford University Press.
CASTLES, S. and WUSTENBERG, W. (1979) *The Education of the Future*, London: Pluto Press.
CROSLAND, C. (1964) *The Future of Socialism*, London: Cape.
DAVID, M. (1980) *The State, The Family and Education*, London: Routledge and Kegan Paul.
DEWEY, J. (1938) *Experience and Education*, New York: Kappa Delta Pi.
ESPING-ANDERSEN, G. (1985) 'Power and distribution regimes', in *Politics and Society*, 14, pp. 223-56.
EVERS, C. and WALKER, J. (1983) 'Knowledge, partitioned sets and extensionality: A refutation of the forms of knowledge thesis', *Journal of Philosophy of Education*, 17.
FLETCHER, C., CARON, M. and WILLIAMS, W. (1985) *Schools on Trial*, Milton Keynes: Open University Books.
FOOTE, G. (1985) *The Labour Party's Political Thought: A History*, London: Croom Helm.
FREEDEN, M. (1978) *The New Liberalism: An Ideology of Social Reform*, Oxford: Clarendon.

GIDDENS, A. and MCKENZIE G. (Eds) (1982) *Social Class and the Division of Labour*, Cambridge: Cambridge University Press.
GINTIS, H. and BOWLES, S. (1980) 'Contradiction and reproduction in educational theory' in Barton, L. *et al* (Eds) *Schooling, Ideology and the Curriculum*, Lewes: Falmer Press.
GIROUX, H. (1983) *Theory and Resistance in Education*, Massachusetts, Bergin & Garvey.
GOLDTHORPE, J., LLEWELLYN, C. and PAYNE, C. (1980) *Social Mobility and Class Structure in Modern Britain*, Oxford: Oxford University Press.
GRACE, G. (1985) 'Judging teachers: The social and political contexts of teacher evaluation', *British Journal of Sociology of Education*, 6, pp. 3–16.
GRACE, G. (1987) 'Teachers and the state in Britain: A changing relation', in Lawn, M. and Grace, G. (Eds) *Teachers: The Culture and Politics of Work*, Lewes: Falmer Press.
GRAMSCI, A. (1971) *Selecting from the Prison Notebooks*, Trans. and ed. Hoare, Q. and Nowell Smith, G. New York: International Publishers.
HALL, S. (1984) 'The crisis of labourism', in Curran, J. (Ed.) *The Future of the Left*, Cambridge: Polity Press.
HALL, S. and SCHWARZ, B. (1985) 'State and Society, 1880–1930' in Langan, M. and Schwarz, B. (Eds) *Crisis in the British State, 1880–1930*, London: Hutchinson.
HALSEY, A. (1972) *Educational Priority*, London: HMSO.
HALSEY, A. (1975) 'Sociology and the equality debate', *Oxford Review of Education*, 1, pp. 9–23.
HALSEY, A. (1983) 'Schools for democracy?' in Ahier, J. and Flude, M. (Eds) *Contemporary Education Policy*, London: Croom Helm.
HALSEY, A. (1986) *Change in British Society*, 3rd ed. Oxford: Oxford University Press.
HALSEY, A. FLOUD, J. and ANDERSON, J. (Eds) (1961) *Education, Economy and Society*, New York: Free Press.
HARRIS, K. (1979) *Education and Knowledge*, London: Routledge and Kegan Paul.
HESSE, M. (1980) *Revolutions and Reconstructions in the Philosophy of Science*, Brighton: Harvester.
HIRST, P. (1965) 'Liberal education and the nature of knowledge', in Archambault, R. (Ed.) *Philosophical Analysis and Education*, London: Routledge and Kegan Paul.
HIRST, P. (1974) *Knowledge and the Curriculum*, London: Routledge and Kegan Paul.
HIRST, P. and PETERS, R. (1970) *The Logic of Education*, London: Routledge and Kegan Paul.
HOOKER, C. (1975) 'On global theories', *Philosophy of Science*, 42, pp. 152–79.
JOHNSON, D. and JOHNSON, R. (1975) *Learning Together and Alone: Cooperation, Competition and Individualization*, Englewood Cliffs, N.J.: Prentice Hall.
JOHNSON, L. (1979) *The Cultural Critics*, London: Routledge and Kegan Paul.
JONES, K. (1983) *Beyond Progressive Education*, London: MacMillan.
KOHN, M. (1977) *Class and Conformity*, Chicago, University of Chicago Press.
LANE, R. (1979) 'Captialist Man, Socialist Man', in Laslett, P. and Fishkin, J., *Philosophy Politics and Society*, 5th series, Oxford: Blackwell.
LAUDER, H. (1987) 'The new Right and educational policy in New Zealand', *New Zealand Journal of Educational Studies*, 22, pp. 3–23.
LAUDER, H., FREEMAN-MOIR, J. and SCOTT, A. (1986) 'What is to be done with radical academic practice', *Capital and Class*, 29, pp. 83–110.
LAUDER, H. and KHAN, G.I.A.R. (1988) 'Democracy and the effective schools movement', *International Journal of Qualitative Studies*, 1, pp. 51–68.
LAUDER, H. and YEE, B. (1987) 'Are teachers being proletarianised: Some theoretical, empirical and policy issues' in Walker, M. and Barton, L. (Eds) *Changing Policies, Changing Teachers*, Milton Keynes: Open University Press.
LIVINGSTONE, D. (1983) *Class Ideologies and Educational Futures*, Lewes: Falmer Press.

McPHERSON, A. and WILLMS, J. (1987) 'Equalisation and Improvement: Some effects of comprehensive reorganisation in Scotland', *Sociology*, 21, 4, pp. 509–39.
MANDEL, E. (1986) 'In defence of socialist planning', *New Left Review*, 159, pp. 5–37.
MILLIBAND, R. (1961) *Parliamentary Socialism*, London: George Allen and Unwin.
MOORE, R. (1987) 'Education and the ideology of production', *British Journal of Sociology of Education*, 8, pp. 227–42.
MOORE, R. (1988) 'The correspondence principle and the Marxist sociology of education' in Cole, M. (Ed.) *Bowles and Gintis Revisited*, Lewes: Falmer Press.
NOLAN, P. and PAINE, S. (1986) (Eds) *Rethinking Socialist Economics*, Cambridge: Polity Press.
NOVE, A. (1983) *The Economics of Feasible Socialism*, London: Allen and Unwin.
NOVE, A. (1987) 'Mandel on planning', *New Left Review*, 161, pp. 98–104.
PETERS, R. (1966) *Ethics and Education*, London: Allen and Unwin.
RORTY, R. (1980) *Philosophy and the Mirror of Natures*, Oxford: Blackwell.
SAMUEL, R. and STEDMAN JONES (1982) 'The Labour Party and social democracy', in Samual, R. and Stedman Jones, G. (Eds) *Culture, Ideology and Politics*, London: Routledge & Kegan Paul.
SHARPE, B. (1980) *Knowledge, Ideology and the politics od Schooling*, London: Routledge and Kegan Paul.
SIMON, B. (1986) *Does Education Matter?*, London: Lawrence and Wishart.
TALIANI, E. (1979) 'The right to study: Worker's demands for an alternative education strategy', in Kloskowska, A. and Martinotti, G. (Eds) *Education in a Changing Society*, London: Sage.
WAINWRIGHT, H. (1987) 'Beyond labourism', *New Left Review*, 164, pp. 34–50.
WALKER, J. (1981) *Autonomy, Authority and Antagonism: A Critique of Ideology in Philosophy of Education*, Ph.D. Thesis, University of Sydney, Australia.
WEINER, M. (1982) *English Culture and the Decline of the Industrial Spirit, 1850–1980*, Cambridge: Cambridge University Press.
WHITE, P. (1983) *Beyond Domination*, London: Routledge and Kegan Paul.
WHITE, P. (1986) 'Self-respect, self-esteem and the school: A democratic perspective on authority', *Teachers College Record*, 88, pp. 95–106.
WHITTY, G. and YOUNG, M. (1976) *Explorations in the Politics of School Knowledge*, Nafferton: Nafferton Books.
WILLIS, P. (1977) *Learning to Labour*, Farnborough: Saxon House.
WOOD, S. (1982) (Ed.) *The Degradation of Work?*, London: Hutchinson.
YARNIT, M. (1980) '150-Hours — Italy's experiment in mass working-class adult education', in Thompson, J. (Ed.) *Adult Education for A Change*, London: Hutchinson.

Chapter 3

Democracy and Fraternity: Towards a New Paradigm for the Comprehensive School[1]

Michael Fielding

Advocates of democracy include those who mistrust ordinary citizens to the point where active involvement in the political process is so slender and so spasmodic as to effectively disenfranchise them; here the public realm of politics is abandoned for the constant clash of private interests and the invisible hand of market forces fits snugly over the mouth of public debate. The beneficence of the invisible hand central to Adam Smith's vision of early capitalism is ensured in its twentieth century progeny by the sheer noise of raucous acquisition enriched by the occasional 'big bang' announcing a new era of pneumatic opulence for the guardians of radical capitalism. In such a world we are told that democracy resides primarily in a competition between elites for the people's votes (e.g., Dahl, 1956). The credibility and the actuality of the notion of representation is strained to the limit and 'the people', whilst having reality as consumers of goods, became almost spectral in their substance as political agents. In such a world the notion of democratic citizenship is virtually non-existent; insofar as it does have life it is passive, reactive and, because the realm of the public is merely an arena for the clash of private interests, myopic and fitful.

A quite different account would regard the elitist theory of democracy outlined above as having little to do with democracy in a procedural sense and nothing whatever to do with it as a system of social and political relations which enshrine liberty, equality and fraternity as constitutive principles of human flourishing. Advocates of a participatory theory of democracy[2] would not only regard voting as a minimally important device of dubious validity, and representation as a straightforward impossibility more conducive to the withering than the nurturing of political and personal growth; they would also argue strongly that a merely procedural device, even it it were to enable fuller and more frequent participation, would not of itself ensure the nature and quality of human relations and practices which democracy intends.

What advocates of both elitist and participatory democracies would agree on, however, is the essentially contested nature of the concept of democracy. What counts as democracy is not something that supporters of the different theories can agree on. The different accounts are rooted in different political traditions, different values, practices and aspirations; different views about the nature of human nature all reside in the linguistic substance of the notion itself.

The standpoint of this chapter is one in which civic participation is seen as fundamental to democratic society. My particular concern is to pursue briefly the fraternal basis of democracy and to suggest certain consequences for education in a society which aspires towards democracy, consequences which point firmly in the direction of a new paradigm for the comprehensive school.

The Real Challenge for the Comprehensive School

'Liberté, Egalité, Fraternité — Ou la Mort'. In the ambiguity of this aggressive greeting of French revolutionaries lie both the hopes and the demise of comprehensive education in this country. For revolutionaries of the 1790s the addition of 'ou la Mort' and the frequent production of a dagger to reinforce the point was a response to a situation in which cries of 'fraternity' were becoming mere mouthings by those whose sympathies lay elsewhere. However paradoxical such a greeting — expressed in even more heightened form in the 'politesse revolutionnaire' of 'Sois mon frère ou je te tué' ('Be my brother or I will kill you') — I find myself sympathetic with the predicament to which it was responding and wholly supportive of what I take to be the profound truth about the human condition to which it, perhaps unwittingly, gives expression.

The predicament was one in which the bright hopes of the revolution which still gave life and hope to the ordinary people were being undermined by those whose political aims were far less revolutionary. The language of emancipation was being expropriated by the forces of reaction. It is arguable that a similar process of expropriation has gained headway in contemporary comprehensive education with the advent of the MSC and other government-inspired developments. Phrases like 'negotiated learning', 'active learning', and 'student-centred teaching' are no longer distinctive of 'progressive' education; and yet from the most right-wing Tory government since the Second World War there seems more likelihood that what we are witnessing is a form of linguistic subversion than the genuine embrace of the pedagogy of liberation. Similarly, the title 'comprehensive school' has come to mean a mere absence of selection at 11, 12 or 13 + rather than providing an indication of the values and educational practices which the institution embodies. The answer is not, of course, to produce real or metaphorical daggers at the throats of all who profess to be working in or supportive of comprehensive schools and demand that their practices match their rhetoric: as the demise of the 'tutoiement' of the early 1790s showed, not only is it impossible both theoretically and practically to impose fraternity, it is also less than reliable to treat the presence or indeed the absence of fraternal terminology[3] as indicative of anything of much significance.

Yet we do need something to do. Writing some three decades after the emergence of the postwar fight for comprehensive education got underway, David Hargreaves argued that: 'For many teachers and most parents there has simply been no explicit and clear rationale for the comprehensive school'. (Hargreaves, 1982, p. 78). If such an assertion still has some resonance it should be a cause for concern. Champions of comprehensive education must, as Brian Simon suggests, 'defend comprehensive schools' (Simon, 1986) — and you cannot defend something which amounts to little more than an umbrella term. The acid rain currently beating down on the public education system in this country is corrosive of more than the physical fabric of the institutions our children attend; the system itself is under attack and with it the democratic way of life which the trinome 'Liberté, Egalité, Fraternité' symbolizes. The additional 'ou la Mort' of my opening sentence takes on a new significance in Britain nearly 200 years later. If we do not defend comprehensive schools successfully, if we do not unmask the pseudo-comprehensive discourse of Tory education policy, the gains which have been painfully won over many, many years will be undermined or reversed. Death is too final, too dramatic a term. But we should be in no doubt as to the nature and severity of the harm that will be done to the education of current and future generations and to our progress as a people towards a truly democratic way of life.

Democracy and Fraternity

If there are some important similarities between the predicaments facing those whose emancipatory aspirations foreshorten the two centuries which separate them, the vision which the exhortation 'Liberté, Egalité, Fraternité — ou la Mort' enshrines seems to me at once more certainly and more profoundly true and as such it provides the key to the way forward not only for comprehensive education but for our increasingly fragmented society. Consider two nineteenth-century equivalents expressed with equal conviction and in more positive a form: 'Fellowship is life and lack of fellowship is death; and the deeds that you do upon the earth, it is for fellowship's sake that ye do them' (Morris, 1973, p. 51) or: 'Only in community with others has each individual the means of cultivating his gifts in all directions; only in the community, therefore, is personal freedom possible' (Marx and Engels, 1970, p. 83). In the twentieth century its most compelling formulation came a further hundred years later:

> The democratic slogan — liberty, equality, fraternity — embodies

correctly the principles of human fellowship. To achieve freedom and equality is to create friendship, to constitute community between men... (The) forces which unite men in fellowship express the ultimate nature of humanity. We can say that we enter into fellowship because that is our nature; that if we did not we should not be human; that if mankind was not united in this way there would be no mankind. (Macmurray, 1950, pp. 74/75, 77).

G.D.H. Cole, now sadly and undeservedly neglected by socialists, wrote in 1941 in his *Essentials Of Democracy* that:

The real democracy that does exist in Great Britain... is to be found for the most part not in Parliament or in the institutions of local government, but in the smaller groups, formal and informal, in which men and women join together out of decent fellowship or for pursuit of a common social purpose... It is in these fellowships that the real spirit of democracy resides (Cole, 1941a, p. 102).

At the root of Cole's remarks is a deep commitment, not only to the Rousseauean belief that: 'One man cannot stand for many men, or for anybody except himself... One man cannot represent another — that's flat' (ibid, p. 99–100), but also the view that fraternity or fellowship is the indispensable basis of democratic practice:

A democrat is someone who has a physical glow of sympathy and love for anyone who comes to him honestly, looking for help or sympathy: a man is not a democrat, however justly he may try to behave to his fellow man, unless he feels like that (ibid, p. 98).

As he says in a companion piece: 'Real democracy, and not... its atomistic perversion (depends upon our) learning to practice democratic fellowship' (Cole, 1941b, p. 95). For Cole the foundation and the justification for democracy resides largely in its personal reality and its faith in ordinary men and women:

Being democratic is not the same thing as holding advanced opinions. It is not the same as believing in democracy. It starts with knowing your neighbours as real persons; and unless it starts here, it does not start at all (Cole, 1941a, p. 100).

Within the last decade there has been a growing awareness of the truths towards which these insights are pointing. Interestingly enough, two of their most explicit proponents are sociologists, both of whom not only have the breadth of vision to realize the importance of an historical perspective in addressing our present needs, but also thinkers who are deeply concerned with the education system as an important element in the creation of our current dilemmas and as a possible agent in their resolution. In his 1978 Reith Lectures, A.H. Halsey argued that:

Michael Fielding

> What is most clearly evident from the British experience, in my opinion, is an unresolved problem of fraternity or basis for social order beneath the clash of egalitarian and libertarian argument... Liberty and equality can operate as social principles only within the bounds set by fraternity... (The way forward for Britain) is taken to its own traditions of citizenship and democracy seriously in all their richness and inspiration. They offer the basis for a new fraternity without which both liberty and equality are impoverished... We should seek fraternity as citizenship in all public organizations (Halsey, 1981, pp. 10, 12, 162, 166).

An important means of nurturing that fraternal base is, Halsey suggests, a reformed educational system:

> An educational system giving balanced expression to the ideal of liberty and equality which would be a practical further development of the slow reform of the class-divided schooling bequeathed to Britain from liberal capitalism in the nineteenth century. The comprehensive primary and secondary school is its fraternal foundation, and could be the nursery of a fully democratic citizenship (ibid, p. 167).

Some six years later in a widely read, exhilarating book by another Oxford sociologist, similar concerns provide the focus of the argument:

> (For Durkheim) true dignity and morality have a social and a corporate aspect. Genuine individuality must be rooted in group life... and group life was not merely a means of giving people the social skills of cooperation and empathy, but of generating solidarity (which is the means of human fulfilment)... (The) solidary base of modern man could not be released unless the spirit of association is already aroused... It (is) the school's key function... to 'breathe life into the spirit of association' (Hargreaves, 1982, p. 111).

The extract is from the key chapter of David Hargreave's seminal *The Challenge for the Comprehensive School*. The chapter itself ends with Hargreave's advocacy that:

> It is for us, in spite of the growth of individualism and the decline of community in school and society since Durkheim's day, to find the means whereby that challenge (to provide the solidary base of modern man through nurturing the spirit of association) can be met in the new comprehensive schools of our own age (ibid, p. 112).

This is the real 'challenge for the comprehensive school'; it is this view both about the demise of contemporary European society and, even more fundamentally, about the conditions of human fulfilment that make Hargreaves' suggestions at once valid and challenging. At present there is scant evidence that the challenge has been adequately understood, still less that it has been taken up seriously. My own belief is that the challenge is worthwhile and that the strengths of the comprehensive school movement can fruitfully be understood by evaluating the extent to which liberty, equality and fraternity have informed its history thus far. I would further argue that an important way forward may well be suggested by an emerging understanding of the relation between these principles, and that of the three, the last is, ironically, although the most neglected and least understood, the most important of all.

From Equality of Opportunity to Equal Value

The history of the fight for and gradual emergence of comprehensive schools as the main agent in the provision of comprehensive education is in some important respects similar to the struggle for democracy in European civilization. Whilst the political aspect of democracy has the earliest roots in time, up until the seventeenth century it remained a largely negative concept with groups of one sort or another protesting their exclusion from a share of power. Summarizing and reflecting on this process, Laski remarks that: 'The basis of democratic development is the demand for equality, the demand that the system of power be erected on the similarities and not the differences between men' (Laski, 1937, p. 76).

A number of aspects of these observations are relevant here. First, the emergence of the aspirations of those fighting for democracy and those fighting for comprehensive education were at once reactive and emancipatory: both fought against perceived injustices which provided the catalyst for their growth; both were concerned to remove those impediments and so widen horizons. The fight for comprehensive schools grew out of the experience of teachers, children and parents at the hands of the tripartite system which not only failed huge numbers of young people both personally and educationally but also rested on a psychological theory (to do with IQ testing) which turned out to be manifestly false. Ironically it failed to deliver the goods from the very meritocratic standpoint from which many advocates of the return to the grammar schools now argue. The morass of problems endemic in the IQ testing scenario were exacerbated by the lack of sufficient movement between grammar, technical and secondary modern schools which the system, by its own admission, required. In their early days comprehensive schools appeared to address this problem successfully. When I first went to Thomas Bennett School in Crawley there were still a number of staff who remembered Tim McMullen, the first head, proclaiming the case of a girl who had gone from the thirteenth to the top stream and ended up at Oxford. Doubtless other pioneer comprehensives could tell the same tale. The exemplar illustrated the strength of the case for equality of opportunity which provided the political context for the early growth of the comprehensive schools which more often that not intended to out do the grammar schools. This last phrase is important because it indicates the strengths and the weaknesses of the early comprehensives: the strengths lay in their capacity to succeed in providing academic success for larger numbers of students, many of whom would have 'failed' in the tripartite system; the failure lay in their inability to recognize the inappropriateness of equality of opportunity as a guiding principle for comprehensive education.

Interestingly enough, although Tim McMullen changed his views and his school, and went on to be the first head of Countesthorpe College in Leicestershire, Thomas Bennett still made the qualitative leap from the reactive to the positive phase of comprehensive schooling. As it turned out this was hardly surprising since the incoming head, Pat Daunt, can legitimately be regarded as one of the outstanding intellectual advocates of the comprehensive movement in the early 1970s. It is his book, *Comprehensive Values* (Daunt, 1972), that contains the clearest exposition of the principle of equal value which gave philosophical strength and form to a comprehensive movement which was beginning to recognize the inappropriateness and straightforward impossibility of equality of opportunity. It is impossible, because even if the starting line is uniform, the arrival of the competitors in various states of fitness points to a prior race which has already been run in quite unequal circumstances. It is inappropriate because the imagery of races, competitors and inevitably few winners posits a mode of life that is in harmony with meritocracy in which the success of a very small number in a narrow field is predicated on the failure of vast numbers of their fellow citizens. It is sharply out of tune with a view of society which seeks to value all its members in all their diversity.

Since the mid-1970s the advance of comprehensive schooling has slowly passed through its reactive phase and is now substantially into the phase of advocacy. Hargreaves' observations that:

> Today we know what the comprehensive schools were designed to be against. Until we ask ourselves what comprehensives are *for* they cannot go beyond the meritocratic principles on which at present they somewhat uneasily rest (Hargreaves, 1982, p. 74).

were over-severe. He seemed curiously unaware that his intervention in *The Challenge for the Comprehensive School* formed part of a debate that Daunt, Marsden and others had started more than a decade earlier. That uncharacteristic historical lacuna does not, however, detract from the importance of his contribution. In many respects the phase of advocacy is the most difficult time thus far in the history of the fight for comprehensive education. The injustices and iniquities of the old tripartite system have taken on new, less immediately obvious forms and many of those issues which need to be addressed find their reference points within the comprehensive schools themselves. Hargreaves' book was more than just another publication from an academic, albeit one whose previous work was actively read at least by teachers in training. It was, by its own admission: 'Directed to the... audience of practising teachers rather than to academic colleagues' (ibid p. x), and its impact on the debate about the nature of specifically comprehensive education was considerable. He reaffirmed the necessity of the comprehensive school going 'beyond meritocracy', gave further practical grip to the equal value principle by highlighting the importance of human dignity and its implications for the outmoded cognitive-academic curriculum, and gave further impetus to the comprehensive community school movement. Above all, as I have indicated earlier, Hargreaves sought not just to reflect on and extend the commitment to the equal value principle and its practical outcomes in terms of the curriculum and the dynamic role of the community school; the over-riding challenge for the comprehensive school turned out to be even more deeply rooted, arguably amounting to something like a paradigm shift — namely, from an individualistic notion of education (exemplified by the 'fallacy of individualism') (ibid p. 93) to one which is communitarian, i.e., one which starts by asking questions about the kind of society we wish to live in and the role of education in its realization, or one which regards individual flourishing as inextricably communal in its manner, its context and its outcome. At root the communitarian paradigm grows out of a different social and political tradition which argues that the atomistic model of human beings on which so much of our contemporary educational and social practice rests is deeply misconceived; which instead argues that: 'It is only in relation to others that we exist as persons... This mutuality provides the primary condition of our freedom' (Macmurray, 1961, p. 213).

The Rejection of Individualism

Establishing a shift in modes of thought and feeling which helps us to establish an alternative educational paradigm is not, of course, an easy matter; it will demand much of our hearts and minds, much courage and considerable commitment. It is not, however, an insuperable task. There is a tradition of social, educational and political thought which Hargreaves and Halsey both draw on and contribute to. That tradition needs to be rediscovered and nurtured. In it we will find pointers to practice and a richness of inspiration which will enable us to respond with more confidence to what we are once again beginning to feel, but which the contemporary educational hegemony denies. Milos Kundura's reminder that: 'The struggle of man against tyranny is the struggle of memory against forgetting' is particularly apt in a society in which the popular memory is too often circumscribed by the media manipulations of a conspicuous present and the partiality of privilege which, for example, cherishes the clarion call for the return to grammar schools on the tacit assumption that one's own children will not find their way into the local secondary modern school.

The values to which our experience begin to point more insistently bring us back once more to Laski's stress in his history of democracy on: 'The similarities and not the differences between men' (Laski, 1937, p. 10). They enable us, too, to appreciate the importance of Halsey's observations that:

> We still have to provide a common experience of citizenship in childhood and old age, in work and play, and in health and sickness. We have still, in short, to develop a common culture to replace the divided cultures of class and status (Halsey, 1981, p. 164).

The driving force of some of the developments in comprehensive schools in the last two to three decades, such as the move towards the common core curriculum, have been fired in part by recognition of this very need. There are signs, too, that Halsey's call for the comprehensive primary and secondary school to provide the 'fraternal foundation' of a reformed education system and take on the role of 'the nursery of a fully democratic citizenship' is being heeded. Bernard Barker's *Rescuing the Comprehensive Experience* has as its final chapter heading 'Towards the Common School?'. The concluding section of the chapter is headed 'Citizenship' and in it Barker argues strongly that: 'Schools could become influential in developing a revival in citizenship and self-government' (Barker, 1986, pp. 148–149). The significance of Bernard Barker's book goes beyond its encouraging grasp of the importance of citizenship and the reorientations such a commitment involves. It fruitfully examines the case for alternative management styles and a more active pedagogy from a perspective broadly in tune with the communitarian tradition which I am suggesting provides the most appropriate framework for the new comprehensive paradigm. The broad delineation of that paradigm and some brief reflections on a number of developments which lead me to offer it as a possible way forward comprise the remaining sections of this paper.

The Fraternal Alternative

What, then, are the broad characteristics of the paradigm I am suggesting as appropriate for the development of comprehensive schools over the next decade? The fundamental principles on which it rests are those of the democratic movement itself best summed up by the French trinome Liberty, Equality and Fraternity. At first glance, they seem vague and only obscurely connected with an undertaking as severely practical as the daily experience of schooling and education for young people. But their power rests firstly in the unfailing persistence with which many human beings draw inspiration and moral legitimacy from their invocation, and secondly in the enormous power of their interconnectedness. Indeed, it is their interconnectedness which give them their emancipatory potential. I would wish to argue that each on its own is only contingently related to democracy and that the excesses of each uninformed by the significant presence of the others may lead, for example, to a freedom which favours only those with wealth and power, or to an equality which mistakes uniformity for fulfilment, or a fraternity whose boundaries are narrowly drawn round the disfigured template of fascism.

The key features of fraternity and similar relations between human beings (whether they are part of what you refer to as fraternity, fellowship, friendship, or community) are firstly that they are caring relationships, not just for some aspect or part of someone, but for them as a person. They are personal, not functional relationships. Secondly, they are characterized by liberty and equality. Fraternal relations cannot exist if they are absent; without liberty and equality their growth is temporary or distorted. If equality, in the sense of equal value, is absent then the relationship, will become lopsided like that of servant and master. If freedom is denied, its restriction and limitation is corrosive of its personal or fraternal character and the more it approximates to one party using the other for their purposes. Fraternity, then, is a form of human unity in which people care for each other as persons, much as friends or families do. It is not, however, a claustrophobic or restrictive relationship; neither is it hierarchical or static. Adherence to the principle of liberty ensures the freedom to speak and to act. The principle of equality guarantees not only the hand of reciprocity, but also the psychological confidence which both supports and conditions that freedom so that it does not become dominating or condescending. Fraternity is a kind of caring — one which is neither restrictive nor possessive of any of the parties to the relationship; it is vibrant and alive; it is emancipatory.

What the detailed implications of this shift towards fraternity are will need to be worked through over time. However, it is perfectly possible to map out briefly some important differences such an approach might make. As a way into exploring some of the consequences of a fraternal paradigm, I will suggest four fundamental characteristics which, taken together, amount to a significant shift in the theory and practice of comprehensive education. These characteristics might usefully be expressed as a commitment to (1) holism which is (2) person-centred. Given the nature of personhood, that commitment must also embrace (3) a communal imperative which should in turn be linked to (4) an emancipatory citizenship and the vital importance of the 'public realm'. Having sketched out in a little more detail what is meant by each of these imperatives, I will then suggest a number of practical implications which seem consistent with them.

Firstly, then, the essentially holistic nature of the new paradigm. Its commitment to ensuring the living presence of the principles of liberty and equality in the daily education of young people can only become truly emancipatory within the context of community. Current comprehensive practice tends to have a centrifugal thrust which, at its best, is exhilarating and imaginative and in many respects liberating for all concerned. It is, however, less effective than it might be because the diversity and energy are too seldom inter-related either to each other or to the totality of the educational enterprise within the school. The fraternal paradigm has a centripetal quality which constantly seeks to relate and give coherence to the multiple facets of life in comprehensive community schools.

A second point of fundamental importance is that the holism characteristic of the fraternal paradigm is person-centred. This is not at all the same thing as saying it is individualistic. The notion of personhood running through this essay rests on the assumption that we only develop as persons in and through community.

Although, strictly speaking, the communal nature of personhood implies the importance of community it is perhaps worth making as a third point that a person-centred holism entails a deeply communal commitment. Just as I assume the communal nature of our human being, so I also assume that a community is not at all the same thing as collectivity. A collectivity is organic or it is functional in its relations. If it is organic the individual has significance only in relation to the overriding totality; if it is functional the atomistic individual relates to other individuals for specific purposes and once these purposes are fulfilled, the unity dissolves. In contrast, a communal relationship is essentially personal in nature, i.e., it is a relation between persons as whole persons, not just in terms of a particular aspect or attribute which they may possess. This person-centred holism has considerable implications, not only for the relations between students and staff, but for the whole organizational structure of the school itself.

Fourthly, and finally, the fraternal paradigm signals up the social and political context of public state education. Fraternity is a notoriously difficult notion to place on our conceptual maps and much philosophical work still needs to be done. Part of the difficulty has to do with the fact that it is often located at different points in relation to other key notions, like 'society' and 'the state'. It is, if you like, at the interface between social and political philosophy and raises problems about the relation and the relative importance of each. A further difficulty has to do with its status as both the grounds and the goal of human well-being. Without attempting to resolve those issues here the commitment to a fraternal paradigm for the comprehensive school involves a commitment to an emancipatory notion of citizenship and, consequently, to the importance of the public realm.

I recognize that to some degree the work of comprehensive schools is informed by these commitments, but only partially and occasionally. The fraternal imperative amounts to something like a paradigm shift because it not only raises aspects of current practice to a new prominence, it argues that those very aspects are fundamental, that the effects of their move from the periphery to the centre of what we are about, combined with the introduction of previously neglected matters, is catalytic in its effects; the conceptual and practical chemistry alters. We are no longer talking about the same thing differently; what we are doing is different.

Even this lightest of sketches setting out something of four of the fundamental characteristics of a fraternal paradigm indicates that each is closely related to the others. Thus, whilst I have schematically divided various suggestions into different categories this should not be taken to mean that an item appearing under one heading could not legitimately, in a slightly different form, appear under another, e.g., 'celebration' could be included under each one of the categories. In fact, in the following section of this chapter I have decided to employ only three headings — (a) Personal Coherence, (b) Communal Life, and (c) The Public Realm — largely because the centripetal pull of holism informs all three. Finally, the remarks that are included under each of these headings are far from exhaustive and they certainly do not amount to anything like a taxonomy. They are merely observations and questions which seek to give some substance to hitherto relatively abstract arguments. My hope would be that they provide stimulus to a deepening and imaginative construction of a democratic, communitarian paradigm for the comprehensive school.

Before looking at each of these categories, it may be helpful to reflect on another passage from G.D.H. Cole's *Essentials of Democracy*. In the earlier extract Cole talked about the necessity of a 'physical glow of sympathy and love' for someone who comes to you in genuine distress seeking your help. Community or fraternity, or in Cole's own words, 'comradeship, friendliness, brotherhood,' are in an important sense prior to justice — 'a man is not a democrat, however justly he may try to behave to his fellow man, unless he feels like that'. The passage continues:

> But — and here is the point — you cannot feel that glow about people, with capacities for doing and suffering — unless and until you get to know them personally. And you cannot know, personally, more than quite a small number of people.
>
> That is why real democracies have either to be small, or broken up into small, human groups in which men and women know and love one another. If human societies get too big, and are not broken up in that way, the human spirit goes out of them: and the spirit of democracy goes out too (Cole, 1941a, p. 99).

The passage is helpful, firstly because it affirms the centrality of community, of being known in a full and rounded way as a person, not partially or as a role occupant. Secondly, it is helpful because this kind of knowing, this communal context of human flourishing, is crucially linked to the question of size. It seems to me that what Cole has to say about democracy applies equally to comprehensive schools as the agents of democratic education, i.e., education in and for democracy. Our means of educating young people must be at once personal, communal, democratic: a fundamental assumption of this essay is that the three are indissolubly linked. Our comprehensive schools must proclaim those values and those modes of living and working together as an educational community and a key factor in realizing these aspirations is the question of size. Education, in the language of Fritz

Michael Fielding

Schumacher, must be on a human scale.[4]

Since each school committed to the kind of values and perspectives advocated in this essay will establish its own practice and pursue its own line of development, it is probably best to gain entry into this new perspective by raising questions. There are, needless to say, no 'right' answers, though there will be wrong ones: some answers will turn out to be more fruitful in the experience of students and staff than others and will undoubtedly lead to the generation of further key questions; other answers may unintentionally betray the spirit of what we are about and/or may prove not to be workable — and in these senses they will be wrong. Having raised a number of questions, I give brief illustrative reponses, sometimes involving further issues. I do so in the hope that the argument of this essay engages with the daily lives of teachers and students and not just with the philosophical debate about the nature of emancipatory education. Inevitably I draw on my own experience at Stantonbury Campus in Milton Keynes, not as in any sense an exemplar, but as part of the concrete grounding of my own advocacy.

(a) Personal Coherence

a.1 What means can we employ to ensure that each student is known well, in their roundedness, by a small number of staff?

a.i Schools sometimes do make a response to this question by, at least in the early years, providing integrated courses covering a substantial part of the timetable and taught by a single member of staff or a small team of teachers. At Stantonbury, 12-year-old students in the Foundation (entry) Year have Shared Time (integrated English, History, Geography, Social Studies, RE, Dance, Drama, Music, Art) for 40 per cent of their time substantially taught by one teacher, wherever possible someone who is also their tutor. The amount of time devoted to shared time in the Third Year is reduced. In the Fourth and Fifth Years we are beginning to introduce a version of Shared Time which includes English, Humanities and Drama, again an integrated course taught substantially by one person working within a small team of staff. The extension of this kind of model eventually leads to a mini-school structure which, at Stantonbury, manifests itself in the form of a Hall organization — something I will return to in subsequent sections of this chapter. The important point about question 1 is that it leads us firmly into a debate about the value of stable, substantial relationships between students and staff as a critical factor in the student's learning. This, of course, includes the question of motivation, though it is not reducible to it. At first glance it would seem to be hostile to the current vogue for modular courses. Certainly the onus is on proponents of the modular curriculum to address, not just the question of the fragmentation of students' experience, but the prima facie difficulty of a modular course taking on board the central place

Democracy and Fraternity

of personal knowledge and the growth of persons in community.

a.2 In what ways is it possible to establish relationships between students and staff which foster mutual warmth and mutual respect?

a.ii This second point is open to a myriad responses. The key words here are 'warmth', 'respect', and 'mutual'. Warmth and respect are predicated on knowledge over time and mutuality depends on ways in which boundaries are drawn less often and with greater hesitancy. It depends on talk and listening, on finding a voice and valuing each other. The stress that Geoff Cooksey, Stantonbury's first director, laid on 'first names and carpets' always draws the expected retorts from those who neither know nor care about what we are trying to achieve. And it is, of course, true that of themselves they achieve little; their significance lies in the doors that are opened, the boundaries that disappear. They point to a commitment to schools as human institutions in which personal knowing is central and in which the physical environment moves away from the noise of the factory to the circumstance of dialogue and the context of conversion.

a.3 How can we enable a student to develop stable relationships with his/her peers?

a.iii Stability of relationships is fundamental. Whilst we must beware of stultification and have the capacity to respond flexibly to circumstances which require change, it remains true that human beings grow in environments in which they feel secure and known as persons. This is not to say that students should remain in their tutor group for the entirety of the school day: it is, however, to say that the tutor group should be the class unit for a significant part of their time in school up to the age of 16.

a.4 How can we ensure that students feel valued?

a.iv My fourth point about students feeling valued is something which schools are increasingly addressing both by offering programmes of work which are perceived to be of value, and by exploring imaginative ways in which a much greater range of student achievement can be recognized and appreciated. The main point I would wish to make here is that we pursue the notion of 'celebration' as central to the work of a comprehensive school. Essentially, celebration is about valuing what we do: it is positive rather than negative; it is communal rather than atomistic; it is active rather than passive; it proclaims values rather than denying them; its objectivity is in its openness and its reciprocity. Above all, it is an essentially practical notion. Elsewhere I have explored the case for celebration as an educational strategy and sketched out some practical outcomes of such a commitment (Fielding, 1985). What I wish to raise here is its contribution to the search for personal coherence and self-esteem.

a.5 Does the school value different kinds of knowing and doing?

Michael Fielding

a.v Breaking out of the severely constricting mould of the traditional academic curriculum is something which secondary schools are now addressing with much greater commitment. Since David Hargreaves's work in the early 1980s, there has been much greater recognition of the inappropriateness of the grammar school curriculum as the basis of secondary education. Students cannot be expected to develop as persons or bring a sense of ownership or personal coherence to activities which are largely irrelevant, narrowly focused and a source of failure rather than success.

a.6 What opportunities do students have for mapping out their own learning paths, thus enhancing the coherence of their knowledge and experience?

a.vi Personal coherence with regard to experience of the manifest curriculum does not depend solely on the ingenuity with which schools construct curriculum matrices or integrate their courses. Both those things are valuable but unless students have some sense of ownership over their studies and activities, unless they are encouraged and enabled to some degree to take charge of their own learning, then we will constantly fall prey to the dangers of confusing teaching and learning, of assuming that what is planned is the same as what is delivered and what is delivered is the same as what is learned. In the end, coherence is a personal construct; meaning is achieved, not received.

a.7 Are these previous questions addressed to teaching and non-teaching staff with the same rigour as they are to students?

a.vii My last point is fundamental to all three categories and serves as a bridge from the first, personal coherence, to the second, communal life. Much good work has been and is being done sensitizing ourselves to the standpoint of the learner, though the well-groomed rodent of National Curriculum soon to descend upon us is bred to foster a bubonic plague of 'received wisdom' which will send us all scuttling back into the cage of pre-war certainties. However, too little attention has been paid to valuing what staff do. There is virtually no recognition that the communal basis of personal coherence applies to staff, all staff, as much as it does to students.

(b) Communal Life

b.1 Have we recognized sufficiently clearly the importance of the hidden curriculum in fostering attitudes and values we wish to encourage?

b.i In a sense, many of the subsequent points are rooted in this general exhortation to spend time, energy and imagination unearthing and examining the existing hidden curriculum and deliberately planning a coherent alternative where appropriate. Most schools acknowledge the existence and the importance of the hidden curriculum as a vital part of the communal life

Democracy and Fraternity

of the institution, but too few carry through that recognition into a commitment which confronts all areas of activity within the institution to include such things as: the gender, race and class of those at the top of the hierarchy; the decision-making structure itself; the provision of social areas for *all* members of the school community, and so on.

b.2 Is our pedagogy conducive to the erosion of privatized atomistic learning?

b.ii The dangers of atomization are beginning to be taken seriously in many schools, if only by force of circumstance. The era of the work card as an educational panacea has, hopefully, worked itself out — and this applies as much to good commercial schemes, such as KMP Maths, as it does to the home-grown variety of fading banda sheets. We need to re-read Dewey. Project work via worksheets has been, for many years, an isolated, privatized activity directly contrary to what Dewey intended. Project work for Dewey was a deeply cooperative undertaking, the idea being that each individual take an aspect of a particular topic and work away on his/her own, or in a pair/small group before sharing his/her work with others. That sharing should be central and is at once a learning experience and an affirmation of social and personal values: the whole undertaking would then have an individual vitality and communal resonance.

b.3 Do we use the stable unit of the tutor group as a means of fostering a sense of identity and commitment to the fundamental values and aspirations of our learning community?

b.iii If schools are not only to signal their values in all aspects of their work but to try to get students to own those values and contribute to their enrichment, then the persistence of a stable group in which students are known and grow as people is very important. This calls into question the firm existence of the pastoral/academic divide characteristic of the vast majority of secondary schools. The existence of a separate career structure and the institutional dissociation of these two aspects of the education of young people, enshrines a false dualism. The centripetal pull of the communitarian paradigm is wholly against such arrangements because they fragment what should be a unity, they undermine the most fruitful ground of learning and foster a view of the educative process which is neither true nor effective. At Stantonbury we are in the process of breaking down two large comprehensive schools, jointly providing for some 2,500 daytime 12 to 18-year-old students into five halls (four 12 to 16 and one post-16). By the early 1990s we hope that each hall of about 500 students will be able to deliver the majority of the curriculum in Hall home-base teams and those subjects such as Science, Design & Technology, Expressive Arts and PE, which require centralized, specialist facilities, would be taught by a team of staff within the Hall concerned. The staffing structure of each Hall also reflects the team-based, unitary approach: virtually all posts of responsibility carry

Michael Fielding

what would commonly be called a 'dual' function, and the Hall itself, not the subject department of the pastoral team, will become the dominant voice in conversations about the nature and direction of the learning experiences of the students and staff. Our responsibility as teachers is to work together with each other and with our students to create a lively, valuable education, and we can only do that if we work as a team and if we focus on the quality of the students' learning. By the Hall structure we hope to achieve what the House or Year structure never could — a merging of the pastoral and the academic into a living unity which proclaims a belief that education is about the development of persons in community and that arrangements which fragment that whole mistake the nature of learning, of knowledge, of wisdom, and of intelligent action in the world.

b.4   Are there opportunities for students of different ages to share mutually beneficial experiences?
b.iv   We have been hidebound too long by considerations of age in our education system. This fourth question suggests we should seek ways of enriching our communal life by enabling ages to mix in a positive, mutually supportive way. At Stantonbury, expeditions and exchanges to India, Tanzania, USA, France, Spain, Germany, and other countries, enable this to happen. Likewise our Day 10 arrangements in which, once a month and for a whole week in the summer term, the normal timetable is suspended and the 150 staff, together with parents, members of the local community and the students, pursue an enormously wide range of activities from Mexican cookery to mountaineering. The emergence of the Hall structure enables the potential for further work within the curriculum.

b.5   Is there active commitment to valuing and positively supporting groups who are the recipients of discrimination and disadvantage, e.g., women, ethnic minorities, working-class students?
b.v   The importance of the richness and diversity of community is something raised strongly by the above question. Two points are worth making here. Firstly, we should seek means of retaining those emancipatory commitments when particularly energetic members of staff, who have worked hard in supporting them, move on. An Equal Opportunities Standing Committee, as part of the decision-making structure in schools, is one possible answer. Secondly, we need to remind ourselves that standing committees and anti-racist policies whilst important are, in the end, only as successful as the substantive relations between all those who make up the school community. Students and staff need to have ownership over what is being suggested, otherwise it will end up being something tacked on to school life instead of informing its daily work.

b.6   Does the manifest curriculum offer sufficient opportunities for 'solidary' experience?

Democracy and Fraternity

b.vi   It is David Hargreaves who has raised the importance of looking at the experience of students in the curriculum and asking to what extent they enable what Durkheim calls 'solidary' experience. It would be interesting to know to what extent his invitation has been taken up. Certainly, it is one that is part and parcel of the communitarian paradigm.

b.7   Are the boundaries between the school and the community to which it belongs sufficiently flexible and mutually responsive?
b.vii   The extent and nature of community involvement in the school is clearly of importance in any consideration of community life. At Stantonbury we have some 10,000 adult students using the campus each week and there is a crèche to enable adult attendance at daytime sessions and the classes which form part of the provision for our 12 to 18-year-old student body. There is a highly successful community drama group and within the formal curriculum there is community placement, work experience and the use of the local community as a learning resource. These are features we share with many schools throughout the country and places like The Dukeries in Nottinghamshire offer examples of ways in which an imaginative commitment can be developed still further.

b.8   Are the different strands of our communal life and activity woven into a unity which gives meaning and coherence to that variety?
b.viii   The weaving together of various strands of communal activity into a living whole is as difficult as it is important. Some schools are more successful at it than others. Most do not seriously attempt it — and the extent to which this is true is a measure of the individualism by which our formal system of schooling is still gripped.

b.9   Do we celebrate the richness and the variety of our life in school?
b.ix   Celebration, as I suggested earlier, is fundamentally a communal notion and it should inform every aspect of our lives in school; it should be part of the rhythm of our daily work. It also applies as much to staff and community as it does to students. Staff development work at Stantonbury operates predominantly in a communal celebratory mode. Our Mutual Support & Observation (MSO) Programme transforms what most teachers remember as an inquisitorial experience into a mode of professional development which is deeply fraternal in character and genuinely emancipatory in outcome. Our Professional Development Partnership (PDP) scheme is grounded on identical principles of mutuality and support and offers an emancipatory, celebratory alternative to staff appraisal.[5]

b.10   As before, do all the previous points apply rigorously to all staff within the institution?
b.x   The fact that I have chosen to illustrate the point about celebration by reference to staff testifies to the importance I would attach to this tenth

question which recognizes the simple but elusive truth that schools are not made up solely of students; the claims of community must embrace *all* who contribute regularly to the life of the school.

(c) The Public Realm

It is perfectly possible to subsume the following six questions about the public realm under the previous section 'Communal Life'. The public realm is after all part of the communal dimension of schools. There are, however, a number of reasons why I have separated it in this way. If we are committed to establishing small-scale structures that enable that participation to take place, we must also educate ourselves in the use of those structures. Generally speaking schools are not organized on a participatory basis, nor do they offer opportunities for most staff to participate in public discussion of matters of importance. What the fraternal paradigm does is to take the public realm, i.e., the site of the practical living out of the responsibilities and opportunities for participatory democracy, seriously. Its virtual neglect is thus the prime justification for its separation from the section on communal life.

c.1 Are there opportunities for students to explore matters of importance: (a) in the mainstream curriculum, (b) non-curriculum issues?
c.i Some schools, such as Quinton Kynaston in London, have sought to provide opportunities, formal and otherwise, for students to feedback on their experience of the curriculum, and the national development of profiling in its formative rather than its summative role can provide another means for those sorts of conversation to take place. The need for an institutional commitment to a form of dialogue that not only allows for but actively seeks student reflection on the courses they have been following is paramount.

Similarly we should provide a forum for students to raise matters of concern about any aspect of their life in school. School councils have lost the prominence they once had in the late 1960s and early 1970s. Often this is for good reasons, largely to do with tokenism and the ineffectual nature of their decision-making capacity. Whilst both weaknesses are real, neither are necessary; both are amenable to concerted effort and imaginative resolve. Arguably we ought also to explore ways in which this participatory process can become a characteristic of the curriculum negotiation between staff and students much as it does in some Danish schools where the topic, the manner, the medium and the peers with whom one works are communally negotiated by the class itself.

c.2 Are there occasions and forums where students and staff together can raise what are perceived as matters of importance?

c.ii The coming together of staff and students on an equal footing to discuss matters of mutual concern has never been other than a rarity in the state education system. Its most famous example, the Moot at Countesthorpe College in Leicestershire, is now defunct. There are all sorts of reasons why such examples are rare and why they seem to have failed. Without going into the matter in detail here, it is nonetheless pertinent to record that one of the five Halls at Stantonbury has recently involved students as active partners in Hall Meetings, the main forum for the discussion of all matters of importance in the life of the Hall and the campus as a whole. It will be interesting to see how the development fares. Certainly in the Hall Meetings, with roughly thirty staff and eighteen student reps (one from each tutor group), we have addressed transition problems of students being unused to the subject matter and the manner of staff meetings via a system of 'sponsorship' and have sought to ensure the meeting retains its 'human' scale by a sensitive use of small group discussion. The sponsorship idea involves students choosing a member of staff to sponsor them and that member of staff committing him-herself to discuss the agenda beforehand, sitting with and supporting the student in the meeting itself, and spending some time afterwards discussing how things went. Our belief is that the presence of students in Hall Meetings is enriching for staff and meaningful and important for the students involved.[6]

c.3 Do decision-making structures invite participation by all staff?
c.iii Schools vary considerably in the extent and the nature of the opportunities for staff to take part in the decision-making process. Most are consultative rather than participatory. There are exceptions, like Quinton Kynaston which operates a system of standing committees that feed in to the full staff meeting where all major school decisions are made. At Stantonbury we have moved to a standing committee structure which, together with the Hall Meetings, has considerable advisory powers. The fraternal paradigm pushes us firmly in the direction of participatory structures and, in the absence of fully fledged practice, the level of participation in the consultative process should be as high as possible.

c.4 What opportunities does the school offer all staff to explore educational issues and development?
c.iv Most schools provide staff with opportunities to discuss matters of educational importance via their membership of faculty and tutorial teams. The extent to which meetings are used for educational as opposed to administrative functions varies considerably. The communal paradigm would certainly require team meetings to provide substantial room for discussion of educational issues. It would also urge other means, such as staff conferences, to be explored. In addition, schools could seek to create occasions in their normal rhythm of work in which discussion and debate takes place. At Stantonbury we produce a Curriculum Bulletin, a series of Occasional

Papers, Broadsheets and a variety of reports on INSET activities. Hall Meetings are also a major arena for discussion.

c.5 To what extent are staff aware of current practice and planned developments in the school outside their own curriculum areas?

c.6 What opportunities are there for colleagues to celebrate their own achievements, those of the teams in which they work, and the achievements of the school as a whole?

c.v/vi Another constructive use of Hall Meetings is the provision of space in which colleagues can share the work of their faculties and teams. In this way staff not only have the opportunity of their work being valued by others, they are able to celebrate the achievements of colleagues in other teams and come to have an awareness of good practice right across the school. With the timely death of the dishonest, divisive charade of Speech Days we must beware of abandoning any kind of celebration of the achievements of the school as a learning community. Undoubtedly, following earlier advocacy of breaking schools down into human-size units the major celebratory arena will be within mini-schools or their equivalents. Nonetheless we should seek to establish emancipatory alternatives to Speech Day which value the enormous variety of achievements of students and staff. An interesting variety aimed solely at staff again comes from Quinton Kynaston: their production of Review Reports provides a communal reflection on the past year's work and the setting of new targets and intentions for the twelve months ahead.

The emancipatory imperative

The link between fraternity, democracy and comprehensive education is important. The composite nature of the principle of fraternity ensures the emancipatory intent which has underpinned the comprehensive school. The comprehensive school movement has always been concerned with challenging orthodoxies; either by championing equality of opportunity and the erosion of privilege; or by the affirmation of the equal value principle and the rejection of meritocracy; or, currently, by the challenge to the individualist model of human fulfilment. The comprehensive school movement is the voice of a democratic, public education and as such it speaks for communities and ways of life that the grammar, secondary modern and public schools could never do. The principle of fraternity is itself the interpersonal grounding which makes possible both public democratic polity and personal human fulfilment:

> Freedom is the product of human fellowship ... Politics is necessary to freedom ... But a democratic polity is possible only for a human community which has established a common way of life upon a

Democracy and Fraternity

basis of mutual trust; and the extent and quality of the freedom it provides depends upon the extent to which those who govern and organise are in communion with one another (Macmurray, 1950, pp. 104-105).

Fraternity or fellowship is the means of our developing humanity and the end towards which it aspires.

A New Comprehensive Paradigm

The challenges which lie ahead for the comprehensive school are the challenges that face us as persons in the different sorts of relations — social and political, personal and communal — which condition our destinies in the last decade of the twentieth century. For those of us whose direct concern is with the nature and the quality of comprehensive education our most pressing need is to reject the contemporary managerialism and address ourselves again to purposes, to the basic question about what comprehensive education is for. Only when we have done that will the appropriate means at our disposal emerge. What is clear from the outset is that they will not be freewheeling techniques applicable to a multitude of purposes; they will be approaches informed by the values which are fundamental to our undertaking.

My own view is that we need an alternative paradigm of comprehensive schooling which has its roots in the communitarian tradition of social and political thought and that central to that paradigm is an emancipatory imperative. Of course, even if we were to develop our practices within that framework the way ahead would not be any less free from contention and disagreement. The authors of the quotations which form part of the opening section of this essay would certainly not agree on a number of issues of considerable importance for educators. But the disagreement is more likely to be productive: what William Morris, Karl Marx and Frederick Engels, John Macmurray,[7] A. H. Halsey, Emile Durkheim and David Hargreaves would all agree on is, not just the 'fallacy' of individualism but its destructiveness of human flourishing.[8]

In all this I am conscious of the problem of language. It may well be that Michael Ignatieff is at least pointing to something important when he says:

Words like fraternity, belonging and community are so soaked with nostalgia and utopianism that they are nearly useless as guides to the real possibilities of solidarity in modern society... Our task is to find a language for our need for belonging which is not just a way of expressing nostalgia, fear and estrangement from modernity (Ignatieff, 1984, pp. 138-139).

Michael Fielding

I am conscious, too, of the importance of a language which is sensitive to the struggles of oppressed groups within our society. It might well be that words other than 'fraternity' or 'fellowship' become more appropriate to our task. And words are important. Those which express deep human aspirations are often contested, always historically conditioned and necessary in a way which is fundamental to our growth as persons: 'We need words to keep us human... Without a language adequate to this moment we risk losing ourselves in resignation towards the portion of life which has been allotted to us' (ibid pp. 141, 142).

Yet the importance of words lies ultimately in the reality which they seek to reflect and create. Near the beginning of William Morris' *A Dream of John Ball*, the narrator ponders on:

> How men fight and loose the battle, and the thing that they fought for comes about in spite of their defeat, and when it comes turns out not to be what they meant, and other men have to fight for what they meant under another name (Morris, 1973, p. 53).

Our fight is for comprehensive schools because they are currently the most appropriate means to the education of all young people. The comprehensive ideal is by its very nature emancipatory and the principle of fraternity sets out the conditions of its success.

Some would argue that calls for fraternity are doubtfully appropriate at a time when the knuckled grip of individualism is throttling the life out of an already emaciated public education system. Why advocate an educational paradigm which speaks of unity and common purposes when the current realities of our society have more to do with division, the partiality of privilege and the secular beatification of greed? Such objections have considerable force. But in the end they fail to convince for at least two reasons. Firstly, the prospect of emancipatory educational provision arising from supporters of comprehensive schools acquiescing in the destruction of the very system they have fought to establish is even less compelling than the alternative it opposes. Secondly, and more importantly, charges of Utopianism must not only be tempered by a recognition that something needs to be done; they must also address more profound questions about the nature and conditions of human fulfilment. What lies at the heart of this essay is a belief about what it means to be and to become more fully human. The conditions that enhance our growth as persons are under attack, but the necessity of those conditions remains absolute. The necessity of loving our children does not diminish in proportion to the increase in the hostility of the social and political world they grow up in. The reverse is true. We love them despite the difficulties and distortions which affect us all. Likewise in schools, the communal or fraternal imperative becomes more not less important as the prevailing climate grows increasingly individualistic. It is true that schools cannot win through on their own: it is also true that they cannot win if they do not enter the fight.

Acknowledgements

Thanks to Graham Benjamin, Roger Dale, Mike Davies, Pat White and John Wilkins for comments on an earlier draft of this paper.

Notes

1. This is a considerably altered version of a previous chapter 'Liberté, Egalité, Fraternité — Ou la Mort: Towards a New Paradigm for the Comprehensive School' which appeared in October, 1987 in *Redefining the Comprehensive Experience*, ed. Clyde Chitty. My hope is that this revised version makes it clearer what the New Paradigm amounts to and what actual differences it would make if it were to inform practices in comprehensive schools today.
2. A very stimulating recent example is Barber (1984).
3. The use of the term 'fraternity' in this paper is not gender-specific. I have retained its use throughout in order to maintain a linguistic thread which, if broken, might well lead to confusion in an already difficult area. It may well be that words other than 'fraternity' or 'fellowship' are appropriate to the emancipatory task I am advocating.
4. See the excellent work of the Human Scale Education Movement who can be contacted at Ford House, Hartland, Bideford, Devon, EX39 6EE, UK.
5. Readers interested in either of these schemes may like to contact the author of this paper who will be pleased to send further information. The address to write to is Stantonbury Campus, Milton Keynes, Bucks, MK14 6BN, UK.
6. As with note 5 above, interested readers may like to contact the author at Stantonbury Campus for further information. We are working hard to ensure Hall Meetings are not merely staff meetings with students present, but genuine encounters in which members of the educational community share matters of mutual concern.
7. John Macmurray's writings on education are outstanding, but not readily available. Of particular interest are the papers: *Learning to be human* (5 May 1958), *Teachers and pupils* (29 November 1963) and *Reflections on the notion of an educated man* (17 November 1965). None of them were published. The author of this article would be happy to make copies available to interested readers.
8. I realise, of course, that the term 'individualism' is itself subject to considerable debate. In his review article 'Durkheim's call to order' (MacIntyre, 1974), Alasdair MacIntyre argues compellingly that:

   The essence of individualism is not so much to emphasise the individual rather than the collective... as to frame all questions according to an ostensible antithesis between the individual and the collective.

   Of the authors mentioned, Macmurray is arguably the most compelling and the most eloquent in his rejection of individualism, Durkheim remained a victim of its distinctive mode of thought.

References

BARBER, B. (1984) *Strong Democracy*, London: University of California Press.
BARKER, B. (1986) *Rescuing the Comprehensive Experience*, Milton Keynes: Open University Press.
BLATCHFORD, R. (1985) (Ed.) *Managing the Secondary School*, London: Bell & Hyman.
COLE, G.D.H. (1941a) 'The essentials of democracy', in Cole, (1950), *v.i.* pp. 96–112.

COLE, G.D.H. (1941b) 'Democracy face to face with hugeness' in Cole (1950), *v.i.* pp. 90–96.
COLE, G.D.H. (1950) *Essays in Social Theory*, London: Macmillan.
DAHL, R. (1956) *A Preface to Democratic Theory*, Chicago: Chicago University Press.
DAUNT, P.E. (1972) *Comprehensive Values*, London: Heinemann.
FIELDING, M. (1985) 'Celebration: Valuing what we do' in Blatchford (1985), ibid., pp. 170–185.
HALSEY, A.H. (1981) *Change in British Society*, 2nd. ed., Oxford: Oxford University Press.
HARGREAVES, D.H. (1982) *The Challenge for the Comprehensive School*, London: Routledge & Kegan Paul.
IGNATIEFF, M. (1984) *The Needs of Strangers*, London: Chatto & Windus.
LASKI, H. (1937) 'Democracy' in *Seligman (1937)*, *v.i.*, p. 76.
MACINTYRE, A. (1974) 'Durkheim's call to order' in *New York Review of Books*, March 7, p. 26.
MACMURRAY, J. (1950) *Conditions of Freedom*, London: Faber & Faber.
MACMURRAY, J. (1961) *Persons in Relation*, London: Faber & Faber.
MARX, K. and ENGELS, F. (1970) *The German Ideology*, Ed. C.J. Arthur, London: Lawrence & Wishart. (Originally written 1845/46).
MORRIS, W. (1973) 'A dream of John Ball' in *Three Works by William Morris*, London: Lawrence & Wishart. (Originally published 1886/87).
SELIGMAN, E.R.A. (1937) (Ed.) *Selections from the Encyclopaedia of the Social Sciences*, New York: Macmillan.
SIMMS, B. (1986) *Defend Comprehensive Schools*, London: Communist Party of Great Britain.

Chapter 4

Costing Democracy: Schooling, Equality and Democracy in Sweden

Stephen J. Ball

The aim of this chapter is neither to eulogise the Swedish education system nor to offer up that system as a model for Great Britain to emulate. Nor will I be attempting a detailed empirical exegesis of that system. Rather I hope to employ the Swedish case, set over and against the British version of school education, as a vehicle for an exercise in disidentification (Pecheux, 1975). That is as a way of challenging the prevailing ideologies and practices which constitute 'good' education. By working antagonistically in relation to dominant educational discourses I shall attempt to displace and transform some key elements within those discourses. In particular I want to raise questions about the frequent claim that a direct and automatic link exists between academic 'standards' in education and economic performance and to displace the concept of 'excellence' from its central position in our thinking about what education is for. In doing this I shall argue for a re-emphasis on the social goals of education, specifically the relation of education to the contents and practices of democracy.

Democratic Discourse in British and Swedish Education

Dewey (Democracy and Education, 1916) argued that a prerequisite for education fulfilling its egalitarian, developmental and integrative functions is that society be democratic. For in a democratic society, the requirements of the citizenry are the abilities to relate to one another equally and reciprocally in controlling their common affairs. Schools that prepare students for this task in life will be necessarily egalitarian. Moreover, full personal development involves precisely the development of those cognitive and other social powers that allow individuals to effectively participate in democratically constituted collectivities and thereby control their lives (Bowles and Gintis, 1975, p. 22).

Stephen J. Ball

The issue of democracy and education has always been a marginal one in educational debates in Britain. Indeed the issue has tended to be dismissed or indeed condemned as a politicization of education and therefore as an unsuitable one for schools to be concerned with, the assumption being as always that what is taught in school is, and should be, politically neutral. In British society people are not expected to show any particular interest in the way in which they are governed or to try to influence directly decisions which affect their lives. Attempts to increase political participation are regarded as aberrant, a threat to stability and a sign of malfunctions in the elite political system. The exclusion of democracy as a topic for or about schools is symptomatic of the minimalism evident throughout the society.

If there seemed to be a moment in the late 1960s and early 1970s when school democracy was on the agenda that moment quickly passed as the fragile, incoherent and disorganised discourse of comprehensivism was quickly and effectively deconstructed by the anti-progressive critiques of the Black Papers. Those few schools which took democracy seriously found themselves beset by an unfriendly media, bemused parents and unsupportive local authority officers. Teachers who attempt to teach democracy and act democratically now have their well-established place in the Sun Hall of Fame of the Loony Left (Fletcher, Caron and Williams, 1985).

In the Britain of Mrs Thatcher's third term, reflecting the two contesting political philosophies of the new Conservative Party (one, neo-conservative, urging the authority of the strong state and the other, neo-liberal, advocating the authority of the market) education is defined explicitly and forcefully in two ways (see Ball, 1988). On the one hand the 'old humanists' cling to and press for a return to excellence and to a concern with 'standards', an elitist, academic version of schooling. On the other, the 'industrial trainers' peddle an arid, instrumentalism which aims to reduce schooling to a matter of skills and attitudes as a preparation for employment (or for 'life'). In either case the (positive and transformative) social goals of education are ignored, the processes of schooling are to be concerned narrowly with reproduction and subordination rather than with regeneration and empowerment. Indeed what it means to be educated is defined simply in terms of the interests of those who already extract privilege from the system. Those interests are powerfully advocated and defended. The redistributive functions of education, even the anodyne concepts of meritocracy and equality of opportunity, let alone those of justice and equality, now have no credibility in public discourse and are left to the concern of those who 'drool and drivel' (M. Thatcher, television interview).

But in *some* other societies, democracy is not a matter for suspicion or of lunacy, the social goals of education are not deliberately set aside. In Sweden education moves to the music of a very different discourse.

Sweden is a highly developed capitalist society, indeed in terms of indicators like concentration of ownership Sweden represents a 'purer' form of capitalism than Britain. By 1975 the fifteen largest firms employed 25 per cent of private sector workers; in 1963, seventeen groups of owners effectively controlled over one-third of all industrial output. The Wallenberg family alone controlled 17 per cent of this output. But since 1932, with the exception of the period of 1976–82, Swedish political life has been dominated by the social welfare policies of the Social Democratic Party of Swedish Workers. In a nutshell:

> Sweden (is) a decentralized market economy dominated by private enterprise, but with an ambitious state policy in public consumption and public saving, including income redistribution, in a publicly owned infrastructure, designed to maximize harmony and in a policy of stabilization. This liberal and democratic welfare state thus operates in a mixed economy and has produced a high capacity to innovate, even against a background of a high employment economic policy (unemployment stands at 3% compared with Britain's 13%). For many people outside Sweden this is a highly enviable state of affairs (Lawrence and Spybey, 1986, p. 25).

In Swedish society the school is both a tool and a goal of social change, it is seen straightforwardly as a political force in the building of a better society. Olof Palme, in 1969, then Minister of Education described schools as a 'spearhead into the future'. This view of the role and purpose of education has long been an aspect of Swedish political culture but it came strongly to the fore in the late 1960s and early 1970s in a number of documents produced jointly by the Social Democratic Party and the LO (the main trade union organization). Equality, participation, self-realization and democracy were the key concepts in the development of all aspects of education (and social and working life). Democracy was defined as:

> ... the opportunity to influence what goods, services cultural experiences and environmental qualities will be available in society. It is a question of economic democracy at the parliamentary level ... and ... democratic conditions at the local level, to influence his or her own immediate life situation, at the workplace, in schools and institutions and in terms of housing conditions (Jamlikhet, 1969, p. 11).

The underlying principle in this conception of democracy was not equality of opportunity but equality of outcomes, again both at school and at work:

> ... the job is not to construct ladders to enable individuals to climb from the role of ordinary employee. The job is to change the role of all employees as a group and their conditions at work and in the community (Lovux, 1976, p. 79).

Basic knowledge and skills for all was to become the foremost goal of the school, and this entailed abandoning curricular differentiation and all forms of streaming.

In the debate on the proposed school reforms of 1975/76 Lena Hjelm-Wallen, the Minister of Schools, argued that it was:

> more important for pupils to have mastered basic knowledge and skills than for them to have gone through everything in the syllabus and all parts of the syllabus, benefitting to varying degrees from the ground they have covered.

And in the same debate she said that:

> strengthening democracy and creating greater social equality are tasks fundamental to the Swedish education system. Consequently education is of major significance in the distribution of prosperity and influence, to the cultural environment, and in preparing people for active involvement in society (Prop 1975/76:39, p. 219).

The predominance of a cognitive/academic version of schooling and the school curriculum was being fundamentally challenged in these reforms. The preoccupation with the academic was seen as a barrier to full participation in schooling, an obstacle in the way of other sorts of goals, and as an unfair discriminator producing biased outcomes in favour of certain social groups. The SIA reform of the late 1970s also attempted to challenge the academic orthodoxies of schooling. Aimed at the early grades in particular, the mental-manual labour divide was breached by bringing aspects of working life and production from the local area into the work of the school. The *SIA* report urged:

> Schools are to be made less academic and teaching must be based on the practical experience gained by pupils. A prominent position must be given to knowledge of value and everyday life, and the community at large must be extensively utilized by schools as a source of knowledge (SIA, 1976).

These extracts in no way capture the complexity of the reforms in Swedish education. From the beginning of the long educational reform period in the 1940s education policy has been characterized by multiple aspirations for the outcomes of education. Thus:

> Equal educational achievement can also refer to the equal preparation within the education system for active participation in society, so that every citizen has the same opportunities to be consulted and informed of the changes that will affect his life style and life chances (Harnqvist and Bengtsson, 1972, p. 206).

The key factor here is that the social goals of education were being validated from within the political leadership, and were related to political traditions in the welfare system as a whole. (Interestingly few Social Democratic politicians were educated in the selective grammar school system, in contrast to the Labour Party in Britain. The vast majority of those influential in the period of reform received their most significant educational experiences in adult education, within the politicised 'popular movements').

The vision of democracy embedded in these various texts is an active rather than a passive one. The school's task is not to teach about democracy but to provide citizenship education in the form of civic and political competence; in Giroux's (1983) terms, to encourage pupils to act as though they lived in a real democracy. The aim is to increase the direct participation of citizens in decision-making. This comes close to what Elster (1983) calls discourse democracy, the development of institutional conditions intended to create a basis for high quality, public exchange of views, leading to the 'best' possible decisions. Discourse democracy emphasizes content rather than form, and detachment rather than self-realization. The goal is to encourage an understanding of politics as a basis for participation. Knight (1985, p. 6) writing from Australia makes a similar point, but goes on to link form and content:

> A democratic school is an integrated school, not a melting pot where differences are filtered away, but a school where differences in race, gender, class and ethnicity can be drawn upon for problem solving and question forming. Students co-operate in order to solve the problems they face in a complicated and diverse world. This process has as its ultimate aim the education of students in order that they become responsible authorities.
>
> It should not be surprising that so many children (and adults) show little sense of social responsibility. They have not been so educated.

Both writers are drawing attention to a set of longstanding debates about the nature and purposes of democracy which oscillate within the form and content division. Stated baldly and extremely the primary emphasis on content views the purposes of democractic politics in economic terms, as the aggregation of individual decisions which are based upon the maximizing of material interests. This is what Elster (1986) calls market democracy, and is represented, to some extent at least, in the consumer-oriented, choice and freedom rhetoric of Conservative neo-liberals. At the other extreme is what Elster (1986) calls forum democracy. Here politics is not *about* anything. It is a combative display of individual skills, or a celebration of collective solidarity. But, it is content-less, and therefore remote from the real course of events. It lacks commitment, except to the principle of democracy itself. Clearly democracy in schools often tends towards the latter extreme, with an emphasis on being democratic in process, and developing democratic competences, without actual influence over concrete decisions and outcomes. Elster makes the point that in the long run democratic engagement can be personally satisfactory only when there is a serious purpose to be achieved. He is clearly sceptical about democracy as a form of personal catharsis or as a way, in itself, of gaining fulfilment. It is a commitment to ends and purposes that is ultimately important, the achievement, rationally and skillfully, of the best decisions. 'If... defined as public in nature, and instrumental in purpose, politics assumes what I believe to be its proper place in society' (Elster, 1986, p 128).

If taken seriously in schools this then leads to a dual emphasis, on processes and skills, and problems and commitments. Students must acquire the skills of citizenship participation, they must also be encouraged to address basic social, economic and political issues. This is what is being attempted in Swedish schools.

Quite clearly in British schools, at the present time, either aspect of democracy, taken seriously, is likely to provoke reaction. As regards the latter, new-right critics of comprehensive education have been vociferous in their attacks upon what they describe as attempts to 'politicise' the school curriculum (Scruton, Ellis-Jones and O'Keeffe, 1985). They regard the 'politicised curriculum' as leading to indoctrination and 'a politics of goals' wherein all 'truth' is seen as ideological and there is a 'lack of respect for all independent purposes' (p. 12).

I do not want to hold up Sweden as an exemplar, but I do want to use Sweden as a demonstration of the possibilities of democratic education, and at least being engaged with the issue of democratic education. Such principles underlie, in part at least, the new compulsory school curriculum (LGR 80) adopted in 1980. Citizenship education is stressed in the goals and guidelines for schools, so too are pupil participation in decision-making and the negotiation of the curriculum. Subjects and subject departments are reduced in importance and the need for teachers and pupils to act in working-groups is emphasized. The aim is to make schools contribute to, and be part of, a social democratic society:

> ... the planning and design of teaching must not be governed by subject boundaries. Teaching questions are dealt with by class committees or at subject conferences. The work unit conference then decides on general planning and design. Teachers and pupils can choose between different ways of arranging subject matter, each way having its own particular advantages and disadvantages (p. 32).

> The organization of a school into work units makes it easier for teachers to co-operate in teaching teams. Co-operation of this kind between the adult members of the school community is an important example to the pupils of democracy in action, and it is essential with a view to the consistent and purposive development of skills in different subjects (p. 34).

> Educational planning meetings summoned by the headmaster or his (sic) nominee must be attended by equal numbers of pupil and teacher representatives, senior level pupil representatives (age 14–16) being also entitled to participate in decision-making. If planning can be done at class committee meetings attended by all

pupils and not only by their representatives, this arrangement is to be preferred. It is important for discussions to be based on alternatives presented by teachers (p. 35).

Schools must be amenable to the manifestation of differing values and opinions, and they must assert the importance of personal commitment. At the same time, schools must assert the essential values of our democracy and must clearly dissociate themselves from everything which conflicts with those values. Thus schools must not adopt a posture of neutrality or passivity concerning the fundamental values of democratic society. Instead they must deliberately promote these values and educate pupils to respect them (p. 11).

Children must be enabled to ponder moral problems and conflicts of norms and also to assume responsibility for solving such problems in practical everyday situations. Our common basic values accommodate many problems and conflicts. Collisions between goals and reality should not be glossed over (p. 10) (LGR 80, 1980).

Here democracy is an active and problematic concept; it is to be presented to children not just as a reified fact of life but as a focus of problems and conflicts and personal commitment.

Clearly the reality of such goals rests in their implementation in the structures and processes of schools. Not all schools seriously attempt this implementation, or achieve it successfully. Not all teachers are sympathetic to these goals (Tornvall, 1987), and they may be reluctant to pursue them. Nonetheless, democratic principles have certainly underlain the processes of comprehensivising the education system, from pre-school through to higher education.

The common compulsory school in Sweden takes pupils from age 7 to 16. It is preceded by a year of pre-school for all children; 99.3 per cent of children attend the state sector and over 90 per cent go on at 16 to the integrated upper secondary school. Participation in higher education is around 25 per cent but also at any time roughly six out of every ten Swedish adults are enrolled in some form of adult education.

There are no public examinations in Sweden and up to the last two years of compulsory school any grading of pupils work is prohibited. Marks are then awarded on a grade point average system across all subjects and this grade point average is used in the complicated system of choosing upper secondary school 'lines'. There is a common curriculum, saving one option choice in the last two years of secondary school, and mixed-ability grouping throughout except for two sets in the last two years in Mathematics and English. As indicated above, LGR 80 has attempted to weaken subject boundaries and by creating teachers' working groups tried to reduce the number of teachers working with each class (ie. by having just one teacher for science and maths, and one for Swedish and social science and civics).

Stephen J. Ball

It should be evident from the comments and description above that social rather than academic or instrumental goals are to the fore in Swedish education. While LGR 80 contains compromises, social outcomes and equality of outcomes are given precedence, in a sense 'at the expense' of the academic and the instrumental. As many pupils as possible are to be educated as long as possible, the idea being to create an all-embracing and favourable environment for young people, dynamically linked to the wider society. The school is no longer to pose as neutral but to take the side of democracy.

Nystrom, a member of a group of influential scholars who were involved in the initiation of the educational reforms in the 1940s, wrote later:

> In fact we had two aims. We wanted to pave the way for workers' and farmers' youth to higher education and we wanted to change the teaching system in school radically. With these aims we wanted on the one hand to break the middle class' virtual monopoly and on the other hand to obtain a more individualized teaching (Nystrom, 1987).

Swedish education policy is centrally concerned with the plight of under-privileged and socially and educationally disadvantaged goups in society. That is, students from working-class homes, adults who have not had the same schooling opportunities as their children, women, the physically handicapped and immigrants and ethnic-minority groups (Marklund, 1980). The provision of education is regarded not only as a moral obligation but an individual, social and economic necessity. The Swedish concept of educational disadvantage, in the sense of not having completed the full cycle of basic and vocational education, has no meaningful equivalent in British political discourse.

A rather superficial but interesting illustration of these trends in Swedish education is given in Table 1. This presents the variance between the schools as a percentage of variance between the pupils in science tests carried out in nine countries at ages 10 and 14 (Comber & Keeves, 1973).

Table 1.
Percentage variance between 10 and 14 year olds in science tests in 9 countries.

Country	Age 10	Age 14
England	19	33
Finland	28	20
Japan	18	20
Netherlands	23	40
Scotland	29	43
Sweden	15	12
Czechoslovakia	27	30
West Germany	40	34
USA	32	28

The point is that the variance between pupils is smallest at age 10 in Sweden and in fact this decreases at age 14. Finland, Czechoslovakia and West Germany also exhibit a decrease in variance between pupils but their initial variances are much larger. The implication is that the performance differences between pupils and between schools in Sweden are minimized by the system of education in operation. In England one effect of the system of education is to increase significantly, over time, differences in pupil performance. In other words the English system of education is oriented to differentiation and thus the maximization of failure. Indeed these figures mark the failure in Britain to make a meaningful transition from an elite, selective, sponsored mobility system to a mass, common education system.

The other aspect of democratization emphasized within the Swedish system, as we have seen, is that of educational participation; the wearing away of middle-class monopolies in education:

> In the dual school system, pupils were directed to lower secondary school according to their marks. In comprehensive school the choice of study programme is free, and the pupils cannot be directed by a teacher or headteacher to take a particular study programme. Free choice of studies became one of the cornerstones of the democratization of education in the 1962 Education Act. An important consequence was that the concepts of 'pass' and 'fail' were removed from the compulsory school system (Jonsson and Arnman, 1988, p. 13).

Such a free-choice system has its effects later when critical separations are made:

> Upper secondary school in Sweden offers education in twenty-five lines with different content. Five of them last for three or four years and constitute the best preparation for further study at colleges and universities. About thirty-five per cent of an age group leaving upper secondary school in the 1980s attended one of these five lines. Another four lines lasting for two years also give a fairly good preparation for university studies, especially at an intermediate level (Jonsson and Arnman, 1988, p. 14).

This 50 per cent involvement in university access courses compares with less than 20 per cent of English and Welsh students doing A-level courses at this stage.

Harnqvist (1988, p. 14) makes the same point, and traces the process of equalization between socio-economic groups which results from the comprehensivization of education and the elimination of differentiation. The trend over twenty-four years for males (comparing those from academic homes, upper socio-economic group 1, with the rest of the male population) is as follows:

Males in 3–4 year lines born in	1934	1948	1953	1958	1963
Academic Background	61	64	69	70	73
Other Background	6	18	25	29	28
All	10	21	28	33	31

While the social characteristics of the higher education population have not changed dramatically the age participation rate has expanded to 25 per cent compared with around 14 per cent in England and Wales. The processes of democratization and comprehensivization are also being extended into higher education. The university curriculum was reformed in 1968 according to labour market sectors and 'social relevance'. Courses are now organized into six broad areas of occupational orientation: technical; medical and nursing; administrative; economic and social work; teaching; cultural and information professions. Imminent reforms are expected to open entry to higher education to any student who completes an upper school programme. In addition, participation in adult education is high; for example in 1985 35 per cent of all adults participated in some way in such courses, 37 per cent of adult women, 24 per cent of unskilled workers. Such figures indicate a high level of continuing commitment to recurrent education. (In Norway the equivalent overall participation figure was 19 per cent, as it was in Canada).

Discourses of Democracy and Discourses of Derision

Educational discourses are by definition self-justifying and self-maintaining, certain possibilities are permitted and others prevented. The predominance of the 'democratic discourse' in Sweden's political culture and political institutions provide for the possibility of the reforms outlined above. But not all attempts at a discourse are successfully brought off, statements within a discourse may not always function to organize and designate all objects in their field. There is certainly no simple consensus in Sweden about the role of education. A whole variety of countervailing discourses are identifiable, some of which are fought out within the Social Democratic Party. The social and economic interpretations of schooling and the primacy of political as against economic purposes remain in contention:

> The schools are an arena of conflict because they have the dual role of preparing workers and citizens. The preparation required for citizenship in a democratic society based on equal opportunity and human rights is often incompatible with the preparation needed for job performance in a corporate system of work. On the one hand, schools must train citizens to know their rights under the law as well as their obligations to exercise these rights through political participation. On the other, schools must train workers with the skills and

personality characteristics that enable them to function in an authoritarian work regime. This requires a negation of the very political rights that make a good citizen (Carnoy and Levin, 1985, p. 247).

Advances and emphases in one sphere may involve costs in the other.

In 1986 the results of an *IEA* test survey of mathematics received considerable attention in the Swedish media. Svenska Dagbladet (a conservative daily paper) reported as follows:

> Sweden has been shocked to discover that its grade 7 students received the lowest test scores in mathematics of the twenty participating countries in the latest round of the survey by the International Association for the Evaluation of Educational Achievement (IEA). A government committee monitoring the tests considers it unacceptable that students can graduate from comprehensive school without a firm foundation in mathematics. In a series of recommendations the committee stresses the need for better teaching-training as a pre-requisite to achieve a higher standard of teaching and learning mathematical skills and concepts.

Pupil test scores in other grades and in other subjects showed a general increase but it was grade 7 mathematics that drew most of the attention. It is out of such events that critiques, discourses of derision can be, and often are, constructed. The point at issue is not a substantive one but an ideological and political one — what is to count as education, as being educated? Are the academic costs of an education system primarily oriented to social achievement acceptable? It may be that an emphasis on social goals, on democratic processes in and through education, is only possible at the expense of other 'valued' outcomes. 'Standards' *may* be at risk, dire consequences may be anticipated by critics and detractors. In Sweden, as in Britain in the 1970s, 'old humanists' and 'industrial trainers' continue to chip away at the democratic reforms enacted by the 'public educators''.

The relative decline of the Swedish economy in the period 1976–82 certainly strengthened the case for a more instrumental orientation to be given to upper secondary schooling. The increase in influence of the employers federation (AMF), over and against that of the LO (the main Trade Union organization), is certainly evident in the recently published report (OGY) on vocational education. The voice of 'old humanism' is also evident in the foundation of the pressure group 'Knowledge in Schools' which aims for a return to a traditional curriculum structure in schools and a re-emphasis on 'standards'. The Social Democratic government is now more willing to respond to arguments which link education directly to economic performance (although given unemployment at 3.8 per cent and a return to a healthy rate of industrial growth since 1984 such a response seems to have little real justification — it is the discourse that counts). Nonetheless, there is no simple acceptance of the sort of crude education/economy arguments that have been mounted in Britain since 1976. The success and long term recovery of the Swedish economy will simply not sustain such an analysis. If the numerous right-wing critics of British comprehensive education were actually right, one would logically expect Sweden to be an economic wasteland. In Sweden, neither 'The pursuit of egalitarianism' nor 'twenty years of experiment in education' seen as so destructive by the British Secretary of State for Education Kenneth Baker (Conservative Party Conference Speech 9.10.87) can be related to any kind of massive and permanent economic decline.

But the argument for academic 'standards' as the basis for evaluating educational processes is not linked solely to the issue of economic performance, it also subsumes a set of social reproduction issues. Notions of excellence and equality, standards and democracy, given the frameworks of power and privilege in which 'excellence' and 'standards' are currently set, are incompatible. 'Excellence' and 'standards' remain embedded in a discourse of subjection, they trade upon and maintain a 'technical matrix' of differentiation, examination and failure. The measurements on which they are based are essentially measures of inequality, they take no account of consciousness and action, only fixed performances.

In Britain in the discursive context of Thatcherism, 'standards' and 'excellence' are intimately related to the notions of possessive individualism and personal initiative. This discursive context, in practice a series of interpenetrating discourses, has at the centre of its interpellative structure, the social-subject of the 'concerned parent'. The 'concerned parent' aims to do the best for their child given the 'harsh realities' of the competitive world. The child needs a 'decent' education and good qualifications which will enable him or her to 'get on'. The emphasis is upon individual betterment, and competition. The parents' duty is to ensure that they 'choose' the best education for their child, even if that means that the children of others will have less than 'the best' education. In this condensation 'excellence' is a competitive aquisition, it is a form of differentiation, of comparison. Education is thus displaced from its political and collective context, notions of 'mass' or 'common' schooling no longer have a valid or logical role to play in this scenario. The 'concerned parent' is thus recruited as a 'discursive subject' of Thatcherism.

Here excellence is articulated within the ideological field of individualism, it is thoroughly ramified with a whole series of conservative, neo-liberal 'philosophies', based on notions of 'self-help', freedom of choice, and 'quality' by competition (strongly counterposed to the possibilities of equality). Also, excellence and standards are thus divorced from qualities of the person, except in terms of discipline and 'behaviour', or qualities of personal relations, and instead are articulated in terms of crudely measured qualitative 'outcomes', such as certificates and examination passes. Much of the discourse of derision aimed at comprehensive education in Britain is articulated in these crudely reductionist terms. Such forms of evaluation are antithetical to any possibilities of equal worth in and through education;

excellence as outlined above is accompanied by failure and standards by stigma. The excellence of the few is measured in terms of the inadequacies of the majority — it requires the production of failure. Daunt (1975, p. 64) argues that:

> The examination system, as we know it, or as it could be improved by mere adaptation, has enormous power simply because it is the only formal system, of esteem. It is easily powerful enough to ensure at worst that many schools do not endeavour to operate an equal value system at all, and at best that those who do endeavour do so in chains.

However, despite conservative critiques, the discourse of democracy still seems to hold the centre stage in Swedish education, even if the heat of debate has cooled since the 1970s. Oppositional discourses seize what opportunities they can to unpick the positivities of social democracy but remain constrained by the powerful *a prioris* embedded in Swedish political culture. Standards and excellence are still being measured in terms of outcomes in citizenship, and the costs of such educational democracy in terms of measures of standards of performance derived from traditional quantative criteria are commonly accepted. In contrast to Britain standards are embedded in evaluations of the society itself. Justice, standards of living, influence over decisions affecting one's life are themselves forms of excellence striven for and valued. Fielding (1985, p. 173) makes the point that:

> Celebration demands not that we applaud everything indiscriminately; rather that our values point out certain things which prompt praise. It follows that we are clear about what is of little or no value and that when we invite students to reflect on their own work, or when we as teachers reflect on it, that very process of reflection involves discrimination and judgement.

The discourse of democracy makes possible one set of values, the discourse of Thatcherism makes possible a very different set. Furthermore, the discourse of Thatcherism is 'naturally' set over and against any meaningful articulation of a discourse of comprehensive education. Socialist notions of collective welfare and cooperative effort which would underpin any meaningful conception of comprehensive education are diametrically opposed to neo-liberal educational notions of market-choice, Darwinistic competition and possessive individualism. The Conservative project to deconstruct and de-legitimate the ideal of comprehensive education is essentially embedded in a political and ideological concern about the transformative potential of emancipatory schooling. This is because comprehensive schooling stands as an institutional challenge to Conservative thought. As Fielding notes:

> The link between fraternity, democracy and comprehensive education is important. The composite nature of the principle of fraternity ensures the emancipatory intent which has underpinned the

> comprehensive school. The comprehensive school movement has always been concerned with challenging orthodoxies; either by championing equality of opportunity and the erosion of privilege; or by the affirmation of the equal value principle and the rejection of meritocracy; or, currently, by the challenge to the individualist model of human fulfilment. The comprehensive school movement is the voice of a democratic, public education and as such it speaks for communities and ways of life that the grammar and secondary modern and public schools could never do (Fielding, 1987, p. 11).

In Britain the *a prioris* which construct and are reconstructed by the dominant definitions of education eschew notions of democracy and progress. Our conceptions of the social role of school remain primeval and divorce it from civil society in any progressive or transformative sense, leaving instead narrowly instrumental relations with 'industry' and 'the economy' and a subliminal task of reproduction through class bias.

I began this paper by referring to the possibilities for democratic schooling and throughout I have used as my counterpoint the case of education in Sweden. As I have tried to make clear, Sweden, like Britain, is a highly devloped capitalist country despite its long standing Socialist government. The extent of 'passive revolution' in Sweden is arguable but the basic structure of the society remains capitalist and unequal. The question this then leaves us with is, what kind of democracy is possible in either Sweden or Britain? Is it to be trapped within the limits of a highly formalistic version of political democracy which rests on a fundamental separation between political powers and rights and economic and social powers and rights? Or might democracy in schools be regarded as part of, and a positive contribution to, a thorough-going socialist transition in society? As Hunt (1980, p. 17) puts it: 'the realization of democracy involves not the smashing of bourgeois democracy but its completion, liberated from the undemocractic framework of capitalist relations'.

What these questions raise again is the nature and purposes of school democracy. Democracy can be regarded as an abstract ideal — for the good of all — or as a concern of special social interests, set within the specific antagonisms of class relations. Wood (1987, p. 133) argues strongly for the inevitability of the latter view and is scathing as to the naïveté and political pointlessness of settling for capitalist democracy:

> We lose sight of the chasm between the forms of democracy that are compatible with capitalism and those that represent a fundamental challenge to it. We no longer see the gap in the continuum of 'democratization', a gap which corresponds precisely to the opposition of class interests. In other words, we are induced to forget that the struggle between capitalism and socialism can be conceived precisely as a struggle over different forms of democracy...

If this tension is to be addressed in a consideration of school democracy then that consideration must include the nature of schools as workplaces, where the interests of teachers and other workers are at stake, as well as a place for learning where the life-chances and skills and commitments of students are at stake.

Clearly, the meaning of school democracy can be colonized from either end of the political spectrum. From the right in terms of a curricula contents (teaching 'about' democracy) and a set of anodyne organizational processes which tie students into the passivity of representative politics. From the left in terms of a 'critical literacy' and a set of social practices which encourage students to act 'as though they lived in a real democracy' (Giroux, 1983). But in Sweden education at all levels approximates much more closely to the latter!

> ... one can probably expect that in the long term perspective the higher level of education will have positive effects on the mobilizing possibilities of the socialist parties. Young people who are educated until the age of nineteen in the Swedish type of education system are likely to have higher expectations regarding working life and equality than did working class youths who until the 1950s entered the labour market around the age of fourteen (Korpi, 1983, p. 218-19).

Debates which critically link education in the nature of a future society, politics to participation in industrial decision-making and economics to workers' control, have been matters of major national significance in Sweden over the past 20 years. The possibility of mass participation and diverse social influences in these debates rests crucially upon the history of democratic education in Sweden:

> ... democracy, by definition, cannot mean merely that an unskilled worker can become skilled. It must mean that every 'citizen' can 'govern' and that society places him (sic), even if only abstractly, in a general condition to achieve this (Gramsci, 1978).

References

BALL, S. J. (1988) 'Comprehensive schooling, effectiveness and control: an analysis of educational discourses', in Slee, R. (Ed.) *Disruptive Behaviour and School Effectiveness*, Sydney: Macmillan.

BOWLES, S. and GINTIS, H. (1975) *Schooling in Capitalist America*, London: Routledge and Kegan Paul.

CARNOY, M. and LEVIN, H. (1985) *Schooling and Work in the Democratic State*, Stanford: Stanford University Press.

COMBER, L. C. and KEEVES, J. P. (1973) *Science Education in Nineteen Countries*, Stockholm and New York: Almqvist and Wiksell, and John Wiley.

DAUNT, P. E. (1975) *Comprehensive Values*, London: Heinemann.

ELSTER, J. (1983) 'Offentlighet og deltaklse. To teorier om deltaker-demokratiet (The public sphere and participation. Two theories of participatory democracy) in Bergh, T. (Ed.) *Deltakerdemokratiet*, Oslo: Litter.

ELSTER, J. (1986) 'The market and the forum', in Elster, J. and Hylland, A. (Eds), *Foundations of Social Choice Theory*, Cambridge: Cambridge University Press.

FIELDING, M. (1985) 'Celebration — valuing what we do' in Blatchford, R. (Ed.) *Managing the Secondary School*, London: Bell and Hyman.

FIELDING, M. (1987) Liberté, egalité, fraternité — ou la mort:' Towards a new paradigm for the comprehensive school', in Chitty, C. (Ed.) *Redefining the Comprehensive Experience*, London, Institute of Education.

FLETCHER, C. CARON, M. and WILLIAMS, W. (1985) *Schools on Trial*, Milton Keynes: Open University Press.

GIROUX, H. (1983) *Theory and Resistance in Education*, London: Heinneman.

GRAMSCI, A. (1978) 'In search of the educational principle', in Norton, T. M. and Ollman, B. (Eds.) *Studies in Socialist Pedagogy*, New York, Monthly Review Press.

HARNQVIST, K. (1988) 'Comprehensiveness and social equality', in Ball, S. J. and Larsson, S. (Eds.) *The Struggle for Democratic Education*, Lewes: Falmer Press.

HARNQVIST, K. and S. BENGTSSON, J. (1972) *Educational Reforms and Educational Equality*, Goteborg: Reports from the Institute of Education, No. 20, University of Goteborg.

HUNT, A. (1980) 'Taking democracy seriously', in Hunt, A. (Ed.) *Marxism and Democracy*, London: Lawrence and Wishart.

JAMLIKHET (Equality) (1969), Stockholm: Prisma.

JONSSON, I. and ARMAN, G. (1988) 'Social segregation in Swedish comprehensive schools', in Ball, S. J. and Larsson, S. (Eds.) *The Struggle for Democratic Education*, Lewes: Falmer Press.

KNIGHT, T. (1985) 'An apprenticeship in democracy', in *The Australian Teacher*, 11, Feb., pp. 5–7.

KORPI, W. (1983) *Democratic Class Struggle*, London: Routledge and Kegan Paul.

LAWRENCE, P. A. and SPYBEY, T. (1986) *Management and Society in Sweden*, London: Routledge and Kegan Paul.

LOVUX (1976) *Utbildning for arbete ock demokrati*, (Education for Work and Democracy), Stockholm: LO.

LGR 80 (1980) *Goals and Guidelines for the New Primary School Curriculum*, Stockholm: National Board of Education.

MARKLUND, S. (1980) 'The democratization of education in Sweden: A Unesco case study', *Studies in Comparative and International Education*, Institute of International Education, University of Stockholm.

NATIONAL SWEDISH BOARD OF EDUCATION (1980) *The 1980 Compulsory School Curriculum*, Stockholm: SO.

NYSTROM, P. (1987) 'Varformisslydeades skolreformera', *Tilden*, 2.

PECHEUX, M. (1975 trans. 1982) *Language, Semantics and Ideology: Stating the Obvious*, London: Macmillan.

SIA (1976) The Reorganization of the Working Conditions in Swedish Schools, Stockholm: National Board of Education.

SCRUTON, R. ELLIS-JONES, A. and O'KEEFFE, D. (1985) *Education or Indoctrination*, London: Social Affairs Unit.

TORNVALL, A. (1987) 'An investigation into the relationship between teacher beliefs and the philosophy of Laroplan 69', *Journal of Curriculum Studies*, 19, 2, pp. 175–82.

WOOD, E. M. (1987) *The Retreat From Class*, London: Verso.

Chapter 5

The Idea of a Socialist Education

Colin Lacey

The purpose of this chapter is to generate a set of coherent notions that together constitute the idea of socialist education. I do not claim that these notions are exhaustive nor that they are a tightly integrated theoretical framework. Education is too broad a phenomen to be treated in this way. It resides within too many aspects of life and properly responds to too varied a set of interests and external phenomena. The idea of a socialist education resides in a set of central concepts seen to be relevant to present and emerging problems at the individual and social level; realistic in the sense that they can be seen to be realisable, starting from present levels of skill and understanding; yet they must be inspirational and compelling to the extent that individuals will commit themselves to 'the cause' beyond the extent of self-interested calculation. In other words, the chapter takes as its starting point the present unpromising scenario for education and contemplates the kind of socialist education that could swim in a 'sea of capitalism'.

The chapter does not stand on its own. It is open to the challenge that it consists of an idealist or prescribed set of components that bear no relationship to real social pressure such as are encapsulated in the descriptive theory of education. For example, social reproduction or the explanation of differential educational achievement in terms of social capital. These arguments will be confronted elsewhere not by challenging these theories but by supplementing them with the need to consider a converging set of destructive trends that will be confronted by this and future generations. The purpose will be to change and broaden the framework of debate about education to include 'real' features of the world economy and environment and the way these features are likely to affect the individual. The idea of a socialist education discussed in the chapter is connected and integrated into this broader argument. Here it stands isolated, torn from its context. The next few paragraphs are an attempt to repair some of this damage to the fabric by describing in shorthand some of the imperatives that emerge from the context.

The deep assumptions underlying education systems throughout the world are relatively simple. Schools need to implant the basic social values, culture and technical systems within the next generation. The social values will then be preserved, the culture will be built upon and enriched and the technical system will ensure future development and enhanced life opportunities as natural problems are overcome by ever more efficient production and distribution. Sociologists have challenged/augmented this basic picture with descriptions of education as a process of social reproduction. These descriptions throw additional light on the inflexible elements of social structure, for example, social class, gender and race relations, that are reproduced in terms of relations of power. These relations give rise to conflicts of interest and marked inequalities in the distribution of rewards of a material and cultural kind.

It is assumed within the first scenario that the interlocking areas of social values, culture and technical systems are in some kind of harmonious relationship and augment each other in the betterment of society. These assumptions have been theorized in functional sociology and challenged by various schools of conflict theory. It has bcome increasingly apparent that in third world countries, for example, the introduction of new technical systems cannot be made without the massive disruption of traditional values and culture and the choice needs to be made between some elements of traditional culture and foreign cultural traits associated with industrialization and capitalist financial systems. Even in these circumstances, however, there are widespread assumptions about the 'rightness' of change in line with modern industrial values of individualism, etc., and that an harmonious future is available in the unspecified future when basic social values, culture and technical systems emerge in their modern form integrated into a growing worldwide industrial/economic system — modern finance capitalism.

The analysis from which this paper is derived challenges the appropriateness of the assumptions underlying the functional, descriptive theories of education. It also challenges the appropriateness and adequacy of the conflict theory attacks on the dominant functionalist idea. They are seen to be almost totally orientated to the dynamics of a national system of competition and social reproduction. While these mechanisms constitute an important bedrock understanding of educational processes they are not a sufficient basis for constructing a socialist education — they give rise to mainly negative strategies for reform and teaching. The key to a socialist education rests in redefining the scope of education to take in the new emergent crises that afflict individuals and social systems.

The 'new' generations must be equipped with knowledge of the dangers that will face them. Quite apart from the practical question of solutions, there is the moral question of the right to participate in decisions that in many spheres have become life-threatening. The issues I have in mind extend from ecological problems of the scale of the destruction of the Amazon jungle with its likely concomitants of climatic change and desertifi-

The Idea of a Socialist Education

cation to the issue of world wide economic polarization where on the one hand one nation with 7 per cent of the world's population absorbs 35 per cent of the world's resources, while the least-developed countries have an average annual income of about $150 per head. They also include issues like the 'arms race', nuclear power energy generation, the military use of space, AIDS, pollution and the effects of fast food and food additives on the teenage diet. The job of a socialist education in these areas is to inform young people of the problems and issues and encourage them to develop the skills and knowledge with which to make their own judgements about the future. Hardly a blue-print for indoctrination.

The Nature/Purpose of Education

The purpose of education should be to equip individuals and each new generation to diagnose and face up to the real problems that they are likely to encounter at an individual level or collective level during their lifetime. This definition might seem on the surface fairly innocuous and indeed that is one of its advantages. On the other hand it opens up a debate about what are the real problems to be faced by the emerging generation and leads into a redefinition of intelligence.

Intelligence reclaimed

No single concept has dominated education in the way that intelligence has over the last fifty years. Even social class pales into insignificance beside it and concepts like 'gender' and 'race' will need to encroach a lot more before they damage the structural roots of the concept. It is my view that the concept needs to be attacked head on and replaced with a completely new understanding. Much of the operational success of the concept rests on the existence of cheap readily-available tests. Children can be conveniently tested, labelled and banded. The concept thus ends up being an organizing principle as well as a dominant factor underlying pedagogy and teacher–pupil relationships.

When intelligence tests are examined they are revealed to be tests of skill and occasionally of talent. They have little to do with judgement and understanding at a deeper level and, more importantly, little to do with the problems faced by individuals within society or the problems confronting societies as a whole.

Skills and talents are concerned with solving problems within already existing paradigms and systems of knowledge. Intelligence has to do with understanding the relationships between complex systems and making judgements about when it is appropriate to work within existing paradigms and when it is appropriate to create new courses of action or avenues of thought. Most fundamentally, intelligence entails the understanding of the relationship between the internal characteristics of the person and external systems. It involves therefore making use of talents and skills; it involves the development of a morality that is capable of guiding action. Intelligence is not the result of impinging external constraints — it is capable of shaping as well as experiencing events. Sometimes this shaping refers only to an individual strategy (a response by and for the individual); more rarely but more importantly it can take the form of organizing a collective response to a situation.

The organization of collective responses involves the exercise of power. The exercise of power and its relationship to intelligence needs careful analysis. I will note here that power enables the setting up of new systems. Intelligence (we have defined) involves the setting up of systems that solve everyday and long-standing problems, that is, not simply using power to maintain individual or small group advantages. We have therefore moved on to the concept of collective intelligence defined as a measure of our ability to face up to the problems that confront us collectively and to develop collective solutions — clearly a concept not open to simple operationalization (testing) but crucial to the health of our society. If we are equipped with a purpose for education and a new understanding of intelligence as a focus for our efforts we must clearly proceed to a compatible pedagogy.

Critical and Constructive Education

Our aim as educators will be to render our students more intelligent. That is, they will need to focus on those problems in our society that will confront them as individuals and those problems with the now integrated world system that will afflict them collectively. These concerns have no resonance with ideas of indoctrination or unscrupulous manipulation of peoples' minds. Clearly it is the duty of the socialist educator to inform about unpopular issues, whether these be AIDS, the health risks of the modern 'fast food' diet, the starvation and genocide of the Nordestinos of Brazil or the destruction of the tropical rain forests, but there should be no doctrinaire or shoddy analysis or slogan making. This would deny the whole purpose of a socialist education.

The central concepts with respect to pedagogy are 'critical' and 'constructive' education. Together they should form a clear strand of an educational strategy starting around 9-years-old with as little as 10 per cent of the curriculum and expanding to 50 per cent in sixth forms and higher education. The disciplines, the creative arts and practical skills should cluster around this central core finding their way into it in terms of application where appropriate. Let us examine these concepts.

The intention behind critical education is not destructive. It is not an excuse to vent one's spleen or engage in self-glorification at the expense of others who are being criticized. The purpose is exactly the opposite. Critical education should lead to deeper understanding and the possibility of constructive action and development. If it is not entered into with this purpose in mind it can give rise to unnecessary conflict and wasted energy. The essential skill within the discipline is to establish the sound elements within previous problem-solving, constructions that are also relevant to the purpose in hand. In this way a necessary base can be built and the preliminary element of a methodology can be established that will point the way towards a means of obtaining the new goal.

Stated in this way, critical education would seem to be an extension of common sense. Who would embark on any undertaking, large or small, safe or perilous, without undertaking this preliminary critical appraisal? Why should an education system give such emphasis to something that anyone in their right mind would undertake as a matter of course. The answer to these questions establishes the importance of critical education. The sad fact is that all kinds of self-interested consideration, social constraints and personal limitations come between the ideal of critical appraisal and the practice of construction. One interesting example of a critical education exercise was recently completed by a group of MA students at Sussex University. Their task was to critically explore the cultural hero Captain Falcon Scott using two main sources:

1 The Ladybird book on 'Captain Scott' written by L.du Garde Peach OBE, MA, PhD.Lit., and
2 a book written by Roland Huntford 'The Last Place on Earth'.

Peach's book was specifically written for children of junior school age and has had a very wide circulation. It is a modern version of Scott's 'adventure'. Using Roland Huntford's text as a basis it was possible to find twenty-two half-truths or complete untruths and an even larger number of important omissions. For example, Scott

failed to realise that fresh meat was the only easy prevention for scurvy (this was the reason that Amundson's party ate their dogs). Scott probably died of scurvy;

failed to understand and make proper use of dogs and skis. Instead he punished himself and his men by manhandling with inadequate rations;

failed to adequately plan the logistic supply and packaging of food and fuel. As a result they lost paraffin through fuel creep and ran out of their inadequate supply of food;

failed to take adequate clothing and tents (no sewn-in ground sheets);

wasted time through poor navigation and poor marking of food and fuel bases.

This list contains less than one quarter of the major short-comings of the Scott expedition. It reveals that Scott did not undertake the 'critical exercise' outlined above and as a result failed to learn from the recorded experience of others lodged in a library close to his London office. In addition, he set up an authoritarian, hierarchical organization that prevented an upward flow of information from men who knew the solution to many of the incredible mistakes that he made. He set up an organization which imprisoned its members, and by not drawing on their skills and knowledge it rendered them less intelligent in the face of the problems they encountered. It caused four of them to die. A book which fails to draw these lessons from the expedition renders its readers less intelligent.

The group then went on to discuss whether schools resembled Scott's expedition or Amundesen's. To their surprise (and horror) they came to the conclusion that they were generally closer to Scott's undemocratic, hierarchical model, which rendered participants less intelligent. The account of this exercise led almost inevitably to proposing exercises for constructive education.

Critical education can develop the facility for forming frameworks of understanding or systematic understanding. It is, however, limited to this function. It cannot on its own yield the fruits of experience or creativity and it cannot deliver the results of experimentation. This element of praxis, of direct personal involvement with problems, can be provided by constructive education. This form of education is not to be confused with practical education, that is practical in a workshop or laboratory (although workshops and laboratories can provide excellent opportunities for constructive education). In practical lessons in most of our schools the essential elements of construction have been removed. Nearly all the decisions about what is to be done and how it is to be organized have been taken in advance by the teacher so that little remains for the pupil beyond following the cookbook instructions and making sure he/she gets the 'right' answer. The whole process has usually been streamlined to speed the process of learning (of facts) so that very little construction remains. So much time is presently spent in cramming pre-ordained structures into pupils' heads that little is learned about the process of constructing a solution to a problem.

The Practical Politics of a Socialist Education

In one sense Thatcher's third election victory would seem to be the death knell of the practical politics of a socialist education. Vocationalism, embodied in the MSC and its TVEI; City colleges; opting out and the differentiation of schools; new exams at 7, 11 and 14; the destruction of Teacher Union power and differentiated reward systems, seem to auger the beginning of a new decade of individualism and competition. Yet there are counter elements in nearly all these proposals. TVEI can be used to expose the shallowness of vocationalism, and the personal and social skills aspects of the curriculum are worth permeating. The demise of the narrow academic curriculum opens up new possibilities not least in the new GCSE. Opting out has to be seen in practice and perhaps some schools will make alternative use of the privilege.

The Idea of a Socialist Education

More important than the national scheme is the 'real politics of the global environment'. This is an area in which it is difficult to dissemble — when a parrot is 'dead' it is fairly obviously 'a dead parrot'. Young people are becoming increasingly aware of the destruction of the global environment. It is doing for the present generation what the H-bomb did for mine. The difference is that the effects of the H-bomb were potential; the effects of industrialization and the effects of the transformation of farming into agribusiness are both happening and potential. The pine forests are dying, the fish are dying, the water is polluted and increasingly people are dying in large numbers. The droughts and devastation of North Africa, parts of India and South America are killing, every few months, more people than died in the Atomic blasts of the Second World War. In the future there is the potential of a hot-house effect, massive redistribution of rainfall and changes in the land–sea boundaries; not a pleasant scenario. The combination of these factors means:

1. there will be room for the socialist educator to put into practice some of the central concepts described above;
2. s/he will do so in the context of a youth generation who will want to know about the 'unpopular' problems because they constitute the 'real' future.

The final issue I wish to discuss in this paper is the issue of the socialist educator.

The Socialist Educator

Once upon a time in the late 1960s there was a piece of research that revealed that some teachers were inspired to take up teaching because they had a vision of society that involved more egalitarianism and because they wished to forward this vision through their teaching and subsequent careers. Shortly after the research came Houghton and the concern for 'career' and promotion seemed to swallow up this generation of teachers without trace. Now the situation has changed again — upward career avenues are blocked and many teachers are looking into themselves for new inspiration and meaning to their careers.

To achieve success and satisfaction the socialist educator will need a number of attributes and need to employ a number of distinctive strategies:

1. s/he will need to be an effective teacher using modern strategies of group work, active learning and non-authoritarian classroom styles;
2. s/he will need to be clear about their goals and only go for promotion, for example, if it is possible to pursue those goals;
3. s/he will need a network of support both within and outside the school. The internal network will be easier to organize as schools

polarise under the new policies. The external network must be put in place and sustained by other agencies. There are an increasing number of suitable organizations ranging from OXFAM to the SEA. However in my view something more specific, more supportive, both emotionally and inspirationally is needed. In addition a broader base is required ranging into a number of fields e.g. research, education, the media, interest groups and voluntary organizations. This base needs to be constructed. This will require resources beyond those available to individual teachers and education. It will require considerable effort from researchers and academics but could repay handsomely by providing an outlet for their work beyond the narrow confines of a research community talking to itself.

Roy Williams and I have recently obtained a small grant for two years to establish an education network similar to that described above.[1] The grant will help set up the sub-structure. We started work in April 1987, but a major commitment in term time has only been possible since the Autumn of 1987. I would like to get a critical response to the idea of a socialist educator as an inspirational teacher, supported by the network. It is my view that democratic socialists and Marxists have neglected the practical and the positive in their critiques of present day systems. They have left the field wide open to the kind of self-confident radical conservatism we are now witnessing. It is not sufficient to wish it away or hope that it will collapse on itself. Nor will a mass of articles and readers make a substantial difference. We need to engage practically in the practical everyday world. We need to construct the idea of a socialist education and identify and support inspirational teachers who stand for an alternative. We and they need to reconstruct our own culture away from the images of the successful 'executive' or the 'history man' toward a recognizable, dedicated and affective personality (cultural image) concerned to confront larger collective problems and learn from bitter experience.

Notes

1 Anyone who is interested in finding out more about the 'Network Project' or getting involved, should contact: Education Network Project, Continuing & Professional Education Area, Education Development Building, University of Sussex, Falmer, Brighton, BN1 9RG.

Chapter 6

Education, Production and Reform

Robert Moore

Since in a modern economy the quality and efficiency of the working population and the degree of vocational and social mobility very largely depend on the educational system, an analysis of its relation to the occupational structure must naturally dominate any discussion of the economic consequences of educational provision or any attempt to assess the effect of education on the national economy (Floud and Halsey, 1961).

What is remarkable about the statement above is that, thirty years after its original publication in 1956, it sounds so contemporary. It would not be surprising to find it attributed to a recent MSC publication or to a member of the current Thatcher administration. This is not meant in any sense to imply that Floud or Halsey had or have any affinity with those positions — neither is it intended to suggest that the reformist tradition with which they have been associated has simply won the intellectual argument during the past three decades. Indeed, the exact opposite is now the case. The broad social-democratic reformist consensus has collapsed, and it is this fact which provides the crucial context for the present discussion of socialist education thinking.

The most striking feature of the debate about education is precisely the extent to which it has been dominated by a particular kind of analysis of education's relation to the occupational structure. The fact that this appears to be also a natural reflex of so many proponents within the debate is indicative of the influence of an underlying principle which structures and orchestrates positions across a range of otherwise opposed ideological perspectives.

This chapter is concerned with those continuities and with the interrelationship between sociological theorising and socialist education strategy in the wake of the collapse of the postwar settlement. It is also concerned with what is felt to be a fundamental rupture with the current situation which demands that these paradigmatic assumptions be explicated and critically assessed. This is necessary in order to re-assess, from a socialist perspective, the reforming of education and the reforming role of education.

The first section will review the changes in the analysis of education's role in social reform and in estimations of its capacity to bring about socially significant change. I will then look at two major sources of structural discontinuity between the educational and occupational systems which, I suggest, fundamentally limit the capacity of educational reform to reform society (at least in the ways envisaged by the model) and also imply the need for a radical retheorization of the education/production relationship in sociology. Finally, I will consider some of the implications of this for socialist thinking about education and reform and for sociological theorizing.

The Sociology of Education and Socialist Education Policy

Education, socialism and sociology are intimately connected. Within the broad social–democratic consensus which dominated Western politics in the postwar period, education was seen as the primary agency for the construction of Welfare State socialism. Education was held to be able to deliver broadly socialistic objectives through what were seen as 'natural' outcomes of its increasing significance within modern society. This view was justified by mainstream sociological (initially functionalist) analyses of the nature of such societies and the role of education within them.

It is the case, however, that the educational reform programme has been structured around what Ken Jones has termed 'the two strategies' of 'equal opportunities' and 'progressive education' (Jones, 1983, p. 1). The latter tended to draw upon psychological developmental theories rather than sociology and to be the province of educationalists rather than sociologists of education. It was not until the seventies and the emergence of the New Sociology of Education (Young, 1971) that these two dimensions of reform were brought together within a single theoretical frame of reference. The New Sociology, proceding from a phenomenologically inspired sociology of knowledge approach, focused upon the 'social construction of reality' in the classroom.

Although the New Sociology of Education concentrated upon educational processes, it required the addition of an ideologically compatible macro theory to sharpen its focus. This was provided by 'the correspondence principle' in *Schooling in Capitalist America* (Bowles and Gintis, 1976). The correspondence principle held that the social relations of schooling correspond to those in production. The differentiation of forms of education within the hierachies of schooling and higher education reflect the differing technical and ideological requirements within the occupational structure. Schooling prepares students for their 'appropriate' class positions in work. This analysis not only provided a general theory of what education did under capitalism, it also provided a rule of method — a principle for guiding the analysis of classroom interaction.

It is also the case that the development of correspondence theory shifted the Left's analysis from an essentially social-democratic concern with inequalities in distribution in capitalist society to a more critical Marxist perspective based in an analysis of relations of production. Whereas the former was optimistic about the possibilities of educational reform reforming society, the latter's view was profoundly pessimistic. Where the former was primarily concerned with 'equal opportunities', the latter is preoccupied with the possibility of 'transformation'.[1]

Hence the mid-1970s can be seen as marking a pivotal point around which the character of the Left's analysis of education shifted from an essentially optimistic, social–democratic reformism concerned with inequality and proceeding from distribution, to a pessimistic Marxism preoccupied with the problematics of transformation and grounded in an analysis of production. Whereas the former tended to ignore the education process in favour of broader institutional relationships, the latter has attempted to integrate process within structural analysis.

Equal Opportunities

The 'equal opportunities' strategy is generally associated with a macro, social structural approach in sociology which is concerned primarily with the educational system as an institution within the wider society. The school is treated simply as an 'input-output system' with little attention being paid to 'the texture of daily life in educational institutions' (Karabel and Halsey, 1977, p. 43). In terms of equal opportunities, sociology informed socialist policy and practice in four main ways:

1. It provided a general theory of modernisation which described a 'natural' development away from 'ascribed' to 'achieved' status which reflected the requirements of an increasingly complex social division of labour based in new technologies of production and facilitated by education.
2. It charted the structure of educational and social inequality — inequalities in the distribution of wealth, status and power, and of opportunities.
3. Educational inequality was presented not simply as one dimension of social inequality in general, but as a powerful determinant of the general structure.
4. The relationship between educational and social inequality was explained in such a way, through the general theory about the character of modern societies, that it followed that changes in educational inequality would automatically generate changes in social inequality.

It is important to stress that the exchange which this envisages between education and the economy is a rational exchange — education provides attributes which industry needs. The approach implied a set of specific and predictable trends in income and mobility associated with the growth in education in response to the increasing technical demands of the economy.

First, as the number of more highly educated people increases, the general wealth of society would increase. This reflected the human capital principle that more educated workers are more productive workers. By virtue of their greater marginal productivity, such workers would also be paid more. Hence not only would society in general be wealthier, but so also, in absolute terms, would increasing number of individuals. However, in relative terms, by virtue of the laws of supply and demand, income differentials would narrow as the supply of more highly educated workers increased and that of less highly educated ones decreased.

Secondly, because social placement becomes increasingly dependent upon education, rates of social mobility would increase and an individual's status would depend less and less upon the accidents of birth. The condition for this is that education itself becomes more open and ceases to reproduce received class rigidities. This move also involved an acknowledgement that the 'pool of ability' is much wider than the traditional pattern of selection in education suggests. The 'wastage' of lower-class talent featured heavily in the rhetoric of postwar progressive educational reform. Associated with this were more sophisticated concepts of intelligence and of genetic inheritance and an increasing emphasis upon the role of environmental factors in conditioning educational success or failure.

Thirdly, not only do the above factors in themselves encourage the formation of a common culture, they require its formation in order to fascilitate their development. Once again the schools have a crucial role to play here. Comprehensive schooling has both the specific role of developing the talents of all children and of overcoming traditional class restrictions in educational selection and also the more general one of forging the common culture by providing a universal experience for future citizens.

This 'package' provided a powerful, coherent programme for social democracy. Though obviously compromising socialist principles to a major degree, it had the considerable advantage of plausibility and practicality — of objectives which could be achieved in a foreseeable time span and without recourse to the more apocalyptic remedies of socialist transition. Everyone could be given equal opportunity to become unequal in an increasingly egalitarian and prosperous society. Reforming education became the means to reforming society.

Within the broad framework of the sociological model of modernisation, postwar sociology reinforced this picture at numerous secondary points — through its re-examination of class structure and culture in notions such as embourgeoisment, privatization, the end of ideology, the managerial revolution, and the 'tightening bond thesis'; through its interrogation of class bias in education, especially in relation to the working-class boy and the grammar school; in its promotion of 'nurture' over 'nature' in the IQ debate and in its prescriptions for compensatory programmes to counter the effects of urban decay and anomie.

In terms of its coherence and the complexities of its implications and ramifications and in its capacity to integrate theory with politics and policies, the social–democratic programme must count as a major intellectual achievement. If its time has passed, it is still comforting to think that its legacy of high minded liberal idealism will have imprinted upon the national culture a basic human decency which will ultimately dismiss the vulgarity of Thatcherism and the new right.

Distribution and Reform

As Karabel and Halsey (1977, p. 3) point out, the 'Fabian social democratic' approach to these issues 'was concentrated characteristically on the analysis of social inequalities of educational opportunity'. This drew upon the established British empirical tradition of social mobility studies combined with a 'socialist influence on the choice of problems'. Although this approach rejected an orthodox functionalist model, it did, as Bernstein says, 'accept the thesis of the increasing subordination of the educational system to the economy in advanced industrial societies' (Bernstein, 1977, p. 165). Major Marxist studies of British society, such as those of Miliband (1973) and Westergaard and Resler (1976), equally exhibited this 'political arithmetic' approach despite their different theoretical base.

Bernstein goes on to describe the position represented by Floud and Halsey in this way:

> Their basic view was that education was contained by the rigidities of an out-moded class structure which deeply penetrated its organizational forms. It is important to understand that Floud and Halsey used a manpower and equality argument as a double-barrelled weapon to bring about change in the procedures of selection and the organizational structure of schools (ibid, p. 165)

Floud and Halsey's view that, 'in an industrialized economy the educational system becomes the prime agency of occupational selection and mobility' (op. cit., p. 84) was essentially a technical argument to do with the development of skill requirements in response to the growth of science and technology. The crucial issue was to translate it into a social prescription compatible with liberal, meritocratic ideals.

> The Welfare State, on grounds both of political principle and of economic expedience, has made a renewed attack through its *educational policy on the problem of securing a close relationship between ability and opportunity (loc. cit*, emphases added).

To achieve this close relationship between ability and opportunity, it was necessary to free the educational system from the rigidities of class. This, in turn, would progressively reduce the constraints of class in society at large. The reformed educational system, standing as a model of the reformed society, could interrupt the reproduction of class inequality by linking social opportunity and reward with educationally developed and credentialized 'natural ability'.

The major strength of the approach was to link, in this way, political principle and economic expediency. The hegemony of the reformist model effectively disarmed reactionary conservatism. It has taken the emergence of the new Right (under a new set of economic conditions) to shatter its dominance. Marxists and Social Democrats on the Left and human capital theorists and technical functionalists on the Right each, in their own way, celebrated the power of education to reform society in a meritocratic direction. In keeping with the technical spirit of the paradigm, the nineteenth century gravediggers of capitalism had been upgraded into twentieth century social engineers.

Ironically it was sociology itself which contributed, at least in part, to the decline and eventual crisis of the model. The change in fortunes has been described by Raymond Boudon:

> For decades both social scientists and policy makers had thought about and acted toward education on the basis of an optimistic philosophy: it was uncritically assumed that education could cure all kinds of social problems and, particularly, that it could bring about more equality among men. As the sociology of education developed, this view was progressively reversed and a new philosophy, a pessimistic one, emerged more and more convincingly. It may be summarised in the statement that schooling is unable to reduce to any considerable extent the inequalities among individuals which result from social background (Boudon, 1974, p. xii)

Sociology contributed to this pessimism by reporting that the changes which were expected to follow on from educational reform did not appear to be occurring. More significantly, the work of Jencks (1972) and, even more profoundly, that of Boudon himself questioned the taken-for-granted assumption that educational reform could generate social reform in that particular manner.

It is important to stress the nature of the problem: it is not that we have failed to reform education — it has changed significantly — but that these reforms have not resulted in the expected changes in society at large. Even if we wish to argue about the 'true' significance of the character of changes in education, there is one central and inescapable fact: as Boudon says, 'in industrial societies, and in particular in liberal industrial societies, educational inequality shows a consistent tendency to decrease' (Boudon, 1977,

p. 187). It is the implications of this fact which provide the critical focus for any meaningful attempt to radically re-evaluate socialist educational strategy.

Production and Reproduction

The focus of concern for both social democratic and Marxist investigators up until the early 1970s was with the distributive relations of capitalism — with issues of inequalities in opportunity, access, allocation and reward. Under the influence of the political economy approach of Bowles and Gintis and of Althusserian and Poulantzian structuralism, theoretical analysis reconstructed itself around a particular view of what counted as 'the social relations of production' under capitalism.[2] This significant shift provided the opportunity for a particular kind of accommodation of the dilemma. The distributive perspective assumed (in keeping with the tenets of the broader paradigm) that because of the way in which education related to production in advanced societies, it had the capacity to reform it. Analyses from the point of view of production, however, argued that for the same reason it was precisely this capacity which education in capitalist society lacked.

The ideological debate around this issue has not concerned that principle as such so much as fundamental disagreements as to the character and status of what it is that industry needs. Basically, orthodox theory views these needs as ideologically and politically neutral, as simple technical requirements, whereas the Left sees them in terms of the theoretical categories of Marxist analysis, as the needs of the social relations of capitalist production.

The parallel between orthodox and Left analyses which follows from this common commitment to the same basic principle can be illustrated by comparing the following two quotes. The first is Randal Collins' description of a central premise of technical functionalism and the second is from a recent Marxist work by Carnoy and Levin:

> Education prepares students in the skills necessary for work, and skills are the main determinant of occupational success. That is the hierarchy of educational attainment is assumed to be a hierarchy of skills, and the hierarchy of jobs is assumed to be another such hierarchy (Collins, 1981, p. 7).

> The reproduction of educated workers means that at each educational level appropriate skills, attitudes, behaviours, and expectations are inculcated that correspond to a particular level of occupation (Carnoy and Levin, 1985, p. 162).

As Simon Frith has observed, 'The importance of the school for labour socialisation has long been a commonplace of Marxist analysis' (Frith, 1980, p. 35. His view that, 'The problem is not to explain this general relationship but to account for its current problems', (loc. cit.) is equally commonplace on the Left. The contention, here, is that it is precisely the current problems which require us to see our assumptions concerning that 'general relationship' as demanding critical re-evaluation.

Whereas the 'old Marxists' and social democrats believed that reforming education could change capitalism, the 'new Marxists' argued that only by changing capitalism could education be truly reformed. The basis for this belief was the 'correspondence principle': the view that the social relations of education correspond to the social relations of production. Gintis and Bowles summarize their original argument as follows:

> We also argued specifically that the current relationship between education and economy is ensured not through the content of education but in its form: the social relations of the education encounter. Education prepares students to be workers through a correspondence between the social relations of production and the social relations of education. Like the division of labour in the capitalist enterprise, the educational system is a finely graded hierarchy of authority and control in which competition rather than co-operation governs the relations among participants, and an external reward system — wages in the case of the economy and grades in the case of schools — holds sway (Gintis and Bowles, 1982, pp. 46–47).

They see this basic characteristic of the education/production relationship as constituting a fundamental limit on the capacity of education to fulfil either its liberal commitment to the individual to develop his or her full human potential, or its broader social reform programme.

This approach takes as its starting point the view that education functions within capitalist societies to inculcate upon individuals the ideological forms of attitude, value and disposition in addition to the technical skills required within capitalist industry. Its is argued that (subject to various contradictory tendencies) the forms adopted at various levels and positions within the educational system 'correspond' to the forms of capitalist social relations in parallel locations within the occupational system. By implication, the key to understanding any particular example of educational organization and practice lies in the requirements of the corresponding occupational site. Individuals are assumed to be located within production on the basis of their educational preparation (indicated by their level of qualification) and this location is legitimated by the credential and its (false) claim to reflect the individual's real ability.

Gintis and Bowles (in the work quoted above) have significantly developed the model of social totality which they originally presented in *Schooling in Capitalist America*. In particular they have both recognized the existence of other systems of oppression (gender and race) in addition to class and have increased the capacity of the model to define sites of contradiction. In both cases this enables the analysis to incorporate the possibility of resistance and oppositional struggle in and through education — a possibility virtually denied in the original presentation.

It is not my intention, here, to review the development from 'simple' to 'complex' correspondence theory in any detail,[3] the relevant point for the present concern is that Gintis and Bowles retain the basic principle within a more sophisticated model of the social totality. It is the model rather than the principle which is critically developed. What is significant is that the approach is still grounded in an analysis of the relationship between the educational and occupational systems which assumes an essentially instrumental exchange between the two. Obviously the nature of that exchange is theorized very differently from that in human capital theory or technical functionalism, but nevertheless its intelligibility requires an assumption of its essential rationality in terms of the technical/ideological requirements of capitalist production.

Resistance and Transformation

The logic of the position which followed from the confluence of the New Sociology of Education and correspondence theory appeared to entail that forms of education which were 'the opposite' of those currently enshrined within the dominant system would automatically be subversive of capitalist social relations. Hence various types of radical pedagogy and libertarian progressive education (including de-schooling) came to be seen as politically as well as educationally radical. Ironically it was precisely certain expressions of this posture (associated with the problem of relativism that the New Sociology inherited from phenomenology) which helped to undermine public confidence in education in the 1970s and which are still appealed to today in the new Right's tirades against '1960s permissiveness' as the source of current social problems.

The idea that there should be some automatic linkage between socialist education and progressive education is now being questioned by some radical writers. Aronowitz and Giroux (1986), in their interesting and challenging analysis of the current situation, have highlighted a number of contradictions within the legacy of 1960s radicalism:

> ... radical school reform of the 1960s adopted an anti-intellectual stance that helped prepare the victory of the right. They surrendered the concept of systematic knowledge acquisition and uncritically privileged an anti-intellectual concept of student experience. This ideology constituted merely the mirror image of the cognitive orientation of school officials which prescribed a set of learnings prior to possible experience. Thus, the radical reformers were prey to the charge that they had betrayed the interests of the poor and

minorities who desperately needed to learn how to read, write and calculate (ibid., p. 7).

Whilst, on the one hand, the Right has used some aspects of radical progressivism to attack the Left, it has also taken up other parts of its programme. It is eerie to hear the echoes of radical attacks on teacher professionalism and demands for community control over schools resounding within the rhetoric of 'the market' and parental choice.

As Aronowitz and Giroux point out, not only has the Right taken over the Left's economic analysis of schooling, it has also used this, in a similar fashion, to attack the tradition of liberal-humanist education:

> They have taken their cue from radical critics who claim that schooling is merely an adjunct to the labour market. But, unlike the left, conservatives criticise the schools for failing to fulfil this function. With some exceptions they are happy to jettison the traditional liberal vision that education must be responsible for transmitting western cultural and intellectual traditions. Instead, they have repeated the 1960s radical attack that schools are not relevant to students' lives (ibid., p. 1).

It is the new Right's attack upon liberal education which is, in my view, the most telling and symptomatic feature of its position; also, perhaps, that most difficult for the Left to accommodate given its own long-established view of the class role of liberal education and its assaults upon it.

It is important to recognize that the conflating of the two dimensions of reform in the mid-1970s was facilitated by a theory which was centred upon an analysis of the education/production relationship — correspondence theory. An understanding of the social relationships of the classroom was sought through an understanding of their relationship to the relations of production. Whilst in sympathy with attempts to critically assess the basis for the linkage between socialist and progressive education, my own view is that the fundamental issue underpinning this remains how the Left sees (and theorizes) the relationship between education and production. It is this question that I wish to address.

The Failure of Reform and the Crisis in Liberal Education

The apparent incapacity of educational change to produce social change could be seen as no more than what should be expected from schooling in capitalist societies. An obvious implication of the reproduction argument is that educational reforms are not 'really' reforms at all, or, perhaps no more than mere reforms as opposed to truly radical transformations. In terms of Bowles and Gintis' original formulation, educational reforms could be seen in terms of the requirement for education to periodically update itself to keep pace with technical developments in production. They expressed this problem in terms of a contradiction between reproduction and accumulation. More recently, Carnoy and Levin (op. cit.) have approached the same problem through a definition of a contradiction between the imperatives of education to prepare young people on the one hand, for the inegalitarian requirements of production, and, on the other, for the (formally) egalitarian rights of citizenship. Gintis and Bowles (op. cit.) have extended the possibilities of contradiction and, hence, of oppositional action in their more recent work.

Mainstream macro sociology contributed to the undermining of the reformist programme by reporting its failures. The new sociology did so through the way in which its position provided material for the orchestrated moral panics that led up to the Great Debate and which are still a powerful feature of the right-wing press's campaign to discredit the Left through its treatment of anti-racist and anti-sexist education. Black Paper writers took up the implications of relativism to attack radical educationalists for threatening academic and moral standards, whilst the media focused upon events such as the William Tyndale affair (the 'wildmen in the classroom') to give substantive, popular focus to these issues.

Parallel to these sensationalist spasms of protest against what was perceived to be happening in education was a more sober concern within the DES with education's apparent lack of responsiveness to the nation's economic needs and the Department's own institutional inability to effectively redirect resources and approaches in a decentralized educational system.[4] Ironically, just as the Left was turning against education because it was seen as too strongly articulated with the economy, the Right was turning against it because it wasn't. The crisis *in* education coincided with a crisis *for* education as the recession set in. It was precisely because so much had been expected of it in the good times, that so much could be held against it in the bad.

The broad movement described above can be summarized as follows:

1 In the period of educational optimism, sociology powerfully supported the view of education as the major agency of social change. Within a broadly social democratic reformist perspective, the Left saw the major problems as to do with the distributional relationships of capitalism. The 'equality of opportunities' strategy predominated. Sociology was relatively indifferent to educational processes within the classroom. Support for progressive education from the Left was relatively untheorised — its inspiration tended to come from the more 'leftish' versions of Leavisite anti-modernism and from 'child-centred' developmental psychology.

2 The reformist programme was gradually undermined by the same mainstream sociology which had initially provided its theoretical foundation. A number of major studies of income distribution, social mobility and of the effects of educational reform indicated that the expected and pledged changes were not occurring.

3   In the period of educational pessimism the general socio-economic and political conditions which had sustained education before were sharply reversed. The New Sociology of Education provided a radical foundation for progressive educational reform at the level of the classroom. With the advent of correspondence theory the Left's analysis shifted from the point of view of distribution to that of production. Whilst correspondence theory provided an apparent explanation for the failure of reformism, the endemic tension between its structural determinism and the subjectivist voluntarism of the New Sociology of Education encouraged radical educationalists to take the view that only the most extreme forms of experimentation could dent 'the system'. Ironically, whereas this confluence of radical strategies inclined the Left to think that education could do very little, it encouraged the Right to think that it could do far too much — and none of it good.

What were essentially social–democratic variants of human capital theory provided the centre of gravity of the Left's perspective in the era of optimism. Although correspondence theory is in many respects its mirror image, their oppositions nevertheless derive from a common principle: of the inherent rationality of an instrumental exchange between education and production. A major implication of the critique of this principle is that the broad strategies which have previously been pursued through supply-side analysis expressed in educational reformism would be more effectively met through action on the demand-side — by directly affecting the institutions within which social inequality is materially present. The concomitant of this is that education will be best reformed and become itself most effectively reforming when discussion of its possibilities is no longer constrained by a principle of its 'natural' domination by the economy.

Education and Production

I now want to consider the fundamental issue of the character of the education/production relationship. The purpose, here, is to focus upon two major sources of structural discontinuity between the two systems. It is important to emphasize that the view being presented here is that the two systems are radically discontinuous rather than that there are simply complexities which result in secondary interruptions and dislocations. This view is grounded in a deeper theoretical argument to the effect that the major problem in the Marxist sociology of education has been the tendency to identify the concept of 'capitalist social relations of production' with the system of social relationships within the occupational system (direct production).[5]

The rationale of correspondence theory (in its simple and complex forms) resides precisely in such an identification. This fails to take account of

Marx's distinction between the 'immediate production of commodities' and 'the system of capitalist production as a whole' (Marx, 1976, p. 1005). Capitalist social relations of production are not identical to and limited to their particular form within the system of the direct production of commodities (the occupational system). The concept of 'capitalist social relations of production' does not, in fact, grant to the correspondence principle the theoretical authority which its manner of formulation implies. Although it is undoubtedly the case that correspondence theory has developed significantly, the correspondence principle as such has remained virtually unexamined. It is now located within a much more complex and sophisticated model of the social totality, but its essential logic remains.

The present concern is more substantive than theoretical, and I will consider in detail, (a) the changing pattern of educational inequality,[6] and (b) the mediating role of the labour market, in terms of their implications for our understanding of how the educational system relates to the occupational system ('production').

The Trend in Class Differentials in Educational Attainment

The issue of class inequalities in education (of opportunity and attainment) is of fundamental significance for the family of theories being considered. In the case of reformism, a clear set of predicted consequences were seen as the correlated outcomes of reductions in educational inequalities. In the historical context, these were seen almost exclusively in terms of (white, male) class with a virtual total neglect of gender and race. As has been pointed out above, the failure of these outcomes to be realized contributed to the undermining of the reformist position.

One of the earliest systematic reviews of data on class differentials in educational attainment was that by Little and Westergaard (1964). Drawing upon official statistics in various education reports, they were able to survey trends in England and Wales over the first half of this century. The following points from their study can be emphasized:

1. The general expansion in provision had tended to benefit all classes with little relative advantage accruing to the working class in particular.
2. The relative significance of those improvements depends upon the perspective from which they are viewed, e.g., whether relative to chances of getting a selective school place or relative to not getting one.
3. The progressive improvement for working-class children at the school level was countered by a regressive trend at the university level.
4. The improvements which occurred (however conditionally) in the situation of working-class children were part of a long term trend

which appears to be independent of major structural reform of the educational system.

Some ten years later, Westergaard and Resler (1976) presented a similar review. This is carried out within a broader analysis of class inequality in British society which was a major and characteristic example of the Left's social analysis of its time. Their summary states that:

> Probably, class inequalities in access to academic secondary schooling continued to narrow in the 1960s: at least the figures for grammar and independent school entry alone suggest that. And the corresponding inequalities in chances of getting to university — stable or even widening, in proportionate terms, until the 1950s despite university expansion — appear also to have become smaller in recent years (p. 323).

Hence we see the continuation of the previously recognized trend at the school level, and a progressive reversal of that at university level.

Westergaard and Resler repeat the basic point that the general expansion in educational provision brought benefits to all classes, but that 'Nevertheless, some element of redistribution followed in the process: the range of inequalities of educational opportunities became rather less extreme' (ibid., p. 324). They go on to reiterate that this is the continuation of a long-term established trend.

Interestingly they note that this improvement in educational opportunity has not been associated with any increase in social mobility. They attribute this to the progressive closure of other mobility routes which were not dependent on education. This view was plausible in terms of the wisdom prevailing at that time and reflects precisely the set of underlying assumptions about the relationship between education, occupation and social mobility which are being examined here. It is probably fair to say that this view no longer holds favour amongst sociologists. It would, in any case, be a remarkable coincidence if the degree of closure in the one area exactly balance the increase in opportunity in the other.

Further detail on the trends in educational inequality is provided by the authoritative Oxford Mobility Study (Halsey *et al.*, 1980). The study was based on four cohorts of men born between 1913–22, 1923–32, 1933–42, and 1943–52 (we must note that even the latest of these left school prior to the raising of the school leaving age to 16, in 1972/3). As with the previous authors, those from the Oxford study note the general improvement in chances for members of all classes which followed from the expansion of opportunities. However, class differentials narrowed 'appreciably' over the period with the chance of an upper-class boy going to grammar school falling from about four to about two times that of a working-class boy (ibid, p. 204). Similarly survival rates within the school system tended to converge over time with the upper-class boy being six times as likely as the working-class boy to be in school at age 16 in the eldest cohort as against less than three times in the youngest.

Those lower-class children who remained in education after the minimum leaving age tended to perform to a similar level as that of upper-class children — 63 per cent of upper-class and 53 per cent of lower-class pupils with at least one 'A' level went to university. However, whilst one in four of the upper class went to university, this was true of only one in forty of the lower class.

On the future projections of the trends, Halsey *et al.*, suggest that there could be:

> ... a striking narrowing of class differentials. The most conservative estimates suggest that in another twenty or thirty years class differences would have narrowed to 20 percentage points... Less conservative estimates suggest that the gap beween the social classes might have been eliminated altogether (ibid, p. 138).

Hence these studies of class differentials in levels of educational attainment appear to indicate a general trend across the century for a narrowing and possible eventual elimination of inequalities, at least at the level of the school. It is essential, however, to take account of the considerable complexities and subtleties embedded within these real and projected trends.

Change and Transformation

In general, British studies of this type have tended to adopt a straightforwardly empirical approach in which comparisons are made over time through a series of cross-sections based in whatever official data happen to be available. Relatively simple measures of inequality and comparative opportunities are applied. In France, Boudon (op. cit.) and Bourdieu and Passeron (1977) have provided sophisticated alternatives to the cross-sectional approach which take account of the complexities of the systematic inter-relationships of the trends.[7] There are direct parallels between their work and that of Bernstein in this country.

In each case we can say that these writers produce transformational, generative models of the educational system. Without developing the features of this approach in any detail here, it can be noted that Bernstein, Bourdieu and Boudon (the three major theorists in the sociology of education) provide between them, as much in their complementary differences as through their basic similarity, an immensely powerful ensemble of theoretical technique.

I want to suggest that a consideration of the systematic features of the trends described above enables us to see changes within the educational system in terms of the endogenous characteristics of the field as such rather than as responses to exogenous influences, e.g., changing technical or ideological requirements of 'production'. The thesis of radical discontinuity between the educational and occupational systems enables changes within each to be seen in terms of their intrinsic transformational principles and possibilities whilst acknowledging that they are (a) conditioned by their systemic relations[8] and (b) ultimately regulated by capitalist social relations of production (i.e., by 'commodification').[9]

The general picture is of declining inequalities of educational opportunity and attainment within a context of, until recently, expanding educational provision. This has been to the benefit of all classes, but somewhat more to the working class. Considerable gross inequalities at the level of inter-class differentials remain. However, this fact should not deflect attention from the implications of the more subtle patterns of change which have occurred within this structure. As Halsey *et al.* suggest, following Boudon, it is important to consider the systematic features of the relative trends in differentials.

Subject to important conditions (see ibid., p. 139), Halsey *et al.* argue that it is possible to represent trend data at a given point in the educational system (e.g., the changing proportion of a social group staying on into the sixth form) in the form of a logistic or 'S' curve. Curves of this type are like long, stretched-out 'S's rising from a low percentage base on the left to a high plateau on the right. This type of trend is often associated with the consumption of commodities. A new product, such as video recorders, comes onto the market and is initially bought in relatively small numbers. As the price comes down and the product becomes both familiar and fashionable, the rate of consumption increases until the market reaches saturation point. The consumption curve measuring the proportion of the population possessing the product over time continues to rise increasingly steeply until a mid-point is reached and then gradually flattens out.

Halsey *et al.* show how educational participation rates for class groups exhibit these formal features — the trend statistics have the form of logistic curves. The curve for each group has its own specific characteristics reflecting different numerical, time and positional bases relative to the educational site and to each other. Over any given period of time, cross-sectional comparisons will reveal apparently arbitrary fluctuations in the positions of the groups relative to each other, e.g., at one level the differentials might be narrowing while at another they will be increasing. This is precisely the situation described by Little and Westergaard (1964) in relation to selective school and university places. Later the differential at the higher level will also start to narrow as the upper-class group approaches saturation point and the rate of increase in the lower-class one begins to accelerate towards the mid (or 'inflection') point, viz. the situation described, at a later date, by Westergaard and Resler (1970).

In terms of changes in differentials of opportunity, chances and attainment, the situation is extremely complex. Halsey *et al.* point out that:

> ...while the rate of increase was greater for the working class, their absolute gains were less. Thus for every 100 working class boys there were an extra twenty-two staying on until 16 or later by the end of our period; but for every 100 service class boys there were an extra twenty-six staying on. In this sense, then, the difference between the classes had actually widened (ibid., p. 205).

Hence we have to distinguish between features such as absolute gains and rates of increase or percentage representations. Some measures will emphasis gross, inter-group inequalities, but at the expense of obscuring educationally significant changes which can occur as a result of radical changes in the social composition of an educational site. Although the increase in numbers relative to the working class as a whole might be seen as slight, within the school itself the working-class composition of a site could increase rapidly in a relatively short period of time. In an expanding system, as higher-class groups reach their saturation points at a given level, new places will be increasingly filled by lower-class groups.

Participation and Pedagogy

In certain cases significant changes in social participation rates at given levels occur as a result of statutory changes in the minimum leaving age, as with ROSLA. Factors such as credential inflation or youth unemployment can 'encourage' young people to stay on at school. Whatever the reason, experience shows that schools tend to respond to particularly critical changes in social composition by radically changing their curriculum and pedagogy. This is very clear in relation to the Newsom programmes associated with ROSLA, but is also apparent today with the 'new sixth' and in FE in response to the YTS.[10] Similar processes can be observed where schools are attempting to break down gender stereotypes in subject choices, as with the notion of 'girl-friendly science', or with 'race' in terms of 'black studies' or certain types of multicultural or anti-racist education.[11]

The general tendency for inequalities in attainment to decline at given levels means that everybody in effect gets more education. However, the purely quantitative changes produce, at certain critical moments, qualitative changes in curriculum and pedagogy as the social composition (the proportions of members of different social groups) of the education site changes.

Although it might well be the case that there are good reasons in principle for changing received forms of education, it has to be noted that the way in which changes occur tends to produce the effect that certain groups are continually pursuing a chimera or conventionally perceived 'high status' education. Whenever they break through into some previously restricted enclave they find it has changed its form into something which, though perceived by well-intentioned educationalists as more 'relevant' to their presumed 'needs', is generally seen by everyone else (including the pupils themselves) as an inferior version of what went before. The process whereby quantitative change in terms of numbers translates into qualitative change in terms of curriculum and pedagogy entails, simultaneously, a devaluation in the symbolic status of the site and its associated credentials — a decline in the worth of their material and cultural capital.

The general trend involves a further effect in terms of the relationship between education, occupation and social status which has to do with phenomena of credentialization and credential inflation. Halsey *et al.* say that:

> ... if a process of 'credentialisation' is occurring in which higher levels of educational attainment are required as more pupils attain the lower levels, the trend towards equality that our logistic curves revealed might be fundamentally misleading. While differentials may be closing at one level, they may be widening at a higher one, and the 'overall' situation may remain relatively static.... There is a process of continual movement. In contrast, if we turn from growth in attendance at different ages to the position of percentile groups, we find a completely static situation. If we assume that there is no change in the size of the IQ distributions of the different classes, then the class differentials among, say, the brightest 5 per cent of pupils will remain absolutely unchanged. The top 5 per cent will be receiving more and more education as the process of credentialization continues, but class differences must necessarily remain as they are (ibid., p. 140–1).

Hence, whilst there is a real decline in inequality in attainment at given levels, the basic pattern of difference in attainment is preserved through being reproduced at higher levels.

Probabilities, Possibilities and Expectations

As Bourdieu and Passeron point out (op. cit., p. 224), these changes in participation rates (which are simultaneously changes in class chances) are also likely to affect 'the agents' systems of aspirations' (ibid., p. 226):

> We know that to different objective probabilities correspond different sets of attitudes towards school and school-assisted social mobility. Even when they are not the object of conscious estimation, educational chances, which may be presented to intuitive perception in the group belonged to (neighbourhood or peer group), e.g., in the concrete number of known individuals who are still at school or already working at a given age, help to fix the social image of university education which is in a sense objectively inscribed in a determinate type of social condition. Depending on whether access

to higher education is collectively felt, even in a diffuse way, as an impossible, possible, probable, normal or banal future, everything in the conduct of families and the children (particularly their conduct and performance at school) will vary, because behaviour tends to be governed by what it is 'reasonable' to expect (loc. cit.).

It is important to note here Bourdieu and Passeron's reference to 'reasonable expectations' relating to changing probabilities. This entails a different view of how educational processes might have effects from that more usually encountered in the sociology of education.

Correspondence theory initially defined those effects in terms of the inculcation of attitudes and values required in production. This view was essentially one of simple socialization. The development of correspondence theory has involved more complex cultural models which have made this process more problematical. It can be disrupted and interrupted by countervailing class values which enable pupils to 'resist' the imposition of 'the ruling ideology'. It is not clear, however, that these counterhegemonic values are not themselves acquired in the same kind of way. It can be argued that the increasingly sophisticated cultural models have not been accompanied by commensurately more sophisticated models of the subject. Such simplistic socialization models can be seen at work today in the assumptions which underpin notions of how school text books effectively develop sexist and racist stereotypes.[12]

From Bourdieu and Passeron's point of view educational processes (whether defined through form or content) do not generate automatic effects (e.g., 'cool-out' the working class, 'feminize' girls, produce 'negative self-images' in black pupils). Their effects at any point in time are conditional upon the state of the entire system of relationships within which they are located (and through which they acquire their specific value) and mediated both the dispositions acquired within the 'habitus' of the home and expectations held under a prevailing system of 'objective probabilities' within key social systems such as the labour market.[13] As with Boudon's concept of 'the educational decision field' (op. cit.), the individual is perceived as positioned with a complex matrix of relationships. The complexities of such 'positioning' and their transformational possibilities have been a primary preoccupation in Bernstein's work.

Credentialization and the Labour Market

Whilst it is the case that radical changes are occurring at particular levels, it is also the case that in other respects everything remains the same. Just as the process of credentialization maintains the general pattern of educational difference, so it also fails to lead to any significant change in social opportunity through, for instance, improved occupational opportunity or social mobility. Essentially what happens is that the reduction in educational inequality at given levels is associated with credential inflation in the labour market so that everyone simply needs more education in order to stay in the same place. The 'upward translation of the structure of the educational chances of the different social groups' (Bourdieu and Passeron, op. cit., p. 224) has occurred simultaneously with a devaluation of credentials in the labour market. Hence everything remains the same as far as the structure of differentials is concerned.

Contrary to the assumptions of human capital theory, the increased spread of higher educational qualifications has not provided improved access to either higher-status jobs or higher incomes. As the 1982 General Household Survey shows, there has been a considerable reduction in the income differentials associated with different qualification levels and the financial returns on extra years of education have declined. The upward translation of the structure of educational differentials effectively continues to reproduce the established pattern of educational and occupational differentiation despite the general improvement in levels of educational attainment.

One feature of this process is for qualifications (especially at the higher level) to be more widely distributed across occupational categories as, for instance, the gap between 'A' levels and certain types of classes of degrees narrows. Paradoxically it could be the case that the saliance of non-academic criteria in employers' recruitment strategies actually increases as qualifications become more widespread and hence less effective, in themselves, in registering social difference.

Summary

The features of the trends in class differentials in attainment, and their implications, are complex. The main aspects can be summarized as follows:

1. The statistical evidence indicates a progressive narrowing of differentials at given levels throughout this century. This appears to be largely independent of specific reforms.
2. At the same time, the general pattern of difference is preserved by virtue of its 'upward translation' into higher levels of qualification. Hence, everyone is getting more education in absolute terms, resulting in the narrowing of inequality at given levels, but the relative differences between groups stay much the same.
3. At those levels where differences decline, radical changes can occur in the social composition of the pupil population (e.g., the ROSLA fifth-form of the early 1970s or the 'New Sixth' and FE today). These changes appear to call forth changes in pedagogy and curriculum (e.g., social education for 'Newsom' pupils, B/Tec in the sixth form, Social and Life Skills for YTS trainees in FE). Such responses can be seen in terms of new problems of classroom control

(hence the legitimating rhetoric of 'relevance' or 'realism').
4   These changes amount to a symbolic devaluation of that level of education's 'cultural capital'.
5   The devaluation of cultural capital is correlated with the qualification level's material devaluation in the labour market. The process of credentialization in the occupational system means that individuals receive no net returns to their extended educational careers. Everyone needs proportionately more education simply to stay put. Hence rising educational aspirations are associated with declining occupational expectations and increased personal costs through delayed entry into the labour market.

This destructive spiral results in an intensifying legitimation crisis for education and its most viscious irony is that in a period of mass youth unemployment it is a particularly sterile form of vocationalism which is deemed to be the appropriate response.

As far as the theoretical presuppositions of the perspectives being considered are concerned (human capital theory, reformism, correspondence theory, etc.), the outstanding features of these trends and their systematic complexities is the almost entirely arbitrary relationship that exists between the hierarchies, forms and levels of the educational system and those of the occupational system. Any appearance of correspondence reflects not a mechanism whereby education is made to serve the interests of direct production, but rather constructions of ideology which regulate the social relations of knowledge production and of educational transmission.[14]

Education, Production and the Labour Market

The previous section looked at the complex ways in which the changing pattern of class differentials in educational attainment reconstruct and reposition educational sites relative to the occupational system. The major implication of this is that the possibility of a synchronized articulation between educational and occupational levels and of the correspondence of their forms (i.e., those of education being derived from the needs of 'production') is non-obtainable in the first instance.

Sites within the systems of education and occupation are only ever in approximate relationships and the manner and degree of that approximation is contingent upon (a) the endogenous development of their internal complexities (b) the strength of the classification (or boundary) maintained between the categories of education and production in the dominant educational ideologies (e.g., how far 'the world of work' is seen as a legitimate part of the curriculum) and (c) the regulation of their systemic relations through official State ideology, policy and practice.[15]

In addition to recognizing the radical discontinuity between the two systems, however, it is also necessary to acknowledge the manner in which the material exchange between them (the movement of people from education into work) is mediated by the labour market.

Strangely, the labour market has been a relatively neglected topic in sociology generally and in the sociology of education in particular.[16] The most interesting feature of the labour market, i.e., its complex structure and segmentation, is also one looked upon with great disfavour by orthodox economic theory and by the dominant form of market economics especially. Essentially this is because the very idea of labour market structure violates the basic tenets of free market theory and of the marginal product theory of wages.[17] It is seen in terms of the 'distortions' of customary and traditional practice and of trade union or professional 'restrictive practice'. In addition, analyses of social inequality from the point of view of labour market segmentation seriously undermine the rationale of Thatcherism's supply-side deficiency attack on education — the view that the nation's economic plight can be blamed on the failure of the schools to adequately equip young people for 'the world of work'.

Work which does attend to the complexity of the labour market has grown out of the tradition of dual labour market theory.[18] Originally this approach proposed the existence of a single division within the labour market between primary and secondary sectors. The primary sector was seen as made up of large, well organized, technologically advanced firms with complex internal structures, high levels of unionization, recognized, formal procedures governing entry and career development and training programmes. Within such organizations, workers (especially white middle-class males) could expect to develop a secure working-life career with incremental increases in earnings, pensions and formal conditions of service. The secondary sector, by contrast, was seen as being in almost every respect the opposite of the primary. It was characterized by its informality and corresponding lack of security for workers. Secondary sector firms were seen as often parasitic upon the primary sector, fulfilling menial or marginal services, such as office cleaning.

A central feature of this theory was that individuals were not assigned to one or the other sector simply on the basis of their education being treated as the indicator of their marginal productivity. Rather, their location was determined by 'non-economic' factors such as colour, gender and age according to institutionalized, customary practices. Hence black and female workers of similar educational level to white males would be severely disadvantaged in terms of access to primary sector jobs and their earnings and status subsequently, would reflect this rather than their educational level. This approach fundamentally challenged the rationality principle of orthodox economic analysis and the marginal product theory of wages, especially the view that the labour market is intrinsically open and competitive.

In the subsequent development of the approach a number of features have been differentiated out which considerably extend, both theoretically and substantively, our understanding of the complexity of labour market structure and the manner in which it mediates both the relationship between the educational and occupational systems and the transition from education into work institutionally and at the level of educational and occupational decision-making. These developments can be summarized as follows:

1 *Labour market segmentation.* The initial dual labour market model has been considerably extended. The attributes of the two labour market types can be found within segments of organizations located within either primary or secondary sectors. Hence certain categories of workers within large primary organizations may be found to be restricted to areas where the normal benefits of primary sector work are unavailable. This could apply to maintenance or low-grade clerical staff for instance and the criteria of membership of such secondary 'ghettos' within the primary sector could include factors such as sex, race and age. Similarly, certain types of managerial work in the secondary sector could approximate primary sector conditions in terms of factors such as security and pay.

2 *Internal labour markets.* Associated with dual labour market theory is the concept of the internal labour market (ILM). This follows from the specification of the features of large-scale primary sector firms and develops the idea that labour market segments are non-competing. The essential idea is that such primary sector institutions constitute labour markets in their own right. The basic characteristic of such ILMs is that entry is carefully controlled and restricted to a limited number of 'entry ports'. Outside these entry ports priority is given to filling posts from within the organization, from existing members of staff following predictable patterns of company-specific career development supported by formal in-house programmes of staff training. The development of ILMs is often characterized as a negotiated exchange to the mutual benefit of workers and management. The ILM structure protects workers from outside competition, provides secure and generally recognized patterns of career development and secures for management a stable and committed workforce which is familiar with the organization's distinctive requirements. It is the idea that ILMs are non-competing in the wider labour market which most radically challenges orthodox economic theory. Educational qualifications are relevant only at the point of entry into the organization.

3 *The Scope of ILMs.* Initially ILMs were seen as located at the level of the firm. It is now generally recognized that such non-competing markets can have other forms. In some cases the ILM might be restricted to certain types of workers within a firm. In others it might be restricted to certain types of workers across firms within a

particular sector, i.e., it is an occupational ILM.[19]

4   *Career paths.* A central aspect of the model which emerges from the combination of labour market segmentation and ILMs is the view that different types of career paths are institutionalized within the occupational system. Depending upon the nature of the market in terms of its scope and exclusiveness, individuals will be able to progress along different types of career pathway. In certain cases the career path might be organizationally-specific, in other cases it might involve an occupational career within a segment across a number of firms or organizations. In certain cases the type of career development facilitated by company staff development programmes will aim specifically at providing a mix of expertise and skills which reduce the 'transferability' of workers' experience. This will involve horizontal movement within company specific 'job clusters' in addition to normal promotion within the organizational hierarchy. Occupational careers, in contrast, will tend to be facilitated by nationally recognized professional qualifications. This raises the issue of the relationship between academic, professional and in-house types of training and credentialization.[20]

5   *Recruitment strategies.* An implication of the complex model of segmentation is that employers in different areas will operate with different types of recruitment strategy depending upon the type of market within which they are located. A major variable is the significance accorded to educational qualifications. Contrary to the expectations of both orthodox market economics and radical correspondence type theories, research indicates that formal educational attributes are only one of a number of criteria that employers use in recruitment and that they tend to be of secondary significance.[21] Work indicates that employers tend to use educational qualifications in a relatively arbitrary and highly generalized fashion with little interest in their specific occupational relevance. Their major value is seen as a screening device to limit the range of possible applicants rather than in terms of any intrinsic occupational relevance.

6   *Employer attitudes to qualifications.* A central argument in current attempts to vocationalize education is that employers are highly dissatisfied with the products of the educational system. It is not usually the case that anything other than anecdotal evidence is used to substantiate this assertion within the political debate. In reality, studies in this area tend to show employers expressing satisfaction with new recruits. Research also indicates that employers tend to be not only largely ignorant about the actual content of educational syllabuses and what particular qualifications signify, but also indifferent to such issues.[22] A remarkable feature of the relationship between industry and education is the lack of exchange of informa-

tion between the two sides. The 'dissatisfaction' theme in the public debate shares with the 'declining standards' myth the lack of any substantive body of supporting evidence. Given the ways in which employers tend to use educational qualifications within the broader programmes of their recruitment strategies, lack of detailed knowledge as to what qualifications actually signify is not incompatible with satisfaction with their contribution. It is necessary to realize the relatively limited way in which qualifications are used by employers in the first place.

7 *Job search strategies.* The significance of employee job search strategies has been emphasized by Granovetter (1975, 1981). In a sample of professional, technical and managerial workers in the Boston (Mass., USA) area, Granovetter found that informal contacts provided a major means whereby individuals came to acquire jobs. He points out that the 'contact' would often occur within a situation which had nothing, formally, to do with seeking employment — through conversations at parties or in bars, for instance. Indeed, 29 per cent of his sample denied carrying out any kind of 'job search' at all in order to gain their present employment. Significantly, 35 per cent of the jobs themselves were actually created out of such meetings. Employers would make jobs in order to employ a particular individual, or would see the individual as providing what they needed in order to initiate a project which had been kept 'on the back boiler'.

Granovetter argues that this informal dimension of the 'matching process' derives its rationality from the need of both employers and prospective employees to gain accurate, detailed and reliable information as cheaply as possible. He points out that for both groups, formal methods are both expensive and limited in information. Advertisements can result in more applicants than employers find sensible or feasible to process (which is why educational qualifications are often employed as a screening device) and employees cannot trust the veracity of employers' own presentations of their companies. For both, inside information (e.g., through personal recommendation of either the company or the worker) is much more reliable. Hence such 'informal' methods are in reality more rational than formal procedures.

Detailed ethnographic studies of information exchange through 'social networks' has been carried out in this country by Grieco (1987). Grieco points out that 'network recruitment' also has an important social control function in that the individual who gains employment through the network has an obligation to maintain the reputation of the person who recommends him or her. From this perspective, the significance of qualifications would lie not at the level of the 'fit' between educationally developed technical skills and job requirements, but in terms of criteria of network membership (which might, in turn, be related to professionalization strategies).

In total studies of this general type develop considerably our appreciation of the complexity of the structures which mediate the movement from education into employment. They also warn against simplifying logics which suggests, as is the case with much of the current vocationalist rhetoric, that the issues can be reduced to institutional adjustments which will improve the alignment between the educational and occupational levels and categories. The major problem with the currently influential supply-side deficiency perspective is its tendency to dismiss as a mere distortion of free market forces what is in reality the definitive characteristic of the labour market — namely its structural complexity.

Labour market processes can be seen as constituting the second major limitation upon the general social effectiveness of educational reform. The phenomenon of credential inflation has the paradoxical effect of reducing educational inequality whilst maintaining the general structure of social inequality. Labour market processes can effectively negate equalizing educational trends within groups located at similar class levels. For instance, lack of access to informal recruitment networks can prevent young blacks from getting jobs even where their educational qualifications are above the mean in the indigenous white youth population. Crompton and Jones (1984) have stressed the importance of the relationship between pre-entry academic qualifications and post-entry professional qualifications in developing gender inequalities in white-collar careers. The educational equality between young women and men on entering work is undermined by the way in which career breaks for child-rearing prevent women from gaining professional qualifications.

The intractibility of labour market processes and their relative imperviousness to the effects of educational change suggests that the reformist objectives which have traditionally been pursued through educational reform would be more effectively realized through measures acting directly upon demand-side institutions. The best known of such measures is contract compliance (i.e., the system whereby Central and Local Government agencies insist that companies to which they award contracts show evidence of the implementation of equal opportunities policies). Evidence from the United States suggests that contract compliance has had a greater impact on opportunities for women and ethnic minority groups than educational reform.[23] The recent experience of women and blacks in this country certainly indicates that educational success carries no guarantee of improved chances in the labour market. The imposition of instrumentalist objectives upon education looses credibility as soon as it is realized that such objectives are largely beyond its capacity to realize.

Conclusion

One way of approaching the current problems for socialist thinking on education is to begin by asking how we explain the failure of reformism. It is important to define the nature of this problem. Significant educational reforms did take place, educational inequalities have been considerably reduced. What has not taken place is the range of wider social changes which it was believed would follow on from such reforms. Correspondence theory provides a particular kind of explanation for the failure of reformism by arguing that education under capitalism is essentially concerned with the reproduction of the 'social relations of production'. The principle of its explanation, however, is, in the final analysis, the same as that which underpinned reformism.

Both approaches operate with a similar view of the basic relationship between education and the occupational system. In the way in which it shifted from the point of view of distribution to that of production, the correspondence argument reversed the polarity, as it were, of the reformist argument rather than radically re-theorized it. The education/production relationship when defined from the point of view of distribution lead to reformist optimism, but from the point of view of production resulted in the pessimism of reproduction.

The central argument being advanced here, is that an alternative approach is available which begins from the principle of the radical discontinuity between the educational and occupational systems. The first major expression of this discontinuity is revealed through the way in which the relationships between specific social groups, educational sites and their pedagogic practices, and occupational sites, are being continually reconstructed, reordered and revalued in the evolution of the structure of places in education as expressed through relative participation and attainment rates. The second is revealed through the manner in which the movement of people from education into work is mediated by the complexities of labour market structures and processes.

Although the presentation of this position, here, has been at a relatively descriptive and substantive level it has drawn upon an already existing theoretical base in the works of Boudon, Bourdieu and Bernstein. My contention is that these three writers provide, already, an alternative paradigm of considerable power. Those sufficiently familiar with Bernstein's most recent writings will be aware of the degree to which this descriptive presentation is derived from his theoretical work. If socialist educational thinking is to continue to be informed by sociological work, then it is clear that a major relocation of its theoretical base is required — to one which can handle in a way that correspondence theory cannot, the complexities of an alternative understanding of education's relationship to the occupational system ('production').

The specific implications of the position outlined above are as follows:

1 The reformist social objectives which have previously been sought through educational reform will be more effectively achieved through demand-side mechanisms which act directly upon the

structures and processes in the labour market which reproduce social inequality and effectively annual progressive gains within education. This is most obviously so in the cases of gender and 'racial' inequality. The best known example of such a mechanism is that of contract compliance.

2 It is also the case that the kinds of skill linkages between education and occupation assumed by manpower planners and very largely taken for granted in society at large should be treated with systematic scepticism. In reality there is actually (*pace* correspondence theory) very little close fit between education and the actual distribution of individuals across the occupational system. In the context of the current imposition of vocationalism upon education it is important to reveal the inadequacies of these assumptions and to demand that industry itself be required to fulfil its obligation to train and to bear the cost of doing so.

3 As far as education is concerned, the most positive gain from the type of analysis presented here is that it frees education from the sterility of vocationalism as well as from meritocratic social reformist objectives. This enables us to get back to education as education. Obviously such an anti-instrumentalist position restates the basic philosophical principle of the Liberal education tradition. For socialists under these conditions what counts is the specific manner in which we accommodate that principle. Socialist educational thinking has produced numerous criticisms of Liberal education (e.g., of its elitist traditional academic form, by (mis)representing philosophers such as Hirst and Peters as 'positivists'), what it has not achieved is a proper critique of Liberal education. Bailey's discussion of the critical role of knowledge in Liberal theory is particularly suggestive for radical theory (Bailey, 1984).

The most remarkable feature of the current situation is the way in which an extreme Right-wing government has attacked and contemptuously dismantled Liberal education. Given the way in which the Left has habitually assigned an obvious class character and function to Liberal education, this fact provides us with a major explanatory embarrassment. What the radical restructuring of education by the new Right's Strong State/Free Market apparatus has revealed is the extent to which progressive education (and by implication putative socialist education) has been parasitic in the past upon a space maintained within a relatively autonomous education system by Liberal education.

In its preoccupation with a particular conservative form of Liberal education, the Left has failed to take adequate account of the manner in which that form, in the first place, represented a (conservative cultural) critique of modernism and, in the second, the manner in which that critique followed from a concern with the character of knowledge in education.

As far as the former is concerned, its anti-industrialism and anti-commercialism has probably aroused more ire from the likes of Thatcher, Tebbit and Young than even progressive education.[24] In the case of the latter, socialist educationalists need to re-approach Liberal education from a consideration of Hirst's proposition that the proper starting point for educational theory is epistemology (Hirst, 1972). It is the epistemological perspective which marks the major break in the conventionally established linkage between socialist educational theory and progressive education (which tends to be grounded in developmental psychology, though see Aronowitz and Giroux's discussion of Dewey op. cit.).

What this means specifically for socialists is a theory of education grounded in epistemological Realism.[25] The Realist view of knowledge can be seen as combining the most significant aspects of the two other major traditions, Positivism and Conventionalism. Whereas the former seeks to provide an absolute foundation for knowledge in the idea of theoretically neutral, presuppositionless 'pure' observations (which ignores both the complexities of human perception and cognition, and the social contingencies of real scientific work) the latter appears to lead to an unrestrained cognitive and moral relativism which suggests, in effect, that 'anything goes' because the truth status of any knowledge is always simply relative to its culture or the conventions of those groups for whom it counts as truth (which ignores the very obvious fact that if it is, say, the Moon you're going to, only things sent up by science tend to arrive). Realism on the one hand acknowledges the intrinsically complex and socially situated character of knowledge, but it also provides a basis for grounding it in terms of the relationship between knowledge and its object, i.e., the (putative) external (natural or social) 'thing' to which it is directed and which, in a provisional fashion it attempts to 'apprehend' in the way appropriate to it.

Australian radical philosophers such as M. R. Matthews (1980) are advanced in this task and give full consideration to the form of liberal philosophy developed by Peters and Hirst. The feature of epistemological Realism which is especially significant in this context is its view of knowledge as a form of material production. The principle argument developed in this paper has been that the educational and occupational systems should be seen as radically discontinuous. Brief mention was made above to Marx's distinction between the system of capitalist production as a whole and direct production as a theoretical justification for distinguishing between 'capitalist social relations of production' and the 'system of social relationships in (direct) production'. The Realist view of knowledge as material production grounds the specificity of the educational system and establishes the material base for its autonomy and hence is a crucial aspect of the more general position being constructed here. My contention is that a theory of education derived from Realist epistemology must be the starting point for socialist education.

This view has clear implications for arguments which approach the idea of socialist education from the point of view of control, i.e., that schools should be controlled directly by representatives of the local community or of working-class organizations. There is nothing in these arguments which is either authoritively socialist or educational. The manner in which education is controlled should reflect in the first instance that which education is specifically to do with, i.e., the production and distribution of knowledge. It is striking how far 'workerist' definitions of socialist education reproduce within their own rhetoric the new Right's arguments about parental choice within the free market. In both cases, models of social relations of control located in direct production are being imposed upon the social relations specific to knowledge production. In the case of the Left, this reflects the failure to see education as practice and as production in its own right.

Notes

1 See Arnot and Whitty, 1982.
2 See Moore, 1988.
3 See Moore, 1988.
4 On various aspects of the official background and of DES policy and concerns see Dale *et al.* 1986; Finn, 1987; Hough, 1987; Jones, 1983 and Roberts, 1984.
5 See Moore, 1988.
6 The term 'inequality' is being used here as if it were unproblematical. However, serious objections have been raised to this form of conventional usage which, it is argued (see Murphy, 1981; Gambetta, 1987) ignores an important distinction between inequality and difference. This argument has fundamental implications for theories of socialization, agency and the model of the subject. Strictly speaking they are crucial to the argument being developed in this chapter, but cannot be treated briefly and, hence, for the sake of brevity, I have 'bracketed' out these concerns within this exposition and its particular focus. However, see Ahier (forthcoming) for a relevant critical perspective upon the widely held but largely unexamined assumptions of simple socialization models which underpin much of radical analysis in education (especially in realtion to gender and 'race').
7 For a comparison of these two different approaches contrast Little and Westergaard, 1964, with the *Appendix* to Bourdieu and Passeron 1977.
8 See Bernstein 1977, ch. 8, on 'systemic relations' and Atkinson, 1985 on Bernstein's work in general. Atkinson's excellent book provides a full, sympathetic and lucid exposition of Bernstein's ideas.
9 See Lauder, 1987 for an interesting discussion of 'commodification' within a particular political context. The new Right strategy of subjecting public sector institutions in general to 'the discipline of the market' can be seen as a programme of systematically eliminating from political and social discourse any intervention of moral principle within the social sphere.
10 See Moore, 1983; 1984.
11 See Stone, 1981, and Cohen, 1987, for critical material in the area of 'race'.
12 See Ahier (forthcoming).
13 See Roberts, 1975.
14 See Moore, 1987.
15 See Moore, 1987.
16 See Blackburn and Mann, 1979; Berg, 1981.

17 See Berg (op. cit.) for critical discussions.
18 See Gordon, 1972, for a critical review of paradigms in the analysis of the labour market.
19 See Ashton *et al.*, 1983; 1986, for a review of the area and a major contribution to it.
20 See Crompton and Jones, 1984a, on the significance of post-job-entry professional qualifications in structuring gender inequalities in white collar employment.
21 See Moore (in press) for a review of some relevant material in this area.
22 See ibid.
23 On 'contract compliance' see Greater London Council, 1984.
24 The broader context of this debate has been fuelled by Martin Weiner's book (1981) which suggests a powerful reason (from the Thatcherite new Right's point of view) for demolishing the liberal form of English education.
25 On 'Realism' see Bhaskar, 1979; Benton, 1977, and Matthews, (1980).

References

AHIER, J. (forthcoming) *Anti-Industrial Lessons for English Children*, Lewes: Falmer Press.
ARNOT, M. and WHITTY, G. (1982) From reproduction to transformation...', *British Journal of Sociology of Education* 3.
ARONOWITZ, S. and GIROUX, H. (1986) *Education Under Siege*, London: RKP.
ASHTON, D., MAGUIRE, M. and GARLAND, J. (1983) *Youth in the Labour Market*, Research Paper No. 34, London: Department of Employment.
ASHTON, D. et al (1986) *Young Adults in the Labour Market* Research Paper No 55, London: Department of Employment.
ATKINSON, P. (1985) *Language, Structure and Reproduction*, London: Methuen.
BAILEY, C. (1984) *Beyond the Present and the Particular*, London: RKP.
BENTON, T. (1977) *The Philosophical Foundations of the Three Sociologies*, London: RKP.
BERG, I. (1981) (Ed.) *Sociological Perspectives on Labour Markets*, New York: Academic Press.
BERNSTEIN, B. (1977) *Class, Codes and Control Vol. 3*. London: RKP.
BERNSTEIN, B. (1982) 'Codes, modalities and the process of cultural reproduction: A model', in Apple, M. (Ed.) *Cultural and Economic Reproduction in Education*, London: RKP.
BHASKAR, R. (1979) *A Realist Theory of Science*, Leeds: Leeds Books.
BLACKBURN, R. and MANN, M. (1979) *The Working Class and the Labour Market*, Basingstoke: MacMillan.
BOUDON, R. (1974) *Education, Opportunity and Social Inequality*, New York: John Wiley.
BOUDON, R. (1977) 'Education and social mobility: A structural model', in Karabel, J. and Halsey, A. H. (Eds.) *Power and Ideology in Education*, New York: OUP.
BOURDIEU, P. and PASSERON, J. C. (1977) *Reproduction*, London: Sage.
BOWLES, S. and GINTIS, H. (1976) *Schooling in Capitalist America*, London: RKP.
CARNOY, M. and LEVIN, H. (1985) *Schooling and Work in the Democratic State*, Stanford: Stanford University Press.
COHEN, P. (1987) *Racism and Popular Culture: A Cultural Studies Approach*, London: Centre for Multicultural Education, University of London Institute of Education.
COLLINS, R. (1981) *The Credential Society*, New York: Academic Press.
CROMPTON, R. and JONES, G. (1984) *White Collar Proletariat*. Basingstoke: MacMillan.
DALE, R. et al (1986) *TVEI: A Policy Hybrid*, unpublished paper, Open University.
FINN, D. (1987) *Training Without Jobs*, Basingstoke: MacMillan.
FLOUD, J. and HALSEY, A. H. (1961) 'English secondary schools and the supply of labour', in Halsey, A. H. *et al*, New York: Fress Press.

FRITH, S. (1980) 'Education, training and the labour process', in Cole, M. and Skelton, B. (Eds.) *Blind Alley*, Ormskirk: G. W. & A. Hesketh.
GAMBETTA, D. (1987) *Were They Pushed or Did They Jump?*, Cambridge: CUP.
GINTIS, H. and BOWLES, S. (1982) 'Contradiction and reproduction in education', Dale, R. *et al.* (Eds.) *Schooling and the National Interest*, Lewes: Falmer Press.
GORDON, D. M. (1972) *Theories of Poverty and Underemployment*, Lexington, Mass.: Lexington Books.
GRANOVETTER, M. (1975) *Getting a Job*, Cambridge, Mass.: Harvard University Press.
GRANOVETTER, M. (1981) 'Towards a sociological theory of income differences', in Berg, I. (Ed.) *Sociological Perspectives on Labour Markets*, New York: Academic Press.
GREATER LONDON COUNCIL (1984) *Ethnic Minority/Contract Compliance Conference Report*, London: GLC Publications.
GRIECO, M. (1987) *Keep it in the Family*, London: Tavistock.
HALSEY, A., FLOUD, J. and ANDERSON, J. (Eds) (1961) *Education, Economy and Society*, New York: Free Press.
HALSEY, A. H., HEATH A. and RIDGE, J. (1980) *Origins and Destinations*, Oxford: Clarendon Press.
HIRST, P. (1972) 'Liberal education and the nature of knowledge', in Dearden, R. F. *et al.* (Eds.) *Education and the Development of Reason*, London: RKP.
HOUGH, J. R. (1987) *Education and the National Economy*, Kent: Croom Helm.
JONES, K. (1983) *Beyond Progressive Education*, Basingstoke: MacMillan.
JENCKS, C. (1972) *Inequality*, New York: Basic Books.
KARABEL, J. and HALSEY, A. H. (Eds.) (1977) *Power and Ideology in Education*, Oxford: Oxford University Press.
LAUDER, H. (1987) 'The new right and educational policy in New Zealand', *New Zealand Journal of Educational Studies*, 22, no. 1.
LITTLE, A. and WESTERGAARD, J. (1964) 'The trend of class differentials in educational opportunity in England and Wales', *British Journal of Sociology*, 22, no. 16.
MARX, K. (1976) *Capital, Vol. 1*, Harmondsworth: Penguin Books.
MATTHEWS, M. R. (1980) *The Marxist Theory of Schooling*, Brighton: Harvester Press.
MILIBAND, R. (1973) *The State in a Capitalist Society*, London: Quartet Books.
MOORE, R. (1983) 'Further education, pedagogy and production', in Gleeson, D. (Ed.) *Youth Training and the Search For Work*, London: RKP.
MOORE, R. (1984) 'Schooling and the world of work' in Bates, I. *et al.*, *Schooling for the Dole?*, Basingstoke: MacMillan.
MOORE, R. (1987) 'Education and the ideology of production', *British Journal of Sociology of Education*, 8, no. 2.
MOORE, R. (1988) 'The correspondence principle and the Marxist sociology of education', in Cole, M. (Ed.) *Bowles and Gintis Revisited*, Lewes: Falmer Press.
MOORE, R. (in press) 'Education, employment and recruitment', in Dale *et al.* (Eds.) *Frameworks for Teaching*, London: Edward Arnold.
MURPHY, J. (1981) 'Class inequality in education: two justifications, one evaluation but no hard evidence', in *British Journal of Sociology*, 32, No. 2, pp. 182–201.
ROBERTS, K. (1975) 'The developmental theory of occupational choice', in Esland, G. *et al.* (Eds.) *People and Work*, Edinburgh: Holmes McDougal.
ROBERTS, K. (1984) *School Leavers and their Prospects*, Milton Keynes: Open University Press.
STONE, M. (1981) *The Education of the Black Child in Britain*, (1981) London: Fontana.
WESTERGAARD, J. and RESLER, H. (1976) *Class in a Capitalist Society*, Harmondsworth: Penguin Books.
WIENER, M. (1981) *English Culture and the Decline of the Industrial Spirit, 1850–1980*, Cambridge: CUP.
YOUNG, M. F. D. (1971) (Ed.) *Knowledge and Control*, London: Collier MacMillan.

Chapter 7

A Socialist Education for Girls

AnnMarie Wolpe

In the feminist literature questions relating specifically to socialist forms of education have seldom been addressed. Our concern has been, primarily, with the inferior facilities available to girls and women in education and how these have militated against their overall intellectual development and employment opportunities. To this extent feminist work on education has taken place within a social-democratic framework which centres on the problem of equality of opportunity within capitalist society (Tawney, 1973).

The assumption in this work is that equality can be achieved through changes in teaching practices and/or reforms of the curriculum, in particular by making the same subjects available for girls that academically-successful boys pursue. At the level of further and higher education some writers have emphasized the need for a support system, such as the provision of crèches for young mothers, to enable women to compete on an equal footing with men.

Where feminists have identified themselves as socialists and set out an agenda for a socialist education for girls they have not deviated significantly from this equal opportunities programme. Their concern has been with the reform of education within the existing system at the expense of the development of a more radical agenda for a socialist feminist educational policy.

What is particularly interesting in this respect has been the overall failure to address the relationship between the education system and the structure of the family. It is a widely accepted argument that it is preeminently, if not only, within the family that gendered relations are defined through the domestic division of labour and that power relationships between men and women are constituted. Yet scant attention has been paid to the part that education plays in perpetuating these relationships.

This chapter will critically review the social-democratic principle of equal opportunity, in general, and argue that it cannot advance the educational facilities for the majority of girls. It will discuss, in particular, the failure of this type of analysis to consider either the class struggle or the relationship between education and the family.

Following this the question of the role of the education system in regard to gender relations within the family will be raised. It is important to draw attention to the fact that changes in the social relations of production will not automatically affect and transform gender relations within the family. It is possible, as seen in many socialist countries, for the traditional form of family relations to remain intact irrespective of major changes elsewhere. In such societies women still perform domestic duties and retain major responsibility for childcare.

Within a socialist context the education system must cease to provide the support it does for these conventional and traditional forms of gender relations in family life. The burden that women bear must be shared. To achieve this a dramatic change in all aspects of domestic division of labour and accompanying ideologies about gender roles must occur, but within the existing structure of some form of family organization. This recognizes that the traditional nuclear family is not the only arrangement that operates at the moment, but is dominant and the one to which the majority of people aspire.

The second half of this chapter will focus, therefore, on questions relating to the family. After a general discussion on the family, the transmission of knowledge and the ideology about the nuclear family in the hidden and overt curriculum will be discussed. It will be pointed out that familism cannot be considered without including issues on sexuality. In addition the mediation of class membership on these aspects will be introduced. The chapter will conclude with suggestions on some strategies which could begin to confront these issues within a socialist context. In the course of this discussion it is taken as given that the education system *can* confront these issues at both an ideological and practical level.

The Social-Democratic Ideal of Equality of Opportunity

The Labour Party's view on education can be traced back to Tawney's classic essay *Equality* published in 1931. Since then the Labour Party's policy on education has been dominated by a social-democratic principle of egalitarianism and equality of opportunity (see Lauder, in this volume). How to achieve such aims has generated a great deal of analysis by educationalists and a range of strategies and policy proposals.

The variety of solutions is illustrated in the statements in *Socialism and Education* (1979). These include the following: 'Opportunity for every child without discrimination and without privilege' (Alice Bacon); the 'abolition of the class structure in schools and post-school education' (Irene Chaplin); the need to examine the curriculum, the defence and expansion of comprehensive schools, and the injection of more funds (Martin Flannery); 'full comprehensive system of primary and secondary education' (Roy Hattersley); the education system 'must lead to careers for all and must cultivate dignity and respect for all' (Eric Robinson). The common link between these writers is the concern to erase inequalities of opportunity through a range of reforms which are assumed sufficient in themselves to effect the desired change. None of them suggests a complete review of the aim, content and form of education.

Whilst not articulated, equality of opportunity is judged by access to jobs in the labour market. It is this relationship between education and work, which is a central issue within the education debate. Moreover, there is an assumption that schools can and should provide basic skills which are needed by the country's industry and commerce. In other words there should be a close fit or match between the products of schooling and the needs of the labour market. It is the apparent failure of the school to meet the 'needs' of industry which comprises, for both the Labour and the Conservative parties, the rationale for present-day educational policies. While the Conservatives[1] employing the 'free market' concept have focused on stimulating competition within the schools, the Labour Party has reiterated the principle of equality of opportunity.

Notwithstanding these differences both parties converge in their aim to provide an adequately trained school-leaving population that would satisfy the needs of industry and which could compete in a stratified labour market. However little recognition is given to the significant differences which exist between female and male school-leavers generally, and in terms of class membership. It has been left to feminist writers to draw attention to some of these differences.

Whilst feminists have brought women to the centre of the stage, surprisingly, the analysis has been conducted in very similar terms to the equal opportunities discourse. The considerable feminist literature which has examined girls' education has been predominantly concerned with allowing open competition between women and men for previously male-dominated professional jobs.

What constitutes a socialist-feminist perspective is embodied in a paper prepared by the Labour Party Collective on the Education of Women and Girls' (*Socialism and Education*, 1982). All the authors set out two main principles — equality of educational opportunity and equality of educational outcome. Both are related to women's employment. The same education could be secured by a common curriculum, abolition of all forms of selection and the 'implementation of comprehensive practice throughout education'. This in turn would challenge 'subject choice' which they say currently disadvantages girls, black student and working-class students. The authors regarded this as a long-term aim and recommended the adoption of positive actions which included 'catch up courses' specifically in mathematics, science and technical fields — those areas from which girls and women have been previously excluded.

They also identified the areas in which new policy should be developed. These are the provision of resources and curriculum development to 'prepare both sexes for equality in later life and work'; extension and development of 16–19 education; establishment of a credit system for combining work and study; extension of the comprehensive principle; spelling out legal rights and monitoring procedures; teacher training to include an understanding and practice of non-sexist education, and the use of the mass media to combat discriminatory practices.

Turning to analyses involving the state provision of education for girls, socialist-feminist writers have worked within similar paradigms of the equal opportunities debate (David, 1980; Deem, 1981; Deem and Finch, 1986; Arnot, 1987). Notwithstanding political party differences, Arnot (1987) has shown how the various arms of the state (EOC, DES and MSC) have been concerned with economic factors and the stated need for a skilled female labour force, particularly in areas such as engineering and science. Through a range of measures and strategies she notes that the various state agencies have:

> an equal opportunities approach (even if only in rhetoric in some instances) rather than a concern for sex equality. For the optimistic, the policies developed by the EOC, the MSC and the support of HM Inspectors indicate positive moves in the direction of change (p. 326).

Deem (1981), in an article examining state policy in relation to the education of girls and women, talks about the state as an instrument for reduction of capitalist and patriarchal social relations. Referring to the 1960s she says that education policy was 'closely linked to the needs of the economy and to prevailing ideologies about women's role in society' (p. 131), with women being encouraged to increasingly participate in the labour market because of the shortage of staff in clerical, manual and professional capacities. This need, according to Deem, can only be met by the recruitment of women. This period — the 1960s — is characterized as one of consensus and consolidation of social-democratic ideals and policies which encouraged women to enter higher education and training courses. She depicts the 1970s as a period when support for social-democratic reforms declined, but does not deal with the effect this has or may have on previous policies.

Throughout her article, the state of girls' and women's education is discussed solely in relation to the labour market and therefore equality for women may only be attained when they have the same job opportunities as men.

In a more recent article, Deem and Finch (1986), emphasize other factors, in an edited volume which considers 'what education after 18 *could* be like and also what it *should* be like if it were to become a coherent part of a social and economic policy which was both democratic and socialist' (Finch and Rustin, 1986, p. 7). Deem and Finch see the need to 'improve and maintain' women's position in higher education as a means to allow women to be 'equal participants with men' in work. They have a number of prescriptions — educational provision for young mothers in 16–19 age group to provide them with some form of training, new types of training of shorter duration and less specialized study for mature women, realistic financial assistance, and, finally, provision of 'good child-care':

> While we would share a strong preference for a society where women were not obliged to be the full-time carers for their own children, we do not believe that we have to wait for that particular social change to happen before we can contemplate improving women's position with respect to education. Our concern here is to offer a vision of the kind of post-school education which does not ignore the reality of many women's lives, but which seeks to offer them maximum access to educational experience despite the limitations which other social arrangements impose.
>
> We believe that the starting-point for this is to create a pattern of educational provision which genuinely makes participation possible for people in employment, those not in paid work and parents of both sexes (p. 134).

These writers are realistic in their appraisal of women's role in family life. They point to the fact that other contributors in that book have concentrated on the relationship between higher education and the labour market. Their contribution is to focus on easing women's entry into the labour market and this, they argue, can be achieved through the above measures. However although they make a promising start by calling for the need to 'unpack carefully the education–economy link and its implications' they do not develop this or what constitutes the 'limitations which other social arrangements impose'. Instead they focus on child-care facilities. Their reason for this is not the consideration of the whole question of parenting and family relationships, but once more the role of the economic. They say that such a move could 'facilitate women parents' more active participation in the labour market' (p. 136).

It is necessary to assess whether all these measures can, in the end, contribute to the diminution and eradication of the inequalities women experience. To do so requires, firstly, an overall review of the strategies of social-democratic endeavours in general and then its assessment in relation to its application to women.

Johnson (1978), in criticizing the equality of opportunity paradigm as Utopian, highlighted the social democrats' avoidance of class issues. He said there was a 'massive over-loading of education as a course of solutions' to economic problems. In calling for a reappraisal of Marxist principles relating to class, he emphasized the limited scope of reforms and how, in the end, reforms cannot alter the capitalist nature of social relations:

> It is here that a more strictly Marxist understanding of class — against which social-democratic conceptions are often defined —

might actually have helped to explain events. What is class is neither residual nor removable... but an ever-present set of relations that are actually reproduced in production itself. From such a perspective the limits of 'social policy' can be grasped, for it can only deal with the symptoms of class and other social division, not with their roots. More absurd still must be the attempt to 'equalise' through an education that seeks to develop capitalist forms of industry. Such an attempt, we might call it 'capitalist schooling', helps to reproduce the causes of the problems which it is supposed to solve (p. 11).

He is correct to emphasize the glaring absence of concern with class issues amongst the social democrats. The question this raises here is: what is the role of education in the course of class struggle and the wresting of power from the bourgeoisie?

Marx and Engels similarly discounted as reformist Owen's work on educational change on the grounds that they were Utopian and doomed to failure. Robert Owen was one of the early socialists concerned with the social conditions of the poor and, amongst other things, set out the principle that 'remodelling of human character' could be achieved through education. Owen considered education as one of the strategies capable of transforming society through a range of reforms directed at altering the 'character' of individuals. For Marx and Engels it was not this aspect that was important. They correctly regarded education as part of the social totality which could not be isolated from other social structures (Castles and Wurstenberg, 1979). They did recognize, however, the importance of education, particularly in the context of training.

Whilst critical of the conditions under which children laboured, Marx assumed they would always be involved in the productive process. He, therefore, took it for granted that children would continue working and combine this with education. He thought that education should be polytechnic and include mental, bodily and technological training to create the 'totally developed individual'.

Although he included all three aspects, it was technological training which he seems to have emphasized. This training included not only learning how to use tools, machines and materials, that is specific skills, but also referred directly to the general scientific and technological knowledge which is necessary for the control of the productive process (Castles and Wurstenberg, 1979, p. 40). In Marx's terms such knowledge was essential to the class struggle. It is one thing to gain control and another to maintain it. For the working classes to do so successfully requires actual skills and scientific knowledge of the technological side of the productive processes. The latter need is particularly important given the ever-changing nature of technology and the consequences this has on the qualities required of the work force:

By means of machinery, chemical processes and other methods, it [capitalism] is continually transforming not only the technical basis of production but also the functions of the worker and the social combinations of the labour process (Marx, 1976, p. 617).

The increasing use of technology is accompanied by the de-skilling of the work force. Yet there is, at the same time, a need for an ever more skilled, technologically-trained workforce. The solution to this is the versatile worker who is adaptable. Although there are contradictory elements about the required qualities of the labour force, it does not negate the need for workers to have knowledge of technological processes.

Thus for Marx technological education was not only necessary for a diversified and ever changing labour market, but, even more importantly, for its control. Marx, then, was concerned with both the reproduction of workers and the issue of control over the means of production. This extends the role of education. It is not only necessary to train the new generation in concrete skills but also in understanding the managerial processes. Likewise Gramsci urged that it was important for the working class to obtain an education similar to that of the ruling class in order that they could understand how hegemonic control was maintained, and how to seize and hold power.

The complexity of the inter-relation between education, work and class struggle is highlighted by these insights. The assumption that the educational provisions within the context of the existing reformist framework could be sufficient to combat fundamental class differences and compensate for the continued denial to so many people of what Bourdieu (1971) termed the 'cultural capital' of the ruling class may be questioned. This is not to deny that the efforts made in Britain (and in America with its Headstart programme of the late 1960s and early 1970s) are worth while but they cannot, by themselves, eradicate class differences. The social democratic measures are, in effect, nothing more than a means of promoting a meritocratic society. Further these measures are not designed to seriously confront the occupational division of labour because this can not be achieved through the education and training of new recruits, but through political struggle. The ideology of equality of opportunity masks the reality and promotes the false notion that through individual effort and the acquisition of a certain level of training and qualification, significant changes in society can be effected. This is not to deny the value of training and education, but to recognize its limitations.

This has important implications for understanding gender divisions in education, and the preoccupation of some feminists with the equal opportunities in the labour market. There are a range of structural factors militating against women working in a whole range of jobs. Having qualifications does not automatically ensure access to work. There are both employers and fellow male employees to contend with. Furthermore, obtaining the same qualifications as some highly qualified boys can only be a partial solution.

Apart from the fact that this can only be applicable to a relatively small élite group of women — after all there are not many 'top' jobs for boys. But also changes in girls' motivations and goals generated either at school or in the home do not alter their chances of employment, (Furlong, 1986). Employment is not determined by aspirations, determination or training, but by the economic structure itself.

Nevertheless, the education system must, amongst other things, provide knowledge and the means to acquire skills. It must be recognized, however, that it is not men who are the main enemies, but the class system which supports inequalities which create the conditions for the continuing domination of women by men.

The Family and Education

Transformations in social relations of production involve many changes. But none of these, by themselves, will automatically affect girls' and women's life-chances. Such alterations will not change the nature of women' employment in terms of wages, access to work and their relationship to male workers and so on. Changes in the education system may open up some possibilities to women but will not alter the structural constraints which determine the role of women in the labour market.

Whatever changes occur in both the education system and the labour market will also not necessarily affect the power relations and gender division of labour within the family, although it could create the conditions in which such changes could occur. Women may continue to work inside the family and hold the same traditional positions even if there are changes in the labour market. It is the particular relationship between education, family life and socialism which will constitute the remaining discussion in this chapter.

The introduction of the family immediately raises a number of questions, only some of which can be discussed here. The nuclear family has undergone significant changes over the years, and whatever form it takes, its roles are multi-faceted. At the general level some of its roles are emphasized and others tend to be overlooked. The family is seen as the main agent for maintaining stability and order in society. As such it is primarily responsible for the transmission and teaching of the parameters of acceptable social behaviour to successive generations. One other effect of the nuclear family is that it provides the conditions for the continuing oppression of women, a phenomenon which is largely overlooked except by feminist writers.

The changes in family life have occurred slowly. The most noticeable changes are the spiralling number of divorces, changes in the age at which marriage is contracted, the number of children born, and the increasing number of single parent families. Moreover, because social commentators, policy-makers and politicans have emphasized the importance of family life for maintaining stability and social order within society, any signs of weakening of the strength of family life is quickly condemned. Since the nineteenth century concern hs been expressed about the increasing disintegration of family life, particularly amongst the working class. State policies have been devised since then to support and bolster the family. At the level of the state, both political parties have clung to 'an ideology of familism', as Wilson (1987) correctly pointed out. And this has been apparent through the 1970s as Deem (1981) has suggested:

> The strengthening of the family was seen as a way of re-establishing and re-structuring social relationships in a period of economic and social as well as political uncertainty. And women's position as domestic labourers and rearers of children within a restrengthened family was seen as of crucial importance (p. 140).

Family life is defined as important because it is here that the moulding of the next generation in socially desirable forms of behaviour and appropriate moral values occurs.[2] Once again, class differences emerge. The capabilities of the working classes to effectively socialize their children has always been questioned. Their influence on their children has been negatively described and their child-rearing practices seen as inadequate. In the nineteenth century, Owen, for one, questioned the ability of the working class in this regard. He clearly did not hold working-class parents in high esteem and thought they were the 'worse equipped to perform the child-rearing task' (Taylor, 1983, p. 51) and his views were subsequently shared by philanthropists and policy makers, providing the legitimation for schools to act *in loco parentis*.

Owen's view of the inadequacy of working-class parents persists, although it is not expressed as bluntly. The model that has emerged is that working-class parents, wittingly or as a result of circumstances beyond their control, have a number of deficits which must be compensated for, through educational policy, and other forms of state intervention.

What is interesting is that so many commentators have ignored the effect of family organization on all women's lives, irrespective of class membership. There has been an assumption that women's roles are important in terms of training the new generation but it is assumed they do so 'naturally'. Their nurturance and caring is seen as unproblematic. Yet it is the nuclear family which is the major site of women's oppression. Engels, who wrote-off bourgeois women because they sold themselves into marriage, likening them to prostitutes, was a rare exception. He identified domestic 'slavery' as a major problem in working-class women's lives and predicted that their increasing involvement in industrial employment would release them from this state. Speaking of earlier socialists he said:

> They considered that the socialization of youth education and, with this, real freedom in the mutual relations between members of a

family, would directly follow from the free association of men and the *transformation of private domestic work into a public industry*. Moreover Marx has already shown (*Capital, Vol. 1* p. 515 *et seq.*) that 'modern industry, by assigning as it does an important part in the process of production, outside the domestic sphere, to women, young persons, and to children of both sexes, creates a new economic foundation for a higher form of the family and of relations between the sexes' (Engels, 1962, p. 436).

The foundation of family life in the future would be inextricably linked to industrial development. Through collectivization family life would cease to be wholly private and it was at this point that working-class women's emancipation from domestic slavery could be effected.

However, as is well known, the increased number of married women working has not reduced their domestic responsibilities nor been accompanied by collectivization of these duties. In America, for example, the percentage of married women with children in the labour force has increased from 19 per cent in 1960, to 28 per cent in 1970, to 54 per cent in 1986 (Hacker, 1986). This increase has not been accompanied by an increase in facilities to reduce women's domestic duties; there is no indication that their drudgery has diminished. In this country, according to a report by The Guardian (16.11.87) women also run the home and do the bulk of the work.

This applies to both working-class and middle-class women. Working-class women who combine work and housework have a much longer working day than their husbands'. Middle-class women, on the other hand, may buy domestic help and may spend less time than working-class women on such chores. Irrespective of class membership, women are responsible for both household management and child care. To this extent, then, the family represents the concrete manifestation of the way in which gender formations in the form of division of labour are expressed and carried out within the privacy of the home.

Aware of the double burden many women bear, there has been a call by many feminists for changes in family organization to circumvent these problems. Barrett and McIntosh (1981), for example, suggest ways of reducing the individual private responsibilities of women.[3] They call for a move towards collectivism:

> especially income maintenance, the work of making meals, cleaning and housekeeping, and the work of caring for people such as children, the old and the sick or disabled (p. 134).

They have put on the agenda some of the early socialist views on family life but their prescriptions for avoiding domestic drudgery are minimal. They recognized that an alternative to family life was limited. They called for women to experience variety in relationships; the avoidance of oppressive relationships and advised women to beware of domesticity.

A Socialist Education for Girls

Yet the ideal of 'traditional' family life prevails notwithstanding peoples' personal experiences of broken homes, single parenting, different forms of arrangement such as homosexual couples and the double burden shouldered by women on the domestic front. Furthermore this ideal appears as strong as ever. A recent survey of social attitudes towards family life (The Guardian, 28.10.87) noted:

> Even the unconventional in the UK yearn for a conventional family life according to the first comprehensive survey of attitudes towards the family. The ideal household is seen to be a breadwinner father, a homemaker mother and two children. Almost four out of five people opt for this 'traditional' pattern if the children are under five.

As this suggests, implicit in the notion of a 'conventional' family life are gender-specific roles. Women are wives and mothers first and foremost and this involves them in very specific household duties and work. Expectations about the way in which this is managed may vary according to class membership and is linked to work outside the home. Irrespective of class membership, though, this is a pointer to the existence of a set of ideologies about family life in relation to gender roles.

The strength of familism, therefore, resides in a set of ideologies and these are transmitted from one generation to another. Furthermore this ideology is held by women irrespective of their oppression within the family. The perpetuation of this ideology is not easily explained, although one of the reasons is, no doubt, because of the link between female identity, sexuality and family life.

What comprises sexuality cannot be simply spelt out. As established by Freud, sexuality is important throughout an individual's life even in childhood. It exists at the level of the unconscious, though learning to behave as a sexual being is not governed only by the unconscious. It involves learned behaviour as Simon and Gagnon (1971) have so adequately established. Sexuality is inextricably linked to the acquisition of gender identity. Being female and feminine involve a prescribed form of behaviour clearly signalling the gender of the individual. In the case of women this may be contradictory, involving the presentation of self as seductive but also maternal. Being male and masculine have their own well-known specific behaviour characteristics.

Adolescence is a period when the questions surrounding gender identity and learning how to behave as a gendered subject are accelerated. Sexuality is high on the agenda of adolescents. In an interesting vignette a successful playwright and author, Boyd, educated at Gordonstoun, recalled in an interview the ever-present concern with sex and sexuality during his school days. He said:

> We were obsessed with sex. Endless conversation, speculation, fantasising, poring over sex magazines, fervid masturbation, there

> is something soul-destroyingly monotonous about that facet of public school life... It is doubtful whether the much leered-at, touched-up and despised school maids at Gordounstoun found much pathos or humour in their work. The mixture of sexism and snobbery with which these local girls were treated brought out the very worst in our natures; it was male lust at its most doglike and contemptuous (*The Guardian*, 20.11.85).

Issues surrounding sexuality are visible in schools as my study on gender formations show (Wolpe, 1988). Boys and girls are continuously concerned with sexual matters: at the erotic level, at an unconscious level and concretely in terms of learning gender-appropriate forms of behaviour. At the interpersonal level they practice how to behave as gendered subjects. Nor is sexual behaviour restricted to the pupils. Some actions amongst the staff involve direct sexual confrontations, predominantly of an unconscious nature. For example, sex and sexuality is discernible in the context of maintaining discipline in the classroom. Sexual matters are ever present and can even be said to have a marked effect on commitment to academic work. Yet not a great deal is known about this, although studies by Lees (1986) Davies (1984) and Wood (1984) have opened up the debate.

Accepting for the moment that gendered subjects are culturally constructed, and that their acquisition is not 'natural' but involves learned behaviour, schools must have a part to play in the course of this learning process. Similarly, they play a part in upholding and teaching the values of traditional family life. How this is achieved will be addressed below.

Education, Family Roles and Sexuality

Although the family is an integral part of the social structure, it retains a semi-autonomous form in that it contains its own dynamics and systems of reproduction. These dynamics include the specific allocation of duties to women and men, supported by a set of ideologies justifying and legitimating these distinctions. In normative terms women's place is in the home and men's out at work.

How does schooling relate to this, particularly as the family is seen as quite separate from the labour market and much of the education system appears to be devoted to training in some form or other of pupils to fit into the world of work? Schools operate at two levels in contributing to the perpetuation of the status quo. One is the level of ideology and the other is in a concrete way of providing training in housewifely craft.

The ideology of family life is incorporated, directly and indirectly, into the school curriculum. It is taught directly in subjects such as home economics, sex education and biology. Indirectly, it is part of the hidden curriculum and as such can be identified in a variety of text books and underlying teacher responses to pupils. Throughout, such teaching covers existing moral codes on the family in which the guiding principle is the inviolability of the nuclear family and the traditional role of women as wives and mothers.

As for sexuality, this is a restricted area largely confined to discussions on moral order and the provision of some sex education. Formally this is taught in specific classes on sex education, as well as in home economics and biology, all of which contain the same guiding moral principle of the inviollability of the nuclear family and the role of woman as wife and mother.

The complexity of the whole area of sexuality, particularly what comprises female sexuality and how this is linked to the representation of wife and mother as an asexual being is seldom tackled. Nor are emotional relationships considered, although these take up a lot of adolescents' time and energy. This exclusion is presumably on the grounds that by definition it relates to personal relationships which are private and located within the home and family. As such it is usually seen outside the scope of formal education.

The feminist response to questions on the family have been largely restricted, as discussed above, to pragmatic solutions to assist women in entering the labour market. Surprisingly, the role of the family in terms of acting as one of the major controlling agents in women's lives has not been consistently addressed, although it does receive attention in some publications. For example the question is addressed in a section of the Equal Opportunities Commission, School Curriculum Development's work on home economics and child development in their publication *Genderwatch*:

> The emphasis in home economics teaching today is upon the basic living skills which everyone needs, on understanding the principles involved in all aspects of the subject and on creativity and decision-making. Pupils are encouraged to leave school equipped for personal independence and for taking shared responsibility for any household unit in which they decide to live.
>
> The main areas of study focus on basic human needs for food, clothing, shelter and personal relationships (Wadsworth, 1987).

Where sexuality has surfaced in feminist discussions on education it has been largely determined by theoretical suppositions relating to male dominance over women, particularly in regard to sexual relations. Given this viewpoint the discussions have portrayed girls as objects of male sexuality and as victims of a patriarchal society in which the domination of female sexuality by males has an adverse effect on their achievement in school (Mahony, 1985).

What part can education play in contributing to the transformation of the traditional form of gendered division of labour in the family? The following discussion will focus on the ideological and practical aspects in which a socialist strategy can be developed to contribute to change. Any blueprint for a democratic socialist education must take serious notice of issues surrounding the family and sexuality.

Domestic Division of Labour

Schools do provide a training in a range of domestic duties which go under the heading of 'vocational' training. Such teaching could be defined as 'really useful knowledge'. The nature of this is largely practical, teaching pupils how to cook, wash, sew and perform child care, among other things. In addition many subjects have an ideological content referring to the domestic division of labour.

'Really useful knowledge' as Johnson (1983) noted when discussing Nineteenth Century education, included acquiring a 'range of resources for overcoming daily difficulties'. Education did provide this, although always in different ways according to class and gender. Owen, for example, called for the separation of boys from girls between the ages of 6 and 10 so they could follow gender specific useful courses of study:

> ... usefulness was the main consideration in the girls' sewing lessons: they brought clothes in need of repair from their homes so that learning and *necessary productive work* were combined. Cooking and housekeeping were learnt and practised in the public canteens (Castles and Wurstenberg, 1979, p. 28, my emphasis).

The Owenite principle of working-class girls learning useful domestic knowledge has been consistently reaffirmed in a number of official documents. There was an assumption that middle-class girls need not be taught such skills: in the Victorian era they would have known how to instruct their servants to do the work and in the contemporary era it was assumed they would have been taught by their mothers.

But the class-based nature of such provision has altered in recent years, particularly at the lower end of secondary schooling. It is probably safe to say that irrespective of class membership, all girls in state schools have been given home economics classes in the first few years of secondary schooling.

However, it is possible to hazard a guess that as girls progress up the school, the more middle class their background the less likely are they to pursue home economics at the senior level. It is regarded as an easy option and does not fall into the category of academic subjects necessary for entry into higher education:

> ... as a practical subject it is linked, in class terms, to manual work and is, therefore, seen as less important than areas of intellectual work in the curriculum (Wadsworth, 1987, p. 180).

What is more, boys at the lower end of the secondary school level have also been taught home economics, although it is not possible to determine how general this is. Where boys have attended classes in home economics and sewing they have been taught such skills simply as temporary aids for bachelordom, or so they could assist their future wives in times of crisis. The defect with such educational provision is the assumption that domestic duties are women's. Their learning is seldom defined in terms of *sharing* domestic responsibilities as adults. This type of teaching has been seen, correctly, as contributing to the reinforcing of stereotypical notions about gender-appropriate levels of responsibility in the home.

Has home economics been successful in contributing towards the breakdown of traditional gender home-based roles? The results are not encouraging. When the ideological content of the courses and the ways in which they are taught are examined it is clear that the conventional masculine and feminine roles in the home are not being subjected to any intensive consideration or criticism. Irrespective of teaching boys specific skills, the ideological components remain largely untouched. It occurs during early adolescence and at a time when boys are immature and not identifying with their adult roles. Furthermore there is, as yet, no way of assessing how successful initiatives taken by the EOC and several local LEAs have been in altering teachers' practices.

There is no doubt that there is a place for the teaching of useful domestic knowledge — good housekeeping, health and nutrition, child-rearing practices and so on — but it should be for both girls and boys. Irrespective of class and gender it could be argued that everyone should learn such skills. But these cannot be taught in a vacuum. The existing traditional forms of division of labour within the family need to be highlighted and challenged so that these skills are no longer seen as 'natural' for women.

Until the question of the allocation of gender responsibilities in the home is given top priority and extended outside the boundaries of home economics there is small chance for successfully altering the ideology of female and male roles in the family. In addition, criticisms have been levelled against the teaching of home economics on the grounds that it firmly locks girls into domestic chores practically and ideologically. The usefulness that such training can provide has not been welcomed.

Education geared towards breaking down gender-specific subject areas could also begin to challenge the hegemonic position of men and pose an alternative view in which joint parenting, and joint housework (particularly when mothers work), should become the norm. This can only be done if the provision is not only in terms of teaching concrete skills but also questioning the ideological components. This means the re-evaluation of what constitutes women's work in the home, the emphasis on the need to upgrade such activities as well as the serious inclusion of men in such work. What is termed 'life skills' must also be upgraded and given a higher status.

Such a task is far from easy particularly as gender identity is so closely interwoven with actual tasks within the family. Such activities can be seen as threatening to boys' masculinity. These issues need to be addressed and will now be discussed.

Ann Marie Wolpe

Sexuality, Gender Identity and Interpersonal Relations

There are obvious difficulties in introducing these factors into the discussion, not least because of the complex nature of what comprises sexuality, gender identity and ideal interpersonal relationships. Within the scope of such a chapter it is not possible to explore definitions of these three elements separately. Suffice it to say that gender identity, formed at a very early age, is mapped out in more detail during adolescence and into adulthood. What comprises gender identity is inextricably linked to sexuality in both its conscious and unconscious forms.

Whilst sexuality may be seen to be important throughout childhood, it is during adolescence that it erupts and becomes influential. Because adolescents are trapped within the education system for a significant part of their lives, concern about their sexuality should be a legitimate area of analysis.

The question that arises is how can education tackle an area as complex as this involving interpersonal relations and bearing in mind the highly privatized nature of sexuality? A distinction will be drawn between 'really useful knowledge' and ideology.

The provision of sex education has a long history, the main emphasis of which has been on teaching the mechanics of biological reproduction, contraception and associated health hazards of sexually transmitted diseases (Wolpe, 1988). One can argue for the continuing provision of such knowledge which falls into the category of useful knowledge. Again there is evidence that the content and availability of such lessons varies according to gender and class membership (Wolpe 1988), for example the evidence is that working-class girls are more likely to be given lessons on contraception than other groups.

Sex education, providing 'really useful knowledge' must continue to be made available, to girls and boys alike and irrespective of class background, and not be dependent on the whims of a governing board which might be the case given the proposed changes in educational policy.[4]

This is only one aspect of the problem because it does not cover the range of issues surrounding sexuality. There is a need to extend teaching into the sphere of emotional and gender-specific power relationships which are derived from sexual encounters whether within the confines of the family or external to it. This moves the discussion into the sphere of the ideological.

Important in this is the recognition that sexuality is the one area in which, up to the present, men have played a dominant role and have exploited women. This view is perpetuated both in youth cultures and in popular culture in which women are represented as sexual objects. Consequently any socialist education on both a short-term and a long-term basis must question sexual relations, including differential power relations between men and women, and place them high on their agenda.

The importance of raising these questions is that all aspects relating to sexuality have an impact in adult life, even though they are hidden in the

A Socialist Education for Girls

'private' world. Socialist programmes should take account of this. For too long questions relating to sexuality, gender identity and women's life inside the family have been debated *outside* the educational world. It is time for these to be brought within the mainstream of educational thought because, no doubt, the education system has a role to play in bringing about social change. It is not sufficient to concentrate on attempting to equip pupils for life as workers. Schooling must also equip them to conduct themselves adequately as adults in family relationships.

If significant changes to women's lives are to be made in these areas then there is a need for open discussion which should cover all aspects of women's lives. Some remedies may be made in concrete terms as, for example, in restructuring the wage levels and removing women's dependency because of their lower earning capacity. This can be partly resolved by equal pay for work of equal worth, and by adequately training girls for the labour force. But this is only half the battle. The rest takes place in the realm of ideology and in the power relations within the home. What is involved is the acceptance and delineation of areas of women's responsibility. A redistribution, reclassification and redefinition of areas of responsibility may result in upgrading domestic responsibilities in the first instance, and secondly, involving men in such duties as well.

It is necessary to put on the agenda of socialist education consideration of those areas which affect adult life. The first is the provision of an education which does teach pupils to think, to question and to adapt to their environment. In the course of this they must learn certain skills which cannot be restricted in the main to a technological world. These need to be applied to their private lives as well. A socialist education should not be concerned with an androgynous egalitarian society, but one in which there is a complementary aspect to gender relations, at home and at work. The contradictions that operate between the ideological components and the external world of work must be tackled head on. It is not assumed that schooling can effect a change on its own, but together with other changes in structural forms relating to the occupational structure an effective change can be brought about.

Notes

1 As could be expected, the overall Conservative position has been one of safeguarding their power base and operating an elitist system which has required a number of deep seated changes in the provisions brought about by both previous Conservative and Labour Party policies. Johnson (1983) says that Thatcherism is concerned with a 'general direction of change' in regard to educational provision, with 'education as a consumer good, acquired and regulated through the market, according to demand in the shape of parental choice'. The Conservative Election Manifesto of 1987 stated that:

> The Conservative Aims are excellence, diversity, and choice.... We reject the left-wing philosophy... which is based on equality, uniformity and central planning.

Thatcher and the present Minister of Education are shrill in their denunciation of the notion of equality of opportunity. They take as given innate differences in regard to individuals' abilities and see any attempt to redress imbalances as the worst excesses of totalitarianism and the denial of individualism. The ideology expressed by Mrs Thatcher, as Wilson (1987) has pointed out, was that women should not go back to the home. The general view amongst the Tories is that 'the battle for women's rights has been largely won', and efforts by LEAs to counter sexist practices in school can be hostilely rejected. Peter Simple in his column 'Way of the World' in *The Daily Telegraph* (3.7.85) called for resistance by teachers to the ILEA guidelines. He accused ILEA of social engineering:

> which would result in schools no longer (being) educational establishments at all. They would be institutions devoted primarily to the mass deformation of children in the interests of the fraudulent ideal — essentially totalitarian — of equality and 'social justice'.

2 An example of this is evident in Coleman's *Equality of Educational Opportunity* (1966) in which he concluded that 'family background was much more important than school characteristics in explaining differential achievement among children' (quoted by Karabel and Halsey, 1977, p. 21).

3 There is no consensus amongst feminists on this question on how the contradictions between the role of women in the labour force and in the family should be resolved. There is a new conservative feminism which has recently emerged in America (Freidan, 1981; Rossi, 1977; Ehlstain, 1981) in which there is support for traditional women's role. Women should value their nurturant, caring role and not compete with men in the labour market. Stacey (1983) offers an interesting critique of this position.

4 However, with the proposed new national core curriculum there is no recommended space for compulsory sex education which may well be the outcome of pressure from a 'moral majority' group which recommends that parents be responsible for giving their children sex education. There will be little time left over for sex education as many subjects will be competing for inclusion in the available space.

References

ALTHUSSER, L. (1971) 'Ideology and ideological state apparatuses', in *Lenin and Philosophy and Other Essays*, London: New Left Books.

ARNOT, M. (1987) 'Political lip-service or radical reform? Central government responses to sex equality as a policy issue' in Arnot, M. and Weiner, G. (Eds), *Gender and the Politics of Schooling*, London: Hutchinson.

BARRETT, M. and MCINTOSH, M. (1981) *The Anti-Social Family*, London: Verso.

BEECHEY, V. (1987) *Unequal Pay*, London: Verso.

BOURDIEU, P. (1971) 'Systems of education and systems of thought', in Young, M. E. D., (Ed.) *Knowledge and Control*, London: Collier-Macmillan.

CASTLES, S. and WURSTENBERG, W. (1979) *The Education Of The Future*, London: Pluto Press.

CENTRE FOR CONTEMPORARY CULTURAL STUDIES (1977) *Unpopular Education*, London: Hutchinson.

COLEMAN, J. S. et al. (1986) *Equality of Educational Opportunity*, Washington, DC: US Government Printing Office.

DAVID, M. (1980) *The State, The Family And Education*, London: Routledge & Kegan Paul.

DAVIES, L. (1984) *Pupil Power: Deviance and Gender In School*, Lewes: Falmer Press.
DEEM, R. (1981) 'State policy and ideology in the education of women 1944-1980; in *British Journal of Sociology of Education* 2, 2.
DEEM, R. and FINCH, J. (1986) 'Claiming our space: women in a socialist alternative post-18 education' in Finch, J. and Rustin, M. (Eds.) *A Degree of Choice? Higher Education and the Right to Learn*, Harmondsworth: Penguin.
EHLSTAIN, J. B. (1981) *Public Man, Private Woman: Women in Social and Political Thought*, Princeton: Princeton University Press.
ENGELS, F. (1962) *Anti-Duhring*, Third Edition: Moscow: Foreign Languages Publishing House.
FINCH, J. and RUSTIN, M. (1986) *A Degree of Choice? Higher Education And the Right To Learn*, Harmondsworth: Penguin.
FURLONG, A. (1986) 'Schools and the structure of female occupational aspirations', *British Journal of Sociology of Education*, 7, 4.
FREIDAN, B. (1981) *The Second Stage*, New York: Summit Books.
GRAMSCI, A. (1971) *Selections From The Prinson Notebooks* London: Lawrence and Wishart.
HACKER, A. (1986), 'Women at Work', *New York Review of Books*, 14 August.
JOHNSON, R. (1978) 'Education and social democracy: A critique', *Socialism and Education* 5, 5.
JOHNSON, R. (1983) 'Educational politics: The old and the new', In *Is There Anyone Here From Education?*, Wolpe M. and Donald J. (Eds), London: Pluto Press.
KARABEL, J. and HALSEY, A. H. (1977) (Eds), 'Introduction' in *Power and Ideology in Education*, Oxford: Oxford University Press.
LABOUR PARTY COLLECTIVE ON EDUCATION OF WOMEN AND GIRLS (1982) 'An inequality policy for Labour' in *Socialism and Education* 9, 2.
LEES, S. (1986) *Losing Out: Sexuality and Adolescent Girls*, London: Hutchinson.
MARX, K. (1976) *Capital Vol. 1*. Harmondsworth: Penguin Books.
MAHONV, P. (1985) *Schools for the Boys? Co-Education Reassessed*, London: Hutchinson in Association with The Explorations in Feminism Collective.
PHILLIPS, A. (1987) *Hidden Hands: Women and Economic Policies*, London: Virago.
POULANTZAS, N. (1975) *Classes in Contemporary Capitalism*, London: New Left Books.
ROSSI, A. (1977), 'A Biosocial Perspective on Parenting', *Daedalus* 106.
SIMON, W. and GAGNON, J. (1971) 'Psychosexual development' in Grummon, D. L. and Barclay, A. M. (Eds), *Sexuality: A Search For Perspectives*, New York: Van Rostrand Reinhold Co.
SOCIALISM AND EDUCATION (1979) 'A forum on socialist education and the Labour Party' 6, 3.
STACEY, J. (1983) 'The new conservative feminism' *Feminist Studies*, 9, 3.
TAWNEY, R. H. (1973) 'Equality', in Silver, H. (Ed.) *Equal Opportunity in Education*, London, Methuen.
TAYLOR, B. (1983) *Eve And The New Jerusalem*, London: Virago.
WADSWORTH, N. (1987) 'Home economics and child development' in *Genderwatch!* (Equal Opportunities Commission) Manchester: SCDC Publications.
WILSON, E. (1987) 'Thatcherism and women: After seven years', in (Eds.) Miliband, R. Panitch, L. and Saville, J. *Socialist Register*, London: The Merlin Press.
WOLPE, A. M. (1988) *Within School Walls: The Role of Discipline, Sexuality and the Curriculum*, London: Routledge (forthcoming).
WOOD, J. (1984) 'Groping towards sexism: boys' sex talk' in McRobbie, A. and Nava, M. (Eds), *Gender and Generation*, Basingstoke: Macmillan.

Chapter 8

Towards a Democratic Science Education

Alison Kelly

Introduction

In government thinking — whichever Government is in power — science education is seen as a 'good thing' which needs to be protected and extended. Science has recently been included in the 'common core' of subjects to be studied by all children throughout their compulsory schooling (DES, 1987). The idea of 'Science for All' is common parlance, although not common practice, within the profession (DES, 1985; SSCR, 1983). The aim is that children of all abilities should study 'broad and balanced' science throughout compulsory schooling. Science is seen as necessary to economic growth and prosperity, but at present Britain is perceived to lag behind other countries in technological training.

So much is broadly agreed among the policy makers. But science is many things to many people, and the content of the curriculum is a matter for debate. At present academically able middle-class boys are much more likely than less able working-class or female pupils to take physics and chemistry (Kelly, 1987a). Black children are less likely to study physics and achieve less well in science (and other subjects) than White or Asian pupils (Kelly, 1987b). There is less class, ability or race differentiation in the distribution of biology education, but biology is taken far more often by girls than by boys.

In this chapter I want to explore some of the curriculum reforms which have been proposed to rid science education of its class, gender and race biases. This will be followed by a description of some recent curriculum work, and an assessment of the extent to which these changes can be helpful in developing an inclusive science education. I conclude by advocating an eclectic mixture of traditionalism, innovation and teacher-based interventions in an effort to produce a more democratic science education.

The Present Situation

Science education in England in the 1980s is very strongly influenced by the Nuffield development of the 1960s. The Nuffield reform was initiated by the Association for Science Education (ASE) although they soon lost control of its development (McCulloch *et al*, 1985). The ASE started life as the Science Masters Association, restricted to graduates teaching in grammar and public schools. Their concerns reflected this. The Nuffield scheme was intended to reform pure science and make it more attractive to the best boys. It was never meant to cover the whole ability range, to teach applied science, or to be for girls. Secondary technical schools were neglected in the development of the scheme, and secondary moderns were not even mentioned. Great emphasis was placed on 'discovery' learning, but the pupils were supposed to discover pure science, not its applications. As Hoskyns (1976) put it:

> In the Nuffield course, although great emphasis is placed on the pupils doing the experiments for themselves, each experiment is designed to teach a very specific and often trivial effect rather than to allow for genuine experimentation.

The Nuffield scheme was very influential. It quickly spread from the elite group of boys for whom it was designed to schools catering for the whole ability range. In the process the scheme was modified, and it is now rarely used in its original form. But the philosophy of Nuffield lives on. Science lessons contain much more practical work, for everybody, than they did in the 1950s. The idea of discovery — or guided discovery — learning is widespread. But science as taught in schools is essentially pure science, with little emphasis placed on applications, either industrial or domestic. This is the context within which critiques must be seen.

The 1960s also saw innovations in applied science. Engineering had influential patrons, notably Prince Philip, who were concerned to make the subject more attractive to the best boys (McCulloch *et al*, 1985). They wanted to avoid the impression that applied science was particulary suitable for lower ability groups, and so, although they started with application, they stressed the intellectual delights of engineering. Among this group reforms which were seen as being closely linked to craft teachers and their concerns, such as Project Technology, were suspect. Perhaps because of this split in the ranks of technology educators, reforms in this area were nothing like as successful as those in pure science. Applied science continued to be marginalized, and associated with the low prestige craft subjects. The current moves towards Craft Design and Technology (CDT) represent a further attempt to upgrade the technical crafts, but in most schools the links to the science department remain weak.

Alison Kelly

Class

The first critiques of post-Nuffield science education, by writers such as Hine (1975) and Young (1976) were, implicitly and sometimes explicitly, to do with class. School science was seen as overly academic and theoretical, presenting disconnected bits of knowledge which were unrelated to pupils' lives. As Hine (1975) puts it:

> even if a lesson starts with a concrete example of pupils' life experience — the way camping gas cookers work, for instance — the *real* problem is learning Boyle's Law and how volumes of gases change under pressure, not the practical problem of storing butane.

Young (1976) shows how teachers emphasize the discontinuities rather than the continuitities between school science and everyday knowledge, by stressing the laboratory as a different place, with its own specialized apparatus and rules. As Keddie (1971) has argued in another context, this can be particulary alienating for working-class pupils, who are less willing than their middle-class peers to take the teacher's definition of the situation on trust. Similarly Hamilton (1975) has suggested that 'discovery learning' syllabuses may operate to the disadvantage of working-class pupils who have less access to middle-class definitions of the kinds of behaviour and skill which are required.

The social implications of science are generally neglected in school science. Hine (1975) comments that 'energy' is a major topic in lower school science, but:

> the concept of the society dependent on particular energy slaves for its existence is not included... presumably because of the open question of the possible radical alternatives that are inevitably posed. Even a topical discussion which must change almost daily, on the enormous repercussions of the oil crisis, is unallowed, presumably because of the political overtones. However ignoring such problems is a political statement, there can be no sitting on the fence. A sensitive teacher must be aware of the futility and irrelevance of the calculation of the energy required to produce a hot bath.

This statement has overtones of conspiracy theory, with its talk of things that are 'unallowed'. Moreover the calculation of the energy required to produce a hot bath can be far from irrelevant to those who have to pay the bills! However, the general point, that science is presented in a decontextualized manner, is certainly valid.

Young (1976) makes a similar point. He argues that:

> science teaching... began and continues with its main purpose to maintain the supply of future scientists. This has two inter-related,

and in effect self-justifying outcomes — the mass scientific and technological ignorance of people in an increasingly technologically dominated society, who see themselves as dependent on experts in more and more aspects of their life, and a community of scientists who see the knowledge which they are responsible for producing and validating as *necessarily* not available to the community at large.

Science education can have many purposes. At present its task is to provide capitalism with the requisite supply of specialist workers, and to ensure a bemused deference from the rest of the population. Most science teachers would not see it like that of course. They would argue that they are providing youngsters with the skills they need to take advantage of job opportunities as mechanics and technicians. But a democratic science education would see its task as that of demystifying the power of scientific 'experts' and providing workers with the information they need to contest their class position. As Young (1976) points out, workers need information, and ways of assessing that information about, for example, the dangers of asbestos, PVC, nuclear power stations and working on VDUs.

Science in school is generally presented as a collection of 'facts', unrelated to the people who discovered them, and their historical contexts and reasons for needing this information. Hine (1975) suggests that:

> the dehumanization makes the material completely different from that in other subjects. It would be meaningless and unthinkable only to present the work of, say, Wordsworth as an anonymous author out of his place in the Romantic Movement.

I seem to remember learning 'I wandered lonely as a cloud' by heart, with no reference to the Romantic Movement, but that's beside the point. A poem is obviously a human creation, in a way that a scientific law is not. When science is presented as decontextualized it appears neutral and unchallengeable and therefore its consequences seem inevitable. Again the consequences of this are more alienating for working-class children, whose future role is as consumers of science and technology, than for middle-class children, who can envisage themselves as potential 'scientists' and creators of knowledge.

Again Young (1976) makes a similar point, in a more theoretical way. He argues that teachers' 'scientific' ways of looking at the world do not recognize pupils' theories, and that this in itself mystifies the production of scientific knowledge:

> What constitutes school science would, I suggest, be very diferent if teachers were to see themselves *and* pupils as scientific theorists. It would be, if you like, an attempt to de-alienate scientific knowledge to recognise that knowledge is inextricably linked to its production by people, in a political context, not only in the school, which is

dominated by a 'culture of positivism' which locates knowing in methods not persons (Young, 1976).

But this sort of decontextualized school science is not inevitable. Hoskyns (1976) describes a physics CSE and O-level course that he ran in an inner-city London comprehensive, which was designed to meet some of these objections to traditional science education and to reduce the pupils' sense of alienation. As the teacher, Hoskyns took care to create an atmosphere in which teenagers could feel comfortable, using pop records and Radio 1. The course was designed around answering 'real' questions, of interest to the pupils, such as how to repair radios and amplifiers, with the aim of giving young people confidence in their own ability to understand and to control their environment. The organization of learning was egalitarian, with lesson plans emerging in discussions between pupils and teacher, rather than being imposed by the teacher, and it was community orientated, with the laboratories being kept open in the evenings, as a facility for the whole neighbourhood. The aim was to show that scientific knowledge is connected to everyday life, not divorced form it. As Hoskyns (1976) says:

> the physics that emerges as real through students being helped to understand everything that they do is different in quality from that which stems from an examination-based course where the content of the course is a commodity which will advance the career of the student. The process through which the physics of our course is established is a humanizing one...

This sort of lesson certainly sounds like a genuine improvement on traditional science education. But it is instructive to compare Hoskyns' account of his teaching with Millar's (1981) discussion of curriculum development for the less-able child in science. 'Less-able' is of course often a euphemism for 'less-successful' or 'working-class'. Millar argues that the greater emphasis on practical works and relevant knowledge for such pupils is a form of control, and comments that:

> one notices how little of the evaluation of such materials by the teacher as 'successful' depends on criteria related even remotely to science, or to any measured or measurable congnitive development. As soon as a course module is refined to the point where its use in the class keeps the pupils occupied, enables a satisfactory staff-pupil atmosphere to develop and therefore permits the teacher to feel unthreatened by an incipient loss of control, it is endorsed as 'satisfactory'.

Hoskyns' rationale for his course is that in traditional science lessons:

> pupils are not involved and interested in what they are doing in lessons. Boredom, indiscipline, under-achievement and truancy are the results of this failure.

By contrast he describes the involvement of students in their work in his physics classes, and the close and friendly relationship between teacher and students. However he admits that:

> It is not easy to assess how successful we have been, though our criteria of success... are clear. (Pupils) want confidence in themselves, and the chance to discover that science need not to be some mystery quite beyond them.

Hoskyns clearly feels that his course is successful, but this assessment is completely subjective. We are not told anything about examination success rates or post-school destinations.

These remarkable parallels between Hoskyns' 'radical' teaching and the mainstream curriculum reform of the 1970s should at least give us pause for thought. Science education can be made more relevant for working-class pupils, the lessons can be made more enjoyable, they can even gain a sense of control over their own work and understanding. But does this represent a real challenge to the class system? Or does it merely enable the reproduction of the social order to take place more smoothly? Hoskyns is clearly concerned to develop a feel for physics in his pupils. But he does not indicate how this translates into either recognized qualifications (which might facilitate individual mobility) or subversive insights (which might challenge the social order).

The articles that I have been discussing in this section are less than 15 years old, but they have dated dramatically. This is partly because this type of curriculum analysis was so closely associated with the short-lived 'new' sociology of education, and its assumption that teachers and pupils together create, and can recreate, educational reality (Young, 1971). But it is equally because they have been overtaken by the 'Science for All' movement, which is centrally concerned, although in a depoliticized way, with making science education accessible to all pupils and with recognizing and using children's ideas (see SSCR, 1983). These articles are also dated by the way they ignore issues of gender and race. Neither is mentioned explicity, but the pupil is always referred to as 'he' and — particularly in Hoskyns' account — the context in which 'relevant' science is discussed is unremittingly masculine. Few girls find 'real' questions in electronics and motor mechanics, but this implicit restriction of physics to half the population goes unremarked. Equally, no mention is made of the way that 'humanizing' science can serve either to reinforce or to weaken the ethnocentrism of white pupils. Both race and gender are areas of concern to which science educators have turned more recently.

Gender

Alternative approaches to the science curriculum are better worked out in the area of gender than in the field of either class or race, and they are more closely grounded in research. Gender differences in socialization and interests form the basis for suggestions for the elimination of gender bias from school science.

Much of the work on girls and science has focused on role models and the way that women's achievements are hidden from history. Textbook analysis has shown that females are consistently under-represented in illustrations in science books (as elsewhere), and considerable effort has gone into providing biographical information about women scientists and taking women scientists into schools to act as role models for the girls (Smail, 1984). While not seeking to diminish this effort, my main focus in this article is on the suggestions that have been made for reform in the curriculum. Bentley and Watts (1986) distinguish three approaches to curriculum analysis with respect to gender and science: 'girl-friendly' science, 'feminine' science and 'feminist' science.

Girl-friendly science consists of introducing topics which appeal to girls into the curriculum, starting from girls' interests so that they are not immediately deterred from science, but aiming to teach traditional content so that both sexes achieve the same qualifications and skills. Research has shown that, at the time they start secondary school, girls are already less interested than boys in physical science, and more interested in nature study, while both sexes are interested in learning about human biology (Smail and Kelly, 1984). Moreover girls' motivation for undertaking technical projects is more likely than boys' to be a social problem (Grant, 1982) and girls like a definite end-product to their science (Ebbutt, 1981). These sex differences are utilized in the development of girl-friendly science.

An example of this approach would be Smail's (1984) map of a curriculum starting from the human body, a topic in which both girls and boys express interest, and developing towards physical science topics which are generally less popular with girls. For example, one track leads through 'smell' to 'particles', 'convection' and 'heat'. Another track leads from 'ears' through 'sound recording', 'tapes, cassettes and records' to 'electricity'.

An alternative example of a girl-friendly approach is the linking of science to everyday concerns. Smail (1984) records that:

> wherever relevance to home life could be spelled out, girls' interest was captured. A unit of work on electricity for one school started by considering a world without electricity. Investigations of record players and tape-recorders led to ideas about circuits. A model electric blanket was made and used to demonstrate electrical safety in the home.

The idea is to start from the application, and develop from there to the scientific theory, rather than the more common approach of using the application to illustrate a principle that has already been taught. A similar philosophy underlies the *Chemistry from Issues* course developed by Jan

Harding at Chelsea College. Modules of this course start with a topical issue, such as lead in petrol, and work from there through the historical and political ramifications as well as the chemical underpinnings. The argument is that if girls can see a reason for studying science they will be better motivated to continue the subject than if it is presented in its traditional abstract form.

This 'girl-friendly' approach to curriculum development has much in common with the 'real' physics that Hoskyns (1976) describes. However there are differences, which go beyond the obvious one of considering problems that are real for girls as well as for boys. Girl-friendly science is explicitly designed to teach principles as well as applications, so that girls acquire the same knowledge base as boys. As Smail (1984) puts it:

> in adapting science to more 'feminine' contexts, care must be taken to ensure that both sexes understand the same underlying scientific principles and can, ultimatley, abstract them from the context and apply them in other circumstances.

Bentley and Watts (1986) distinguish between this girl-friendly science and feminine science, as they define it, concentrates on creating a context 'in which the classroom atmosphere is one of a caring supportive web of relationships'. Like girl-friendly science, this approach is based on research. The primary source is Gilligan (1982), who suggests that girls' developing sense of morality is focused around the understanding of responsibility and relationships, rather than the rights and rules which concern boys. With respect to science education this means making much of:

> feelings and engagement with issues and with cooperation in working groups. In such groups ideas would be welcomed because people have the courage and commitment to put them forward, and would not be evaluated and then dismissed by other individuals almost as a matter of course. The ambience would be one of caring, not overt competition (Bentley and Watts, 1986)

Feminine science emphasizes the importance of cooperation and collaborative work in science classrooms. This is in contrast to the more traditional, and masculine, emphasis on competition. Feminine science also emphasizes the social, moral and ethical issues in which science is embedded, and sees these as an integral part of the subject.

This sort of discussion shifts the emphasis away from the curriculum developer, and back to the individual teacher in her or his classroom, whose job it is to establish the atmosphere in which pupils work. Teachers are also responsible for the classroom interactions in science, and work in this area has shown that most of the teacher's attention and most of the best equipment is monopolized by boys (Crossman, 1987; Kelly, 1985). Although much of this inequality appears to stem from the behaviour of the pupils, it is up to the teacher to develop classroom management strategies which eliminate the disadvantage that girls suffer. Boys have more than their fair share of contact with the teacher in all school subjects (Kelly, 1987b), but this may have particularly severe consequences in science. There is more freedom of movement in a laboratory situation than in many other lessons, which allows greater scope for gender roles to be developed as boys comment on girls' work and persuade the girls to fetch and carry for them; and the presence of equipment allows boys to demonstrate their toughness and girls their timidity in a very concrete way (Kelly, 1985). Teachers who attempt to implement feminine science are concerned with the extent to which girls feel welcome and at ease in a science which accommodates their concerns and their ways of working.

Feminist science, according to Bentley and Watts, goes further than girl-friendly or feminine science in that it aims to change the nature of science itself. The argument here, based upon the writing of 'gender theorists' like Keller (1985) and Easlea (1981), is that science, with its characteristics of objectivity, rationality and disinterestedness, is an embodiment of patriarchal values, which have been used to oppress women, and which are fundamentally at odds with women's way of viewing the world. Bentley and Watts (1986) argue that a feminist science education would value science primarily as a means of personal growth, which helps the individual to enrich her/his own life; it would re-value subjectivity, seeing it as just as valid as objectivity as a way of knowing; it would be holistic rather than reductionist; and scientific knowledge would not be privileged over other forms of knowing. As they put it:

> in a feminist school science, feelings, reactions, values and intuitions become important starting points for the development of principles and theories. Evidence can be unique, anecdotal, partial and partisan, and seen to be so... to us this methodological and epistemological approach challenges the masculine heart of science, and brings to it the positive virtues of a feminist view of scientific enquiry.

This type of argument has seldom been applied to science education, although it has enjoyed considerable popularity among scholars concerned with the relationship between women and science (see for example Dahms *et al*, 1986). Bentley and Watts (1986) do not spell out in any detail what a curriculum based around their definition of feminist science would look like. Nor do they give any examples of teachers who have adopted this approach or discuss how it works in practice.

The gender theorist's critique of science as intrinsically male has come under attack from other feminists. Koblitz (1987) has shown that it is historically inaccurate to argue that there is something inimical between women and science. Women's position in science has changed massively over the centuries, and women have by no means always been excluded from the scientific way of thinking. Moreover this view of feminist science

Towards a Democratic Science Education

tends to exaggerate the differences between males and females in a way that can easily slip over into biological essentialism, and lead to reification of the very distinctions that feminists traditionally wish to eliminate.

Race

The discussion of multicultural and anti-racist perspectives in science education in Britain is very much in its infancy. As late as 1981 the association for Science Education, in its response to the Rampton Comittee on the Education of Children from Ethnic Minority Groups, could comment that 'it was thought to be unlikely that any discrimination existed in schools' and that 'science is regarded by the majority of science teachers as an international study, with no particular national bias, and with its own neutral terminology which is also culture-free. (ASE, n.d). Nott and Watts (1987) remarked on the lack of any multicultural or anti-racist considerations in the DES policy document *Science 5-16* (DES, 1985). They pointed out that 'no document can be devoid of cultural assumptions' and highlighted the assumption that 'British science is also Western European science, which is also "world science" — an assumption that implicitly denies the cultural diversity of science and the contributions of non-European peoples.

Within the last few years some science centres and individual teachers have begun to work towards reviewing the curriculum to make it less ethnocentric (see, for example, Brandt *et al*, 1985; Chamberlain, 1986; Gill and Levidow, 1986; Hollings, 1985; Jones, 1985; Lindsay 1985). Many of the critiques of contemporary practice which have emerged from this work are similar to those made about gender and science when this was first debated. For example, Black people are under-represented in science textbooks, and when they are shown it is in the stereotyped roles of nurse and athlete, or as impoverished and dependent people in developing countries. As with gender, stereotyping is more severe in textbooks which attempt to humanize science. Traditional abstract science, with its equations and diagrams of apparatus, does not include people or any race or gender, and so shows little overt bias towards white males!

Black people's contribution to science, like women's, generally goes unrecognized. Siraj-Blatchford (1987) argues that:

> historically the major advance of scientific knowledge occurred in the Middle East, China, the Indian sub-continent and Africa. Subsequently the Greek and Arab civilisations made major advances and this was passed on to Europe where it was significantly developed in the period, roughly, from 1550 to 1900. Since that time the predominance of Europeans and North Americans in Scientific work has become less marked, and yet most school science syllabuses

are concerned almost exclusively with European and North American innovations. One serious implication of this is that students are liable to see some credibility in the still prevalent racist ideas of innate inferiority.

In an attempt to redress the balance CIBA-Geigy in the United States produced a series of posters featuring the achievements of Black Scientists. The Equal Opportunities Commission in Britain did the same for women scientists.

The distinction is not always clear-cut, but there is a tension between multi-cultural and anti-racist approaches, in science, as in other subjects. Multi-cultural science education aims to reflect the diversity of ethnic groups in Britain today by looking at things like nutrition, and the different types of diet adopted by different communities. It attempts to counter the notion that science is a product of the superior Western intellect by considering topics such as the history of astronomy, emphasizing the contributions of the ancient Chinese, Muslim, Egyptian and Greek astronomers. It considers the contemporary world by including discussions of appropriate and intermediate technology for developing countries.

Some of the issues which multi-culturalism raises for science teachers are trivial — for example the fact that dissecting a cow's kidney is problematic for Hindus. But others are more serious. Many Muslims (and fundamentalist Christian groups) object to the teaching of evolution. But, as recent controversies in the United States and Norway have shown, if science teachers compromise on this issue their integrity as scientists is called into question. Similar dilemmas arise over the discussion of reproduction, which is generally seen as progressive, but which is opposed by many religious groups. Moreover, as Siraj-Blatchford (1987) points out:

> many of the current resource lists for 'multicultural' science include... materials which offer third world applications of technology. If applied uncritically in the laboratory these materials may well serve to reinforce racist stereotypes of 'primitive' technology and be counterproductive.

Multi-cultural science syllabuses which discuss technology in developing countries run the risk of stigmatising Black people as poor, unable to help themselves, and lacking in initiative. They may perpetuate the myth that Black people belong 'there' and not 'here'.

By contrast, anti-racist approaches to science education tend to emphasize whole-school policies and issues such as how to tackle racism among pupils. They discuss the concept of race and arguments about its biological basis, and explore the links between science, industry, capitalism, third-world exploitation and racism (Hollins, 1985; Lindsay, 1985). In short the message of anti-racist science is that science lessons should include more history, geography, economics and sociology.

Many science teachers have understandable reservations about this approach (see the reports of some of the discussion groups in Brandt *et al*, 1985). They wonder whether science teachers either can or should take on the role of general studies teachers, and where they are going to get their information. But this is not inevitable. One of the few attempts to put anti-racist science education into practice as a curriculum is a booklet written by the Head of Science at a largely black, inner city school (Jones, 1985). The *Seeds of History* booklet covers half a term's works for 3rd year pupils in integrated science. It sets out, amongst other things:

> to demonstrate that the most important scientific discoveries were made, not by élite scientists, but by ordinary men, and particulary women in the countries of Asia, Africa, Southern Europe and Meso America . . . and . . . to experience science in a discovering, practical and interesting way.

In this booklet science is contextualized, but it is still recognisably science. For example a discussion of primitive agriculture leads to works on seeds sprouting, measurement, fermentation, and tests for starch, sugar and protein — all topics covered in most science syllabuses for the early years of secondary school. Similarly works on the discovery of metals leads on to the traditional topic of the reactivity series. Its anti-racism is expressed in its insistence that it was Black people who made many of the fundamental discoveries.

This would probably be something that most science teachers could feel happy with. It is similar to 'girl-friendly' science, in its implication that science, as it currently exists, is a powerful body of knowledge, to which all pupils, Black and White, female and male, should have access. The context in which science is presented is altered to make it anti-racist, but the content remains largely unchanged.

There are of course alternative traditions of science stemming from different cultural backgrounds. Sardar (1980) discusses the Islamic tradition which emphasises 'humility; recognition of the limitations of scientific methods; respect for the object of study'. He suggests that:

> the scientific tradition of Islam is based on the profound intuition of the inter-dependence and inter-relation of all things in the Universe, let alone our planetary environment. The rediscovery of this tradition will remind man (sic) among other things, of the necessity of humility and respect in preserving the harmony and equilibrium of nature, if his science is not to lead to the destruction of its own object of study.

This discussion has some similarities with the gender theorists critique of reductionism and preference for holistic methods of enquiry. However its implications for the science curriculum in British schools are unclear.

One of the most far-reaching suggestions for changing science education in an anti-racist way is Siraj-Blatchford's (1987) assertion that an anti-racist teaching model must... reject open-ended or guided discovery. His argument is that if we present pupils with simple experiments from which they can 'discover' important scientific principles such as the existence of atoms they end up thinking: if its so simple, why didn't people understand this centuries ago? And, in particular, why didn't black people do this simple experiment and make scientific discoveries? It must be because they are stupid.

There is undoubtedly some logic to this argument, and it applies equally to women and to working-class people. The idea that scientific truths can be 'discovered' by simple experiments disguises the way in which real discoveries are historically, culturally and economically situated, so that discoveries happen when there is a need for them and when they fit into existing frameworks of thought. But it is doubtful whether children actually make these connections, either consciously or unconsciously. The rejection of open-ended and guided discovery teaching would reverse twenty years of curriculum reform in science. It seems unlikely that Siraj-Blatchford is actually advocating a return to the 'talk-and-chalk plus teacher-demonstration' approach to science teaching, but that must be the implication of his remarks.

Science and Society

The unifying thread in these various critiques of science education is the plea to humanize science and make it more relevant to children's lives by placing it in a wider historical, sociological and philosophical context. Although not directly refering to issues of class or race, and making only oblique reference to gender, this is summed up in a short article by Newton (1986) who says that:

> for too long we, as science teachers, have been too self-indulgent. We aim only for the goals which distinguish science from other disciplines. The goals which make school science a part of the wider process of education we largely ignore.

Newton argues that science teaching, like all other teaching, is about *people*. Our aim in science teaching should be to produce more rounded personalities, better able to cope with their environments.

One way in which this could be done is through the introduction of Science, Technology and Society (STS) courses in schools. One of the first and most widely used of these courses is the ASE Science and Society course, published in 1981. This was designed for sixth-form science specialists, and it claims to take a 'neutral' line and present 'both sides' of the case. The contents of the course and its development have been analyzed by Walford (1985) who suggests that:

in most of these articles industry and management are presented as paternalistic, being wealth producers for the good of society overall and looking after the health and welfare of both workforce and public. Nowhere is there a discussion of the inequalities in society and the ways in which the capitalist system helps to perpetuate these inequalities. There is no discussion of class, race or gender inequalities. There is no discussion of the conflict of interests that exists between responsibility of industry towards society and the needs of employees, and . . . the basic aim of any company to make a profit.

Walford traces this bias in the Science and Society materials to the origins of its developers. At the time the course was initiated in 1976 the ASE was still dominated by masters from boys' public schools, and their ideas were reflected in the course content. Walford concludes that the radical power of social studies of science is decapitated by a definition of the contents of the course. Moreover by aiming it at sixth-formers any insights which might be derived from the study of science and society are denied to pupils who are going to end up on the factory floor. Walford explicity rejects any conspiracy-theory explanation for this move of development, suggesting that it was the result of an attempt by traditional natural science teachers to define the area of social studies of science as 'their' territory, rather than that of social scientists.

My intention here is not to add to the critiques of this particular course. Rather it is to suggest that the introduction of material on the social implications of science into the school curriculum is not necessarily a radical move. The idea of introducing STS materials into the science curriculum is steadily gaining in acceptability and such material now forms a part of many GCSE syllabuses. Some STS courses, such as the Science in a Social Context (SISCON) materials, do provide a critical perspective on science. But, as Newton (1986) points out, the thinking behind these courses has not really permeated into school science courses. He suggests that:

> there are a number of possible reasons for this. These include self-indulgence, inertia, and a view of school science as having only economic and technological ends.

but points out that:

> merely padding science syllabuses with lists of potential topics, names of scientists and examples of 'good' and 'bad' social consequences of the application of scientific knowledge seems likely to be self-defeating. It would encourage a sterile and didactic exposition of, for example, the history, philosophy, psychology or sociology of science, severed from the teaching of the science content itself. Teaching *about* science would then be as formalised as the teaching *of* science and it would form nothing more than yet

> another task to be completed before the examinations... The most appropriate way of achieving (humanizing) aims seems to be less through a detailed prescription of content and more through the *way* in which science is taught.

Newton argues that activities such as role playing, imaginative writing, and discussion of topical issues should be introduced into science education. After discussing the role of examination reform he concludes that:

> a slower, but probably effective, way of bringing about change is through in-service and initial teacher training. Science teachers need to be introduced to humanized science teaching as a method, to be shown how to humanize their teaching, to be encouraged to produce material which does so, and to be seen to use it in their practice.

It is crucial to change teachers, and to consider them as active agents in the mediation of science to their pupils, if any real change is to come about. The best curriculum materials can be presented in a way that renders them sexist, racist, classist and rigid, while a good teacher can challenge the stereotypes that exist in traditional materials and turn them to her or his advantage.

Inevitably, many teachers will resist any attempt to humanize science. This is evident from the Letters colums of *School Science Review*. For example, Darnton (1987) commented on Newton's proposals that:

> while one can readily agree that education should enable students to be more human this has never been the role of Science *qua* Science. The successful scientist has generally been the one who leaves out the natural human feelings and in so far as he (sic) is unable to do so then his observations are less objective. The scientific ideal would seem to be to approach as near as possible to the vanishing point of pure objectivity where the human element disappears.

Most science teachers have been brought up with, succeeded in and presumably enjoyed, traditional abstract science. They feel threatened by the criticism of their traditional way of working and either cannot or will not cope with a change of approach. The idea that 'science is science' is widespread, as is the idea that knowledge is discovered not constructed. Change can only take place if such teachers can be persuaded to alter their attitudes.

Recent Developments

The Association for Science Education has been in the vanguard of recent innovations in the science curriculum. In 1979 a discussion document summarized the two existing traditions of science education, associated with grammar schools and secondary moderns as follows:

> the former tradition placed a high premium on academic scholarship involving a deep and systematic concern for the content of science; a concern with the latest developments in the subject; and a search for the ways and means whereby new knowledge could be incorporated into teaching schemes. Leaving status issues aside the alternative tradition was much more overtly concerned with pedagogy; the study of ways and means whereby science, in whatever form could be effectively mediated between teacher and taught. In the 1950's both traditions lacked a clear analysis of *process*; the analysis of the nature of science and how it is created (ASE, 1979).

It is suggested that, with the move to comprehensive education, a new approach emphasising process skills (how to think scientifically, how to weigh evidence) was necessary. This was in contrast to the previous focus on knowledge of scientific facts. Science should be made accessible to the whole ability range, throughout the whole of compulsory schooling, and should be person-centred, with a full integration of science and society issues into the curriculum. The discussion document identified six contexts for science education:

a. science as science
b. science as a cultural activity
c. science and citizenship
d. science in the world of work
e. science and leisure
f. science and survival

and argued that 'to achieve a balanced science education within the context of general education requires the consideration of all the above factors as being of comparable status and importance' (ASE, 1979).

Two years later in the policy paper (ASE, 1981) the last four contexts had been condensed into one, 'science and its applications'. This was downplayed even further in the DES document that followed (DES, 1985). This dilution of the social aspects of science could be seen as back-tracking in the face of opposition from the establishment. However as West (1983) pointed out it is not a simple matter to identify the major advocates of change or supporters of the status quo. Most agencies contain within them both innovative and conservative tendencies. For example West states that:

> the pressure for change from industry and commerce appears to be in the direction of more broadly based studies with a greater emphasis being placed on applicability and capability

while simultaneously many schools anxious to broaden their approach to science studies... have been frustrated by employers insisting on O-level physics he notes similar paradoxes in the responses of central government, higher education, Local Education Authorities, the Inspectorate, the Schools Council (RIP), the Association for science Education, examination boards and society as a whole.

Nevertheless significant changes in the science curriculum *are* taking place. An emphasis on process skills, on using the children's experience and on 'Science for All' has been a constant theme of recent pronouncements (ASE, 1979; 1981; DES, 1985). The consensus among science educators is that we should be moving towards a broad and balanced definition of science, including elements of all three science subjects, and occupying approximately 20 per cent of curriculum time in the last two years of compulsory schooling. The main vehicle for implementing reform has been the Secondary Science curriculum review (SSCR, 1983), which was one of only two Schools Council projects to be reprieved when the Council was abolished in 1983. Their aims include

> working towards science courses that are:
> *open* to all students irrespective of their ability, aptitude and career aspirations or intentions;
> *fair and unbiased* in terms of the gender of the student and his or her ethnic, cultural or socio-economic background;
> *encouraging and enabling* with regard to students with handicap (SSCR, 1984).

The way in which this highly democratic vision is to be operationalized is spelled out in a series of vignettes of the science education of 'average students from different backgrounds' (SSCR, 1984). These are clearly influenced by the 'alternative frameworks' school of psychology (Driver, 1981) which stresses the need to take children's prior knowledge into account in teaching scientific concepts. There are constant references to the out-of-school experiences of the pupils, although these are resolutely individualistic and do not consider the political implications of viewing children as members of differing social groups.

The philosophy of the Review was described by its first director, Dick West (1982) as:

> supporting science teachers as they attempt to create a better match between what they now do and what society wants them to do, i.e., to teach all young people something of the value and importance of science as a way of looking at, and understanding, the world. I put it this way for I am firmly of the view that whilst educational *policy* can be enunciated from outside the educational system, educational *practice* can only change from within the system.

In accord with this view the main focus of the SSCR has been on locally based groups of teachers coming together to work on curriculum development. Many of these groups have now reported, and the project has entered its dissemination phase (SSCR, 1987).

An emphasis on teacher groups is certainly consistent with the view that curriculum change only comes about when teachers are convinced of its necessity. But teacher involvement, although necessary for change, may not be sufficient. One of the features of the SSCR is the clear contrast between the materials developed by the central team, which are consistently radical, and those produced by local groups, who have frequently made only small changes in existing procedures. Teachers need to be politicized, as well as involved, if we are to make genuine progress towards a more democratic science education.

The Conservative government has recently announced its plans for a national curriculum whose aim is to ensure:

> that all pupils, regardless of sex, ethnic origin and geographical location, have access to broadly the same good and relevant curriculum and programmes of study which include the key content, skills and process which they need to learn and which ensure that the content and teaching of the various elements of the national curriculum bring out their relevance to and links with pupils' own experiences and their practical applications and continuing value to adult and working life (DES, 1987).

This is a remarkably egalitarian statement. It implicitly recognizes that some pupils are disadvantaged on the basis of gender, race and geography, and that academic education is irrelevant to many students. Science is to be part of the core curriculum for all pupils throughout compulsory schooling (DES, 1987). The details of the curriculum has not yet been decided, but a working group has been set up to advise on the science curriculum. Many of the professional educators who comprise this group have been involved in earlier debates over the future of science education, and it seems unlikely that their report will reverse the trend towards a more inclusive definition of science. Nevertheless, as I have argued elsewhere (Kelly, 1988a), a truly uniform science curriculum will entail a reduction in the amount of physical science studied by elite pupils, and there are already signs that any such change will meet with severe opposition from teachers at private boys' schools (Kahn, 1987).

Two Steps Forward and One Step Backward

The present situation is full of contradictions. The issue of a core curriculum came under discussion in the wake of the 'Great Debate' initiated by a Labour government which felt that the DES should have more influence in the 'secret garden' of the curriculum. But in the area of science it resulted in the very decentralized SSCR project. This was nurtured by the Conservatives, although much of the SSCR concern with the 'average' pupil is in conflict with Conservative rhetoric about 'standards'. The SSCR stands in stark contrast to the Nuffield reform, which took place outside direct government influence, but was highly centralized, and concerned with élite pupils. The Conservatives, the party of individual enterprise, are committed to the idea of a national curriculum, while Labour, traditionally the party of uniform provision, are ambivalent or hostile towards this goal.

The content of a national curriculum in science is still a matter for debate. Despite eight years of Thatcherism, science education is currently moving in a democratic direction. There is a steadily increasing concern with extending science education to the whole ability range, with multiculturalism, and with gender differentiation. In some quarters this may be purely instrumental—'we can't get enough good White boys into science, so we'll have to take other people'; 'our industrial competitiveness is lagging behind that of other countries because we don't train enough'. But to attribute all the current changes to this type of motivation is unduly cynical. Radicals can take — and have taken — advantage of these concerns to debate more far-reaching changes in the nature of science education. The emphasis on process skills and on the social implications and applications of science is now well established.

I believe that a common curriculum is a necessary condition for a democratic education. The individualized curriculum has been one of the great false turns of progressive education. As Hargreaves (1982) has pointed out, it is premised on the idea of the free individual, and ignores her or his social context. Whenever choice occurs the disadvantaged use it to disadvantage themselves further. Thirteen-year-old working-class girls happily choose a curriculum consisting of human biology, child care, home economics, drama and typing — and then we wonder why working-class women are confined to unpaid or underpaid service work. Middle-class boys take physics and chemistry and so provide themselves with the necessary qualifications for élite technological jobs. Providing a common curriculum will not eliminate inequality; but it will remove one justification for inequality, and thus strip away one layer of the mystification surrounding the process of differentiation.

However a common curriculum is not a sufficient condition for a democratic education. We must also consider the content of the curriculum. Paradoxically it is some of the radical proposals for changing the nature of science education which seem to me to pose the greatest threat to the current egalitarian tendencies. In particular the argument that scientific thought is intrinsically masculine, and that feminist science should emphasize subjective and holistic approaches strikes me as positively dangerous. Can subjectivist scientists build bridges or design circuits? Will children taught in an holistic way be employable? Cockburn (1985) has demonstrated clearly that technology is an extension of male power, and that women are disadvantaged by their exclusion from this power. Women are not unwilling or unable to learn technological skills; however men are consistently reluctant to allow them to acquire these skills. As Gramsci argues (Entwistle, 1979), disadvantaged groups need access to the most powerful forms of thought society has developed; in our society this includes science. To confine girls, ethnic minorities or working-class children within the boundaries of a science defined in accordance with their existing subcultures is to confine them to a position of subordination. I am suspicious of curriculum reforms that stress relevance at the expense of content, or subjectivity at the expense of objectivity.

The national curriculum will be recommended but not enforced in private schools. This could be — and has been in some quarters — interpreted as allowing schools for the élite to continue to 'educate' for leadership while the bulk of the population receives only 'training' for subservient roles. I think this is an unnecessarily sinister interpretation. The exemption is more likely to have been designed to allow for the distinctive curricula of, for example, Rudolph Steiner or orthodox Jewish schools, than for Eton or Harrow. But if a radical redefinition of the meaning of science were to become established in state schools we would almost certainly find that the public schools continued to teach traditional content. To quote Reynolds and Sullivan (1980):

> the socially shrewd bourgeois regard some forms of knowledge and thought as superior and therefore worth learning simply because they *are* cognitively and intellectually superior.

Such superior forms of thought include the scientific method. Radical changes which are intended to assist disadvantaged pupils may end up disadvantaging them still further if the effect is to exclude them from such successful modes of thought.

But this is not to say that the science curriculum should remain unchanged. It is crucial to work towards a more contextualized science, one which includes the implications and applications of the subject as a fundamental part of the syllabus. The present emphasis on the technical aspects of the subject produces future scientists who are technically competent but socially naive. When science education neglects the social aspects it is hardly surprising if professional scientists pursue their subject as a technical puzzle. The disastrous results of this approach are visible all around us.

A contextualized approach is also essential if disadvantaged groups are to be included in science. The curriculum must take the starting point of its pupils as a base, and use their existing interests to develop an interest in science. And it is here that the greatest progress can be made — and the greatest obstacles lie — on the way to a democratic science education. By the organization of topics and control of classroom interactions teachers can create an atmosphere in which female, Black or working-class pupils feel at home, or one from which they feel excluded. They can use examples which draw on a range of interests and experiences, or ones which implicity assume a White, middle-class and male clientele.

This emphasis on the power of teachers to change their pupils' ideas is strongly reminiscent of the 'new' sociology of education of the 1970s (Young, 1971). The Secondary Science Curriculum Review (SSCR, 1984) and the Children's Learning in Science Project (Bell and Driver, 1984) both emphasize the importance of taking the pupils' prior experience as a starting point for curriculum development. But they do so in a depoliticized way that emphasizes individual rather than group differences. Whatever its faults, the 'new' sociology of education did recognize the links between social reproduction and the curriculum. This is an understanding that needs to be revived within science education.

The next few years will bring far-reaching changes in science education. However it seems unlikely — indeed impossible — that teachers will lose control over the day-to-day tasks of the management and presentation of material. We are a long way yet from the textbook-dominated classrooms of France, or even the United States. Unfortunately too many science teachers still see their subject as immune from social influences; the notion the 'science is science' dies hard. If pupils do not learn the science that is on offer then that is their own fault, or that of their parents and homes which have socialized them incorrectly. The subject itself is seen as neutral, and therefore unchangeable.

In order to create a democratic science education, which is genuinely open to all pupils, we need a massive investment in in-service education emphasizing anti-sexist, anti-racist and anti-classist techniques of the sort described at the beginning of this article. Such in-service education must be subject-specific, otherwise experience suggests that science teachers will dismiss it as irrelevant. The goodwill may be there, but the understanding of the problem is absent. Unfortunatley it is just this type of in-service education which arouses the greatest suspicion among our present political leaders, and which is least likely to be forthcoming.

In conclusion I think the pressure for a democratic science education should take place in three directions simultaneously. We must support moves towards a common curriculum which will equip all children with the scientific skills traditionally reserved for the élite; we must insist that these skills are taught in a humanized context, so that future scientists automatically consider the social as well as the technical consequences of their actions; and we must demand an extensive programme of in-service teacher training in egalitarian classroom management so that girls, ethnic minorities and working-class pupils are no longer marginalized in science lessons. Only then will we be able to claim that we have truly developed a 'Science for All'.

Acknowledgement

This chapter was written while I was on study leave, supported by a Nuffield Social Science Fellowship. I am grateful to the Nuffield Foundation for its assistance. However the opinions expressed in this paper are mine alone.

References

ASSOCIATION FOR SCIENCE EDUCATION 1979) *Alternatives for Science Education*, Hatfield: ASE.
ASSOCIATION FOR SCIENCE EDUCATION (1981) *Education through Science*, Hatfield: ASE.
ASSOCIATION FOR SCIENCE EDUCATION (n.d. est 1981) 'Response by the Association for Science Education to the Committee of Inquiry into the Education of Children from Ethnic Minority Groups', Hatfield: ASE.
BELL, B and DRIVER, R. (1984) 'The children's learning in science project' *Education in Science* 108, pp. 19-20.
BENTLEY, D. and WATTS, M. (1986) 'Courting the positive virtues: A case for feminist science' *European Journal of Science Education* 8, pp. 121-34, reprinted in Kelly, A. (Ed.) (1981 *Science for girls?* Milton Keynes: Open University Press.
BRANDT, G., TURNER, S. and TURNER, T. (1985) (Eds) *Science Education in a Multicultural Society* Report on a Conference at the London Institute of Education.
CHAMBERLAIN, P.J. (1986) 'Science education in multi-cultural Britain' *School Science Review*, 68, pp. 343-8.
COCKBURN, C. (1985) *Machinery of Dominance: Women. Men and Technical Know-How*, London: Pluto Press.
CROSSMAN, M. (1987) 'Teachers' interactions with girls and boys in science lessons' in KELLY, A . (Ed.) *Science for Girls?* Milton Keynes: Open University Press.
DAHMS, M. *et al.* (1986) (Eds) *Contributions to the Women Challenge Technology Conference*, Denmark: University of Aalborg.
DARNTON, J.H. (1987) 'Letter to the Editor' *School Science Review* 68 p. 776
DEPARTMENT OF EDUCATION AND SCIENCE (1985) *Science 5-6: A Statement of Policy*, reprinted in *Education in Science* 112, pp. 21-36.
DEPARTMENT OF EDUCATION AND SCIENCE (1987) *The National Curriculum, 5-16*, London: HMSO.
DRIVER, R. (1981) 'Pupils' alternative frameworks in science' *European Journal of Science* 3, pp. 94-101, reprinted in BROWN, J. *et al* (Eds) *Science in Schools* Milton Keynes: Open University Press.
EASLEA, B. (1981) *Science and Sexual Oppression: Patriarchy's Confrontation with Woman and Nature*, London: Weidenfeld and Nicholson.
EBBUTT, D. (1981) 'Girls' science: Boys' science revisited' in KELLY, A. (Ed.) *The Missing Half: Girls and Science Education*, Manchester: Manchester University Press.
ENTWISTLE, H. (1979) *Antonio Gramsci: Conservative Schooling for Radical Politics* London: Routledge & Kegan Paul.
GILL, D. and LEVIDOW, L. (1986) (Eds) *Anti-Racist Science Teaching*, London: Free Association Books.
GILLIGAN, C. (1982) *In a Different Voice* Harvard: Harvard University Press.
GRANT, M. (1982) 'Starting points', *Studies in Design Education, Craft and Technology* 15, pp. 6-10.

HAMILTON, D. (1975) 'Handling innovation in the classroom: Two Scottish examples', in REID, W.A. and WALKER, D.F.W. (Eds) *Case Studies in Curriculum Change: Great Britain and the United States* London: Routledge and Kegan Paul.
HARGREAVES, D.H. (1975) 'Political bias in school physics' *Hard Cheese* Nos 4–5, reprinted in WHITTY, G. (Ed.) (1977) *School Knowledge and Social Control*, E202 Units 14–15, Milton Keynes: Open University Press.
HINE, R. J. (1975) 'Political bias in school physics', *Hard Cheese* nos. 4–5, reprinted in WHITTY, G. (Ed) *School Knowledge and Social Control*, Milton Keynes: Open University Press (E202, units 14–15).
HOLLINS, M. (n.d., est 1985) (Ed.) *Science Teaching in a Multi-Ethnic Society: a Handbook of Suggestions and Resources*, London: North London Science Centre.
HOSKYNS, A. (1976) 'An experiment in the teaching of physics', in WHITTY, G. and YOUNG, M. (Eds) *Explorations in the Politics of School Knowledge*, Driffield: Nafferton Books.
JONES, L. (1985) *Revolutionary Science: The Seeds of History*, Birley High School, Manchester.
KAHN, A.J. (1987) 'Letter' *Education in Science*, No.125, pp. 41–2.
KEDDIE, N. (1971) 'Classroom knowledge', in YOUNG, M. (Ed.) *Knowledge and Control: New Directions for the Sociology of Education*, London: Collier-Macmillan.
KELLER, E.F. (1985) *Reflections on Gender and Science*, New Haven, Conn.: Yale University Press.
KELLY, A. (1985) 'The construction of masculine science' *British Journal of Sociology of Education* 6, pp. 133–54, reprinted in KELLY, A. (Ed.) (1987) *Science for Girls?* Milton Keynes: Open University Press
KELLY, A. (1988a) *Who gets science education? An analysis by class, ability and gender*, in McNEIL, M., VARCO, I. and YEARDLEY, S. (Eds) *Deciphering Science and Technology*, London: Macmillan.
KOBLITZ, A.H. (1987) 'An historian looks at gender and science' *International Journal of Science Education*, pp. 399–407.
LINDSAY, L. (1985) *Racism, Science Education and the Politics of Food*, London: ALTARF Occasional Paper No 1.
McCULLOCH, G., JENKINS, E. and LAYTON, D. (1985) *Technological Revolution? The Politics of School Science and Technology in England and Wales since 1945* Lewes: Falmer Press.
MILLAR, R.H. (1981) 'Curriculum rhetoric and social control: A perspective on recent science curriculum development' *European Journal of Science Education* 3, pp 272–84, reprinted in BROWN, J. et al. (Eds) (1986) *Science in Schools* Milton Keynes: Open University Press.
NEWTON, D.P.L. (1986) 'Products, processes and people' *School Science Review* 68 pp. 350–5.
NOTT, M. and WATTS, M. (1987) 'Toward a multi-cultural and anti-racist science education policy', *Education in Science* 121, pp. 37–8.
REYNOLDS, D. and SULLIVAN, M. (1980) 'Towards a new socialist sociology of education', in BARTON, L., MEIGHAN, R. and WALKER, S. (Eds) *Schooling, Ideology and the Curriculum* Lewes: Falmer Press.
SARDAR, Z. (1980) 'Can science come back to Islam?', *New Scientist* 23 October, p. 212.
SECONDARY SCIENCE CURRICULUM REVIEW (1983) *Science Education 11–16: proposals for action and consultation*, London: SSCR.
SECONDARY SCIENCE CURRICULUM REVIEW (1984) *Toward the Specification of Minimum Entitlement: Brenda and Friends*, London: Schools Council Publications.
SECONDARY SCIENCE CURRICULUM REVIEW (1987) *Better Science* London: Heinemann
SIRAJ-BLATCHFORD, J. (1987) 'Creating an anti-racist ethos', *School Science Review* 68, pp. 756–8.

SMAIL, B. (1984) *Girl-Friendly Science*, London: Schools Council/Longman, part reprinted in KELLY, A. (Ed.) (1987) *Science for Girls?* Milton Keynes: Open University Press.

SMAIL, B. and KELLY, A. (1984) 'Sex differences in science and technology among 11-year-old schoolchildren: II — affective', *Research in Science and Technological Education*, 2. pp. 87–106.

WALFORD, G. (1985) 'The construction of a curriculum area: Science in society', *British Journal of Sociology of Education* 6, pp. 155–71.

WEST, R.W. (1982) 'The secondary science curriculum review', *Education in Science* 99, pp 29–31.

YOUNG, M. (1976) 'The schooling of science', in WHITTY, G. and YOUNG, M. (Eds) *Explorations in the Politics of School Knowledge* London: Nafferton Books, reprinted in BROWN, J. *et al.* (Eds) (1986) *Science in Schools* Milton Keynes: Open University Press

YOUNG, M. (1971) (Ed.) *Knowledge and Control*, London: Collier Macmillan.

Chapter 9

Body Matters: Towards a Socialist Physical Education

John Evans

Ruled by Games

It seems like an aeon since, as a small, cold and blue-kneed schoolboy, I took (or more precisely, was taken) to the rugby fields at my Welsh valley grammar school. There I learned not only the act of running leaning sideways without trying, such was the incline of the pitch at the time, but to dread and fear the violence of The Game as much as the possibility of revealing such cowardice to my teachers, peers and friends. Worse still in a school where rugby ruled, my distaste for The Game was matched only by my delirious attachment to that other boys' sport — soccer — a game ruthlessly, religiously, outlawed by the culture of my school. To play soccer was to go looking for trouble, to court instant ignominy and invite the status of deviant. It was, especially if one had the ability to play The Game, a denial of one's duties, a betrayal of one's school, friends, community and country. After all it was The Game that celebrated our school's and country's status, that demarcated the boundaries and announced the qualities of our subculture and our precise class position. It was The Game that would help us mingle with both the posh and the proletariat, that told us we were the 'tidier' (the more respectable) within our working class. Just down the road four miles away, the unfortunates in their secondary modern school, who had unluckily failed to master the massive meritocratic hurdle, the hated 11-plus, could play the commoner game — soccer — a game of no passion, no quality, requiring no courage or character. And for all we knew and cared, in our sister single-sex grammar, as in the co-educational secondary modern, girls into sport didn't go.

Then as now sport mattered greatly in the process of schooling; it signified and it celebrated, elevated and excluded, it layed down the rules of belonging to our gender and our class fraction. Given the massive centrality of sport and Physical Education in the lives of young people, especially but not exclusively in those of young males, it is odd and disappointing to those of us working in the field of PE that so very little of the energies and interests of either British sociologists of education or politicians of any persuasion, have been drawn to the analysis of PE and sport in schools. This lacuna in the discourse of educational sociologists and politicians is not unimportant in any quest to promote either democracy in schools, or the cause of equal opportunities. Both depend upon a capacity and willingness to inspect and challenge existing social categories and status hierarchies. The silence is, then, not altogether surprising. As others have pointed out in Foucaultian fashion, any discourse concerns itself with certain objects and puts forward certain concepts at the expense of others (Macdonnell, 1986). The selections and the silences in respect of PE are neither arbitrary nor culturally value-free, they reach out to wider social, cultural and economic contexts which we have long imputed differential status and associated rewards to the practical and the physical as opposed to the abstract and the academic. These differences suffuse the world of educational research, public consciousness, the minds of politicians as well as the process of schooling.

For many, sport is what Physical Educationalists teach. Despite its deep cultural significance it is often seen as unimportant when considered against the more serious activity of school work. Sport signifies enjoyment, fun, freedom from constraint. It is at best only a highly organized form of play. Anyone can do it, everyone has a view on it, even if they have never experienced physical involvement. This conceptual conflation of PE and Sport has damaged and seriously limited academic, political and public debate concerning PE in schools in Britain and elsewhere. As Hargreaves (1986, p. 2) has pointed out, it is precisely because 'sport is so impregnated with common sense' that it is in one particular respect problematic: 'As a socio-cultural, historical phenomenon sport remains profoundly opaque. It has proved strongly resistant to critical analyses...'. To assert this of course does not run counter to any argument that PE in school or sport inside or outside it can do you good. But it does remind us that PE, like sport, is a cultural formation and as such it can:

> never be adequately explained purely as an instrument of social harmony or as a means of self expression, for this ignores the divisions and conflicts and inequalities of power to society which if we care to look closely register themselves in sports both outside and inside schools (ibid., p. 2).

Both have largely missed the sceptical gaze of the radical left in recent cultural and educational analyses. As Whannel (1983) has pointed out, most Socialists do not take sport very seriously; because it is simply not seen as a site of class struggle, nor even a significant part of 'social life' (p. 12), it is overlooked in the labour movement's traditional focus on economic and political struggle. In this respect there is little difference between the thinking of such socialists and that of the 'radical Right'. In the view of both, putting people back to paid work is seen as a necessary precondition to getting them into leisure. Sport and PE are largely irrelevant in a process of schooling orientated primarily towards a future of employment. PE has at best been positioned on the margins of educational and political debate centered on the relationships between schooling and the world of paid work. When it has been brought inside, it is only on terms laid down by a powerful vocational discourse.

Whilst this focus on the preparation of children for paid work, on the relationship between schooling and the economy may be important, it is also thoroughly incomplete and potentially very conservative in its implications. As feminist critiques of both leisure and educational theory have repeatedly pointed out, access to leisure is neither solely determined by the level of either State or private provision of leisure services and resources, or on an individual's economic position, particularly whether he or she is in paid work or not. It is constructed within a nexus, a complex co-mingling, of both occupational and familial relationships and beneath an ideological carapace which govern and regulate where, what and how men and women, boys and girls ought to be. Thus if we are interested in effecting anything approximating radical education and social change we need as teachers to be as interested in the question of how we prepare children for their futures in unpaid family work in the household context as we are in their preparation for paid employment, and in how these contexts interact to facilitate and constrain, condition and define their access and opportunites for 'free time' and leisure. Children do not encounter either the occupational structure or leisure directly, but construct subjective definitions of both through their family and school experiences. In this process:

> Teachers and parents (and other children) are not only the mediators of typifications of external sex and social macro structures, but relate to children, sex and social class differentially in the micro structures of home and school (King, 1987, p. 298).

PE teachers can play an important part in this process. They may contribute greatly to the way in which children and young people think about themselves and each other, about their bodies, abilities, and opportunities for involvement in school and post-school sport and other forms of leisure. Granted this, as socialist educators, is it possible to construct a form of curricular practice which brings to the surface and confronts conventional rules and roles, challenges established social categories relating to ability, race, sex and class and status hierarchies, and begins to institute those which are non-sexist and non-racist, less elitist and more co-operative, and which ultimately heralds the arrival of a 'Physical Education for all'?

In the next section I want to consider whether such a situation in PE has already arrived.

The New Physical Education: Moving the Goalposts?

There have been recent signs, in Britain as elsewhere (Kirk, 1987: Greene,

1987), that PE and sport are achieving a newly important position in the public consciousness, at least as this is represented by the popular press. We would have searched in vain through the archives of our national press to find a time when PE had captured so much space in the popular unsporting media. Yet, in July 1986 *Today* published a leading front page article, entitled 'Barmy Britain' vilifying the actions of those PE teachers (characteristically insinuated to be all of them) who were attacking and damaging the place and importance of competition in the PE curriculum. The finger was pointed at one Head Teacher, Mrs Hardless, who had banned the egg-and-spoon race from sports day because it was too competitive and who 'did not want children upset by losing'. Her actions were described as 'barmy' by the Conservative Education Minister, Chris Patten, while the Tory Chairman of Avon County stressed:

> You cannot protect children from the harsh realities of winning or losing. It's a vital part of their education and development. How are they expected to get good jobs without being competitive . . . ? (see *Today*, 1986)

This attack by one of the milder organs of the popular press, which in this case centre on the teaching of games in the primary school curriculum, was only one amongst many to have issued from the media (both the popular and specialist press, like *The Times Educational Supplement*, eminent sporting persons, the Central Council for Physical Recreation, and political sources in recent years. One could be forgiven for thinking that something both radical and widespread was already happening in PE departments throughout Britain's schools. For the most part, criticism centred on the teaching of competitive team sports in the PE curriculum. At times it looked as if PE teachers were exclusively to blame for the Nation's consistently bad performances at cricket, rugby, tennis and football as well as a large measure of moral and industrial decay. 'Positive stances' by the major political parties, and prominent sports organizations and associations on competition in schools have become the order of the day if only to separate themselves from press images of looney or radical elements in the PE teaching profession.

In many respects, the idea that traditional games-teaching in schools is being dissolved by the radical, progressive philosophy and practices of PE teachers, is largely a media creation (which in Britain had much to do with a coming General Election). 'Murdoch (1987, p. 6) reminds us that 'although the extra curricula programme of competitive games has sometimes been badly depleted' still they form the staple diet of within-lesson-time PE programmes in most secondary schools. Shifts away from the provision of a traditional games programme have had more to do with the chronic shortage of resources (the sale of playing fields, sub-standard pitches) and teachers' industrial action than any radicalization of the paradigmatic mentality of the PE profession. In this respect, criticisms such as *Today's* have functioned to obfuscate the root causes of PE teachers' problems in schools as part of the means of attacking and exaggerating elements of progressivism in the curriculum, itself part of maintaining the established boundaries of acceptable educational practice. They have, however, brought the PE curriculum well into debates both about 'standards' and school, work, and to a lesser degree leisure, which we now conventionally date back to speech-events at Ruskin College, 1976, and which for most of the time has been directed at the academic curriculum. Callaghan's concerns about standards and behaviour in schools and the supply of skilled manpower have been developed and aired most noisily ever since by the 'old humanists' and the 'industrial trainers' of the political Right (Davies, 1987; Ball, 1988) unhindered and now even joined by the beaten Left. Schools are blamed for failing to equip pupils with the necessary skills and attitudes to cater for industry, employers are 'appalled' at the quality of school leavers applying to them for jobs — they seemed not to have the right attitude to work, nor the right social skills to cope with the process of finding work. *Today's* critique brought PE into this debate on the terms defined by the vocational discourse, for failure to deliver the social skills and attitudes necessary to sustain Britain's position in the national and international market place. At the heart of this critique is the notion that Britain's economic success or failure rests upon the development of *individual* drive/ambition and a competitive spirit, the will, the longing, the desire to win. Physical Educationalists, like others, were presented as being so caught up with fashionable egalitarian educational theories and progressive practices that they are failing in their responsibility to the nation's economy. The neglect of competitive games becomes a move against popular tradition, nationalism, and the production of quality sport performances. Faith all round is shaken in the view that PE as a subject is socially neutral and ideologically unsullied. Not for the first time, a little moral panic goes a long way to exposing a site of struggle, in this case for competing definitions of what 'the body', the individual, the school and society is and ought to be.

Changing the Laws?

Granted that there is a good deal of confusion — some quite deliberate — at the issue arising from the fact that there are less games (especially out of school hours) being played as a result of resource reduction and teacher action, I now want to consider the substance of recent initiatives in PE which have caused such outrage. Do they herald the arrival of a 'Physical Education for all', a form of PE curriculum and pedagogy in which conventional social categories and hierarchies are challenged and every individual, irrespective of race, class, gender or ability is equally valued and given the same chance to realize their full potential both within the school PE programme and in their post-school leisure? Are these initiatives as emancipatory or as radical as the official discourse of the new PE and indeed its critics would sometimes have us believe?

At the heart of recent criticisms is the view that competition is being relegated, marginalized or at worst dispensed with altogether in the PE curriculum. While highly inaccurate in relation to the PE curriculum at large, it certainly has some claim to validity as far as it relates to the image of practice contained in two innovations — Health Related Fitness (HRF) and Teaching Games for Understanding (TGFU) — which have featured most prominently in the official discourse but much more marginally in schools' practices of PE in recent years. While it would not be true to say that these innovations ask the profession to dispense with competition altogether, they do strongly challenge its nature, status and place in the PE curriculum and in schools they may have occupied space previously given to competitive team games. Within the 'official discourse', TGFU and HRF display a number of common features and prescriptive themes. Both start from a critique of conventional practice in PE, both challenge the content of the curriculum, especially its emphasis on skilled and competitive games and its authoritarian pedagogical mode. At times, they have certainly gone for the throat of the skill-based sports especially dominant in boys' PE; both claim to offer a curriculum which is not only more beneficial but also more accessible to the majority of pupils (Bonniface, 1986).

In the case of TGFU it is claimed, in contrast to traditional games, that success can be achieved more easily by the majority of pupils and their aims are more relevant and desirable for children within today's society where it is desirable for all pupils to be offered equality in terms of experience. The term 'equality' seems to imply the provision of a curriculum content and pedagogical mode which not only permits equality of access to each and every individual irrespective of their levels of physical ability or skill, but also some measure of equality of outcome. It is intended that everyone should experience a genuine (but not necessarily the same) level of success, achievement, satisfaction and enjoyment, along with an understanding of the principles which underpin different game forms.

All this presupposes that is is not possible through the teaching of traditional games for all pupils to be offered an equality of experience, because poor physical skill acts as a barrier to further learning. Thus the emphasis is placed upon the cognitive rather than the technical aspects of the game; on 'knowing that' rather than 'knowing how'. While learning the full adult version of a game may present a long-term goal, in the eyes of those advocating an 'understanding' approach, it is not the main purpose of games teaching in schools. Mini-games with adapted rules and equipment are more likely to provide all pupils with opportunites to make decisions concerning their play and the game itself, whatever their physical ability. In this context all pupils are given more opportunity to take responsibility for their own learning and to experience the satisfaction of achievement and success. It is hoped that these experiences of positive achievement, satisfaction and enjoyment, will form the motivational bases for post-school involvement in physical recreation and sport.

The HRF literature also carries an image of educational practice in which organizational forms and curriculum content avoid the creation of losers and failures. Characteristically in this innovation, the principle of equality of outcome is stressed even more strongly. It is against selection and the creation of ability hierarchies and for 'non-authoritarian', 'non-didactic' approaches to teaching. At the heart of this innovation (at least as officially espoused by the Health Education Council) is a concern for the development of each and every individual's 'health career', their positive 'self esteem' and 'decision-making skills' (Payne, 1985, p. 5). The aims are to create the habit of exercise and the belief that this can be fully integrated into one's life style. Within the context of PE, as Kirk (1987) points out, emphasis is placed upon the development of individual, personalized activity programmes designed to ensure a consistent involvement in physical exercise of an intensity which improves level of fitness (especially cardio-vascular functioning). In philosophy and content, both the TGFU and the HRF initiatives seem radically child- rather than subject-centred. The focus is on 'individual needs rather than activities and on individual responses to exercise rather than marks of achievement' (Payne, 1985, p .5). The emergence of a Health Education emphasis in PE is neither arbitrary, nor unsurprising. HE initiatives have been constructed within and against a broader social and political ideology which in Britain, France, Canada and Australia, has already defined Health as an individual rather than a social concern and responsibility. In this discourse, as Kirk (1987) points out, the emphasis is placed upon prevention rather than cure, on the individual avoiding the negative consequences of an inactive, unhealthy (drinking, smoking, etc.) lifestyle.

HRF and TGFU initiatives have (in recent years) vied for a place not simply within, but as the dominating, curriculum in the official pedagogic discourse of PE. At their heart lies an allegiance to the principle of equal opportunities which seems to mean opening up access to a physical education experience in which each and every child can experience success, satisfaction and enjoyment. The dominant motivation of those professing this discourse and attempting to realize it in schools (see Evans, J. 1987) tends to be ameliorative and hedonistic rather than socially transformative. There is an identifiable concern to alter the conditions of work for teachers and pupils, so as to improve the lot of each child. The goal is to generate interest, secure enjoyment and in this way lay the motivational bedrock upon which, in later life, each individual would build and develop their sport, leisure and health careers. But their discourse neither strongly confronts existing conventional categories of ability nor conceptions of the body, or social class or gender categories, nor does it challenge the social rules and roles governing social relationships inside and outside classrooms.

All for one without one for all?

In some respects HFR and TGFU herald little that is new for the PE curriculum, especially for those involved in the teaching of girls PE. The educational gymnastics, dance and movement education initiatives of the 1950s and 1960s were also explicitly child-centred in philosophy, curriculum content and pedagogical mode. They were also heavily classed and gendered. They were, as Hargreaves recently pointed out, methods for developing in the individual child the 'qualities of flexibility and adaptability, the ability to explore and solve problems independently and to co-operate with others', (1986, p. 162), qualities which, in a strong echo of Bernstein (1977), he claims are required for a competent occupational performance amongst the new middle class. Hargreaves's critique of these earlier initiatives are very pertinent to our present analysis. He argues that movement education, which (with its origins and strongholds in the women's PE colleges) was always strongly gendered was never wholly accepted in the PE fraternity. It always had to co-exist with the fitness/skills, competitive games tradition which was deeply entrenched in the men's teacher training colleges and in boys' secondary schools, 'which more strongly articulates with and is more attuned to male working class culture' (p. 63). I would argue that the two traditions now often happily co-exist in colleges and in comprehensive schools.

To some extent HRF and TGFU, with their commitments to individualized teaching and to fitness, health and games playing have succeeded in straddling the male/female traditions which Hargreaves describes. This may productively signal the beginnings of the dissolution of long-established gender divisions between staff within the PE curriculum and a liberalizing and drawing together of gender interests within the PE profession. It would remain to be seen whether this coming together of interests heralds any re-distribution of status and reward. If Hargreaves' analysis is correct, these initiatives, far from offering something radical or new, may index instead a more widespread imposition of new middle-class values, through practices which indeed may be very satisfying and status-giving to teachers, but may be also highly disconnected/removed from the experience and interests of a large number of pupils. This squares with what we have noted as the accommodative rather than transformatory practices of the initiatives. Issues of class, of gender, ethnicity and ability rarely enter explicitly into the 'official discourse' of recent HRF and TGFU initiatives as they have been constructed in both Britain and abroad (cf. Kirk, 1987). It is, to use Bernstein's (1986, p. 2) words, as if both message and media are somehow 'bland, neutral as air'. These silences can seriously impair the ambitions of teachers who are trying to influence and change the attitudes and decisions of children towards each other and their school and post-school involvement in sport and leisure. We have noted these particularly with respect to teachers who have to teach boys and girls together (sometimes for the first time) and deal with the ways in which they are differently predisposed to relate to the curriculum on offer (Evans, 1987). Again, we must not be surprised. The predominant value underpinning the discourse of PE (and all school knowledge) is 'individualism' which as ideology unites many across the profession and ultimately accomplishes:

> the virtual disappearance of the social structure, that is social processes and social phenomena are radically individualised, reducing them to the attributes of persons and interactions between them. The school as a social organisation, knowledge of the nature of the social context of the educational process and of the cultural characteristics of the pupils forms no part of the discourse (Hargreaves, 1986, p. 165).

We might for the moment dwell briefly on the person conceptions which feature in the HRF, TGFU, official discourse. We find repeated reference to 'young people', the 'individual', the 'person', and of course the 'pupil' or 'the child'. This abstracted individual, this generalized 'youth', does seriously disguise a 'profound set of differences' (Clarke and Willis, 1984) in the origins, the predispositions and the destinations of the children in our care. The transition from school to work, and leisure is:

> not a common process, it is differentiated by the social divisions of British society: by class, gender and race. The transition is differentiated in its starting points, the experience of the transition itself and in its destinations.
>
> Class affects how young people enter it (school) and where they are expected to go when they leave it. Class also shapes the process of transition itself — its length (at which age do people leave it?) and the sorts of institutions in which it is experienced (school; school plus college; school plus university). Gender, too, differentiates the transition. The different destinations assumed for boys and girls structure how they enter it, the sorts of experiences and direction they encounter within it, and the manner in which they leave it. Finally race impinges on the transition, again partly on the different experiences with which groups enter it and partly on the different destinations presumed for them. These social divisions, then, produce not a transition from school to work (and leisure), but a whole variety of transitions. They bear on the process of transition in two ways. First by locating individuals in different starting points and secondly, through the social divison of labour, they determine the different destinations to be arrived at: skilled worker, white collar worker, manager, wife and mother, or unemployed, (Clark and Willis, 1984, p. 7).

Perhaps nowhere is this 'abstraction of youth' more evident than in the use of the concept of 'Health Career' in the HRF literature. This concept sometimes creates the impression that progress along the 'health career path' (towards a healthy life style) is both unproblematic and dependent only upon a positive interaction between a person's self esteem, really useful health knowledge and decision-making skills. It is not stressed that careers have both subjective and objective dimensions, that the concept denotes not only the subjective experiences of the individual (their aspirations, ambitions, ideals, etc.) but also the conditions (social, cultural, material) which may frame (set limits to, frustrate or facilitate) those experiences. Taking this view we would need to at least consider that progress along a 'health career' pathway towards the adoption of healthy habits may be more or less problematic for different people, depending upon their age, their ethnicity, gender or social class and the material conditions of their life. No matter how ambitious or highly motivated to get fit or stay healthy some people are, they may not be able to progress along the health career path because factors in their life styles, over which they may have little control, do not permit or at least inhibit such a development (see Barrell *et al.*, 1987). In short, the dominance of individualism in the discourse even of PE may constitute a massive barrier to any form of practice which would/could help children consider how, for example, their health is socially, politically and economically structured. Kirk puts it nicely when he states:

> If we are overweight, drink excessively or catch AIDS, physical educators would tell us that we only have ourselves to blame, we have simply mismanaged our lifestyles and need to refrain from eating cream cakes or promiscuous sex (1987, p. 9).

Issues of advertising, social conditions or ideology itself as significant contributions to ill health do not enter into the story.

The development and nurturing of individual achievement, enjoyment and individual responsibility — which feature strongly in the new official discourse may be worthy goals indeed. My point here is simply that this discourse remains incomplete, insofar as it fails to articulate a 'philosophy' and practice, which also considers how these qualities of responsibility and autonomy might be fostered in and through the practices of teachers, and enacted within the social and material conditions of a person's life. Years ago Aneurin Bevan (1952, p. 26) made the point that 'responsibility without power is the most dangerous of all situations', whether it be for a 'political party with progressive pretentions' or for the individual. The 'person may be more conscious of the responsibility than they are the lack of power'. To acknowledge this is to concede that giving pupils 'responsibility' may mean very little to them unless at the same time they are provided with the knowledge and the opportunity to identify and challenge those social and cultural rules, roles and interests which may curtail its enactment. Those rules and roles will relate to their gender, their class, ethnicity or ability and which together form the social fabric of the educational work place (or more locally, life in the gym), the family, or other out of school work and leisure contexts. These rules and roles receive very little attention in the official discourse of the new PE.

Beyond Critique: Towards a Socialist Physical Education?

There are elements of the new PE which do seem radical. It has constituted a sustained and well-orchestrated attack on an élitism, on the high status and place given to the provision of a narrow range of traditional games, on the time and effort given to a few able performers, and on the limits of PE teachers' didactic teaching. This critique echoes well with a socialist discourse on sport (see Whannel, 1983). The new curricula have broadened the curriculum of PE and made more sophisticated the profession's teaching methods, and as such they have altered the conditions of work for pupils and teachers in schools. Indeed there is some evidence to suggest that they do provide the means of better realizing the potential of every child, and of opening up opportunities for their within- and post-school involvement in physical activity and sport (see Evans, J., 1987). But while the new PE produces more and maybe increasingly satisfying participation, is it capable of realizing the value of each and every individual and of challenging the ideological and material conditions which are likely to set limits to their actions? My reluctant conclusion is that the official discourse of the new PE has been socially and culturally neutralized and as such it may impede the formation of collective action (see Apple, 1986) both inside and outside school. At the same time as it celebrates individualism, person power, control and responsibility it remains largely silent on issues of class, race, gender and ability and how these elements enter into the curriculum not least via the identities of children. (Indeed a discourse on gender and PE has existed alongside but largely separate from others on the initiatives of the new PE). These omissions may well ultimately only serve to 'distort the text' of these new initiatives and the practices to which they give rise, 'in favour of already dominant groups'. With others in this book, I want to stress that:

> ...dignity and morality have a social and corporate aspect. Genuine individuality must be rooted in group life... and group life was not merely the means of giving people the social skills of cooperation and empathy, but of generating solidarity (which is the means of human fulfilment)... The solidarity base of modern man could not be realised unless the spirit of association is already aroused... It (is) the school's key function to 'breathe life into the spirit of association'... (see Fielding, 1987).

How is this spirit of association, of cooperation and collectivity, to be achieved in the practices of PE; what are the principles upon which they are to be based? The slogan 'Physical Education for all' has undoubtedly figured prominently as a theme in the discourse of the New PE, and this may have productively challenged the practice of over concentrating attention (resources, time, money, effort) on only the élite performers in the PE curriculum. But it has to be acknowledged that neither élitism nor competition are being totally rejected. As others have pointed out (Sherlock, 1987; Hargreaves, 1986) the values of competition are being challenged because it is this component of the PE curriculum which is deemed to contribute towards turning children away from sport not because physical educationalists are critical of competitive individualism. In this respect, new initiatives have only shifted the emphasis in teaching, but they have neither challenged or reformulated social categories and status hierarchies (relating to ability, gender, class) which have long featured in the practise of PE. In this respect the New PE is egalitarian in intention and orientation; it remains strongly committed to meritocracy in schooling and the wider social order (a commitment which lies well with the principles of individualism), one in which every individual is given equal chance to get to the top, achieve satisfaction and pleasure at the limits of their potential. This commitment to equal opportunities may well be an important starting point towards a more radical PE (and serve as a point of contact for liberals and socialists) if it implies the right of access to a common PE curriculum for every child, irrespective of their class, colour, sex or ability. But with others in this volume I would want to say that the adoption of an equal opportunities policy does not necessarily herald the arrival in either practice or intention, of a 'Physical Education for all'. The concept and practice of equal opportunities is and has always been highly problematical for social and educational reformers. As Fielding (ibid) explains, citing Dent:

> It is impossible because even if the starting line is uniform (if all pupils have access to the same PE curriculum) the arrival of the competitors in various states of fitness (social attributes, physical abilities, competence, etc...) points to a prior race which has already been run in quite unequal circumstances. It is inappropriate because the imagery of races, competition and inevitably few runners points to a mode of life that is in harmony with meritocracy in which the success of a very small number in a narrow field is predicated on the failure of vast numbers of their fellow citizens. It is sharply out of tune with a society which seeks to value all its members in all their diversity.

For Fielding this means rejecting individualism and the shibboleth of meritocracy, for the principle of equal value, a commitment which at once brings to the surface the question of how one implements a form of curricular practice which both brings children (boys, girls, black, white, etc.) together towards a common culture and humanity and, at the same time, respects and values 'all its members in all their diversity'. The adoption of an equal opportunities policy and the provision of a common PE curriculum for all children irrespective of social category or background and cultural origin, ensuring, for example that boys and girls have access to activities (football, cricket, netball, etc.) which were once the preserve of only males or females may be an important step towards the first of these goals, bringing children together. But unless a common curriculum and an equal opportunities policy are supported by other forms of organizational curriculum and pedagogical change, the resulting social changes in how children think about and act towards each other, knowledge and teachers are likely to be insubstantial indeed. I can here only begin to offer some first thoughts on what those changes and the principles which underpin them might be.

While any radical PE would embrace the initiatives of the New PE, especially if imbued with an educative and critical edge (see Kirk, 1987) it would neither outlaw nor oppose the quest for individual excellence, achievement or merit within the context of individual or team competition. Competitive team games are after all deeply embedded in the cultural worlds of many individuals (especially males) and to exclude or undervalue this element from and in the PE curriculum would be to make its residue or replacement both deeply alienating and uninteresting for a great many children. It would also badly undervalue their culture. As Forbes and Street (1986) point out:

> The transition to socialism must start from the analysis of people as they are (and concomitantly must be sensitive to existing forms of thought and behaviour) not as they might be. Whatever particular vision of the future that socialists adopt their first step has to involve them in linking the world as they find it with the world as they would like it to be (p. 17).

Competition of course takes many forms, (against self, others, time, etc.) and as a social construct it is inevitably imputed different meanings in different cultural contexts. Competition (the Game) structured by capitalism (and the ideology of individualism) and realized within a social order and school system bent on selecting and differentiating children may not be the same as when it is structured by socialism and realized within a school system which fosters cooperation, collaboration and the 'spirit of association'; where the principle of action is the goal of bringing children together rather than setting them apart. Any competitive game is potentially Janus-headed. It has the potential to foster both togetherness and selfish individualism but the function is determined not by any qualities inherent in the game or activity, but by the ideological carapace which surrounds and supports it. As such there is little justification for denying competitive games a place alongside the more obviously cooperative and the individualized forms of activity which have found a place in the new PE towards the development of a socialist PE.

Commitment to the principle of equal value will, however mean much more than the provision of a common PE curriculum. It would actively confront and challenge actions and values in the process of schooling which foster or support the creation of differential statuses based on ability, sex or race. Accusations have repeatedly been made that PE is one of the more sexist of the school subjects. It has, especially in the secondary sector, long separated male and female departments — often with a male Head overseeing both — and offered differential curriculum to boys and girls. This practice still very often is legitimated with the view that girls/boys are naturally suited to certain sorts of physical activities (Carrington and Williams, 1988; Scraton, 1986). In recent years, however, sexism has become a case suitable for treatment. Some have found it difficult to justify the separation of boys and girls and have begun to effect mixed-sex grouping. In some cases this has been a concomitant of the curriculum initiatives described earlier. However, simply effecting organizational change, opening up access to boys and girls to a common range of physical activities, does little to alter the traditional, stereotyped conceptions which they have of themselves and each other. In a radical PE, organizational change has to be supported by a curriculum and pedagogical change which is capable of taking into account the physical and social differences which children bring to the classroom (see Evans, M., 1985). Teachers have to be able to effect not only mixed-ability teaching, but also a form of personal and social education in their classrooms which is capable of dealing with and confronting the often negative attitudes and inhibitions which children hold towards each other. We are some way off knowing what form of educational practice this would be (but see Evans, M., 1985; Humberstone, 1986).

Without such changes, the practice of letting boys and girls 'mix' in a curriculum which was previously strongly gendered and differentiated, can have the effect of exacerbating rather than dissipating differences between them. Such a practice (mixed-sex grouping) thus may not in the first instance be the best or the only way of bringing boys and girls together, indeed it may be highly insensitive particularly to the cultural value and interest of some categories of children, (for example, Asian girls, see Carrington and Williams, 1988). It may well be the case that the task of effecting equal opportunities in PE has firstly to be founded on a policy of positive discrimination (see Scraton, 1987). This practice may neither contradict nor oppose the principle of equal value or equal opportunity; it could constitute a strategic action towards the goal of a PE for all. Both feminists and socialists have taken this view. For Whannel (1983), for example, positive discrimination is needed to undo a long history of sexism and racism (in sport) and will be part of the fight for genuine opportunity for all, while Scraton argues a strong case for 'space in the curriculum' for girls/women to develop their confidence and interests, especially in coeducational schools. Clearly in any radical PE, the practice of teaching children apart will need to be based on clear and unifying organizational principles. In a context where these are integration and cooperation, where the ultimate aim is to bring children together to value and respect each other, the practice of separating children on the basis of their gender, ability, colour or for that matter their confidence may be both a necessary and legitimate short term means of achieving longer term integrative goals.

In this discussion I have only begun to touch the surface of this endeavour as far as it relates to the principles and practice of physical education in school. Clearly any radical alteration in peoples' post-school work and leisure opportunities will require much more than curriculum change inside schools. Reform at this level will be constrained or facilitated by changes in the extra-school setting and will need to relate to the struggles against racism, sexism and élitism in the wider leisure and sporting scenes. The realization of principles of equal opportunity and equal value will ultimately depend upon changes in both the thinking of educationalists and politicians and concomitantly the resourcing of educational practice. In Britain we now enter a period when, in reality, the place and position of the subject in the State secondary sector of schooling is more insecure than ever before. A recent discussion document on the National Curriculum contains proposals which if implemented could cut by half, in some schools, the already limited amounts of time available to physical education. Yet we continue to learn (Walford, 1986) that children in the private school sector who will be exempt from the rigours of the current legislation, enjoy a level of resource (in the form of time, equipment and opportunities for PE and leisure) which would be the envy of most physical educationalists in the State secondary sector.[2] Moreover, at a moment when secondaries dominate the stage, one must add that a radical Physical Education would begin in the primary sector. Physical Education in this sector of schooling has hardly received the attention of British politicians of any persuasion. Most teachers in this sector are only minimally trained in the teaching of PE and at best can only offer the most limited and usually the most conventional of Physical Education practices. The upshot of this is that what is provided is often strongly classed and gendered. At a time in children's lives when they are not only eager and enthusiastic about involvement in PE but also relatively willing to work and play with others regardless of their colour, sex or ability, the quality of curricula and pedagogical provision is at it's worst.

The existence of a form of educational practice in PE which is capable of providing 'an education for all', remains then, in my view, some distance away. The commitment to education for health or education for leisure, is, as has already been outlined above, unlikely to be realized unless, within the classroom context, teachers are resourced with a form of pedagogy which is able to help children to better understand and then challenge the expectations they hold about themselves and each other. That is what some practitioners of mixed-sex grouping are already trying to do (see Evans, M., 1985). But of course the quest to help children better understand each other and the social aspects of their lives is no simple task and cannot only be the preserve of any single approach, or only the school. To take this task seriously inside schools will mean not only weakening the boundaries between different sorts of debate and innovation, HRF, TGFU, and mixed-sex grouping, but also moves towards integration or at least better communication between the work of PE teachers and that of other subject teachers, who may also be addressing issues of race, class, culture and of family, work and leisure in their curricula. This will require teachers bringing both the personal and the social aspects of childrens' lives into their classrooms. Social class, race and gender have to become concerns of the profession and perhaps especially of those adherents of the New PE. HRF and TGFU do carry enormous potential and scope for pupils to work together cooperatively and to generate data about themselves, others and their life styles (through keeping diaries, fitness and activity profiles, etc). This may be one way into a discussion of complex and sensitive issues about the social roles and rules which influence people's lives and of the powerful economic, political and ideological interests which set limits to leisure, work and health expectations and behaviours. Ultimately, to bring class and cultural issues into both the official discourse and the classroom practices of PE teachers is to consider that progress in the lives of individuals towards a situation in which each is empowered to achieve amongst other things a healthier or more active life style will depend upon the taking of collaborative and cooperative action. It will mean starting from what people have in common rather than from what already sets them apart. The identification of common interests, shared responsibilities, mutual problems and some understanding of the reciprocity of human actions — my leisure, my health is dependent upon your attitudes, your willingness to compromise or share — will need to be as high on the agenda of the official discourse, as is the quest for the development of individual autonomy.

Acknowledgements

I am indebted to Professor Brian Davies for his comments on an earlier draft of this paper, and to Pam Webster and Ann Freeland for their patience and expertise. The faults and limitations in the paper are all mine.

Notes

1 Sociological perspectives have long been brought to the study of sports (such as football or rugby) as they are organized and played outside schools, and to the behaviours which people display while watching them. This literature has valuably illustrated the social class and cultural origins and significances of these activities (see for example, Dunning *et al.*, 1988). I am simply claiming that sport in schools and all else that passes for a PE programme still has to be subjected to the analytical gaze of critical theorists. Though Hargreaves (1986) and Kirk (1988) have made an invaluable start in this direction.

John Evans

2   I am reminded of a more distant debate (and I thank David Kirk for drawing my attention to this) on the Physical Training and recreation Bill (1937) when 'Mr Bevan and Mr Maxton accused the Government of providing Physical Education for the masses on the cheap, while the upper classes enjoyed lavish facilities at their Public schools' (McIntosh *et al.*, 1981, p. 213). Clearly both the form and level of PE provision have long been strongly classed, though they have rarely appeared so obviously high on the agenda of political debates.

References

APPLE, M. (1986) *Teachers and Texts*, London: Routledge and Kegan Paul.
BALL, S. (1988) 'Comprehensive schooling, effectiveness and control: An analysis of educational discourses, in Slee R. (Ed) *Education, Disruptive Pupils and Effective Schooling*, (forthcoming), Melbourne: Macmillan.
BARREL, G.V., HOLT, D. and MACKEAN, J.M. (1987) *The Marathon Phenomenon*, The University of Southampton.
BERNSTEIN, B. (1977) *Class, Codes and Control*, London: Routledge and Kegan Paul.
BERNSTEIN, B. (1986) *A Sociology of the Pedagogic Context*. Unpublished Mimeo. Institute of Education, University of London.
BEVAN, A. (1952) *In Place of Fear*, London: William Heinemann Ltd.
BONNIFACE, M. (1986) *The Changing Physical Education Curriculum*. Unpublished paper. The Department of Physical Education, University of Southampton.
CARRINGTON, B. and WILLIAMS, T. (1988) 'Patriarchy and ethnicity : the link between school physical education and community leisure activities', in Evans, J. (Ed.) *Teachers Teaching and Control* (forthcoming), Lewes: Falmer Press.
CLARK, J. and WILLIS, P. (1984) 'Introduction', in Bates, I. *et al.* (Eds) *Schooling for the Dole*, London: Macmillan.
DAVIES, B. (1987) 'Halting progress — some comments on recent British educational policy and practice', in *Journal of Education Policy*, 4, pp. 349–61.
DUNNING, E. *et al.* (1988) *The Roots of Hooliganism. An Historical and Sociological Study*. London: Routledge and Kegan Paul.
EVANS, J. (1987) *Teaching for Equality in Physical Education? The Limits of Progressivism in the 'New PE'*. Paper presented for the Conference, Ethnography and Inequality, St. Hilda's College, Oxford.
EVANS, M. (1985) *An Action Research Approach to the Innovation of Mixed Physical Education in a Secondary School*. Diplomas in Professional Studies dissertation, Kingston Polytechnic.
FIELDING, M. (1987) 'Liberté, egalité and fraternité — ou la mort. Towards a new paradigm for the comprehensive school', in Chitty, C. (Ed) *Redefining the Comprehensive Experience*, No. 32. Bedford Way Papers, University of London.
FORBES, I. and STREET, J. (1986) 'Industrial Transition to Socialism', *Theory, Culture and Society*, 3 pp. 17–33.
GREENE, M. (1987) 'Teaching as a project: Choice, perspective and the public space', in Carnes, M.M. (Ed.) *Proceedings of the Fourth Conference on Curriculum Theory in Physical Education*, The University of Georgia, Athens, Georgia 30602.
HARGREAVES, J. (1986) *Sport, Power and Culture*, Cambridge: Polity Press.
HUMBERSTONE, B. (1986) 'Learning for a change: A study of gender and schooling in outdoor education', in Evans, J. (Ed.) *Physical Education, Sport and Schooling, Studies in the Sociology of PE*. Lewes: Falmer Press.
KING, R. (1987) 'Sex and social class inequalities in education: A re-examination', in *British Journal of Sociology of Education*, 8, 3 pp. 287–305.
KIRK, D. (1987a) *Barriers to Change in Physical Education: The Influence of Teacher*

Biography and Ideology. Paper presented for the British Educational Research Association Annual Conference, September 1987.

KIRK, D. (1987) *Studying the Change Process in Physical Education. A Proposal for a Socio-Historical Study.* Unpublished Paper. Department of Human Movement Studies, University of Queensland, St. Lucia Q4067, Australia.

KIRK, D. (1988) *Physical Education and Curriculum Study. A Critical Introduction*, London: Croom Helm.

MACDONNELL, D. (1986) *Theories of Discourse*, Oxford: Blackwell.

MCINTOSH, P.C. (1981) *Landmarks in the History of Physical Education.* (Revised edition) London: Routledge & Kegan Paul.

MURDOCH, E. (1987) *Sport in Schools*, London: The Sports Council Publications Department.

PAYNE, S. (1985) 'Physical education and health in the United Kingdom', *British Journal of Physical Education, 17*, 1, pp.4–9.

SCRATON, S. (1985) 'Images of feminity and the teaching of girls' physical education', in Evans, J. (Ed.) *PE Sport and Schooling*, Lewes: Falmer Press.

SCRATON, S. (1987) 'Boys muscle in where angels fear to tread — Girls sub-cultures and physical activities, in Horne, J. *et al.* (Eds) *Sport, Leisure and Social Relations* London: Routledge and Kegan Paul.

SHERLOCK, J. (1987) 'Issues of masculinity and feminity in British physical education', *Women's Studies International Forum, 10*, 4, pp. 443–5.

TODAY (1986) *Barmy Britain*, front page, *Today*, 18.7.86.

WHANNEL, G. (1983) *Blowing the Whistle. The Politics of Sport*, London: The Pluto Press.

Chapter 10

The Playground Project: A Democratic Learning Experience

Patricia White

Working in the education service in the UK in the late 1980s is hard. It becomes more and more difficult, even for the most committed teachers, to work in the belief that through their efforts they are doing something to improve the quality of life of all members of the community. For the current political climate is basically hostile to this aspiration, with government-backed divisiveness between schools and children and a squeeze on those studies which broaden horizons and inspire constructive social criticism. Increasingly beset and beleaguered in their professional aspirations, it is, in turn, hard for teachers to encourage in their students the kind of wholehearted commitment to the values of equality, cooperativeness, compassion, honesty, and courage which is essential in a democratic community.

Hard, but not yet impossible. In the department where I work, a couple of us have been involved with Laycock School, an inner-city primary school which, against all the odds, has improved the quality of life for staff and students, within a civilised framework of democratic discussion involving the whole staff, children and parents. How has this come about?

The origin of the project

The staff of the school had been concerned for some time about the children's moral development. They applied for a grant to the School Curriculum Development Committee and invited two members of the department to work with them on a consultancy basis.[1] In a first informal discussion about how we might focus the rather amorphous project of 'doing something to improve the children's moral attitudes and behaviour' we decided to concentrate on improving the quality of life in the playground. This was for four main reasons. First, life in the playground can be grim. Children can hurt themselves; they can experience bullying; they can be excluded from games or friendship groups; they can get into fights. Second, life in the playground very much affects life within the school. (In work done during the course of the project children described graphically their very different attitudes to classroom activities depending on whether they had enjoyed good or bad playtimes). Third, the playground is a public space and so attitudes and behaviour there can more easily be the focus of a whole-school policy than, say, attitudes and behaviour in classrooms. Even in reasonably open primary schools, classrooms can still be rather private places where each teacher is in his or her private space with his or her class. The playground therefore seemed a good focus for a modest project. Finally, following on from the last point, we felt that the playground was a good choice in another way, in that it easily involved everyone connected with the school — all staff, children and parents. This would allow for the participation of everyone connected with the school.

A few background details about the school

The staff is a large one for a primary school — twenty-six teachers, four nursery assistants, two full-time helpers, seven lunch-time playground staff and eight kitchen staff. The school, covering an age-range of 3 to 11, comprises junior and infant schools, a full-time nursery and a partially-hearing unit. There is a community play-centre and a nursery extended each day unil 18.15.

The school is deemed to be an educational priority one. Fifty-five per cent of the approximately 240 children are on free dinners and approximately 50 per cent do not live with both of their parents. There are pupils from many different ethnic origins. Its Head did a Masters degree in Philosophy of Education in our department a few years ago, with a dissertation on moral education. Once before she had invited two of us from the department to the school to lead a discussion of the teaching staff on their views about the aims of education.

The progress of the playground project

In an initial informal meeting in November 1986 with the Head and the proposer of the project, the teacher responsible for Curriculum and Special Needs, John Bown, we discussed the idea of focusing on life in the playground. We then started the project proper with a meeting in February, 1987. All staff, teaching and support staff, were invited. The Inner London Education Authority paid for the support staff to attend and in all about forty staff came along. There was an elected chair, as at all staff meetings at the school.

John Bown and I introduced the session. We asked staff to consider, amongst other things, whether they wanted to concentrate on encouraging children to engage in/avoid certain specific kinds of behaviour in the playground or whether they wanted to put more emphasis on encouraging the children to become generally more reflective about their behaviour. There was no question of a sharp either/or here but there was one of emphasis. Then we broke up into five groups to discuss a list of five issues which produced conflict in the playground. The list had been determined by John Bown through informal discussions with the staff and, in outline, it ran as follows:

1. Instances of disobedience, e.g., children ignoring requests to come down from the roof.
2. Parental attitudes, e.g., children being told to fight back or protect younger siblings.
3. Hierarchy, e.g., children taking little notice of support staff.
4. Exclusion, e.g., the domination of football to the exclusion of other activitites.
5. Violence, e.g., physical and verbal.

The report-back and summing-up of this meeting produced the following conclusions. It was generally thought that it would be a good idea to have a code of conduct for the playground which many people thought should be backed by sanctions. It was agreed that the project should seek the views and ideas of all concerned at all points and always move forward in such a way as to maintain the support of all those involved.

Our next meeting was the following month and again it took place after school. There was no money to pay for support staff to attend this meeting but they were encouraged to do so and some of them did. Our brief was a large one: to try and see if we could achieve agreement at least on the principles of a code of conduct for the playground and the necessity or otherwise for sanctions — some said an ultimate sanction. Once again we divided into five groups and reported back on our discussions. Most groups spend all their time on a discussion of what they understood by moral education.

The plenary session revealed many different views and approaches. Let me try to suggest something of the flavour of it. The following answers to the question 'What is moral education?' were offered:

> Teaching children the Golden Rule; teaching children to discriminate right from wrong; getting children to respect one another; getting children to make reasoned decisions; getting children to weigh up the consequences of their actions; socialising children; training children in a socially acceptable way, getting children to adopt socially acceptable behaviour patterns, making children into socially acceptable individuals; getting children to form a personal code of behaviour; encouraging people to feel good about themselves...

In so far as discussions had ranged over what to do about fighting, bullying and so on in the playground a similar diversity of issues came up:

Should aggressive behaviour be banned? Should we have sanctions, because sanctions say 'we care about what you do'? Do some children set themselves up as victims? Is it right to sacrifice some children for the benefit of others? Would things be easier in a church school with God as the ultimate sanction? Could there not be agreement at least on rules to do with safety? Do we make too many allowances? For instance, for children with difficult home circumstances? Do we reward bad behaviour? Do we have any right as adults to interfere in the children's 'private' time?

This was a necessary meeting but it was at the same time a very frustrating one for the staff. They felt that we were going round in circles, not getting anywhere and also unlikely to get anywhere. How were we likely to determine and agree on the true nature of morality and moral education in a few weeks or months?

At this point we felt that the time had come to try a fresh approach to the issues. We decided to bring the children fully into the picture and ask them for their views and feelings about the playground and playtime and try to use that material as the basis for a code. The whole school spent some time in class in the next couple of weeks discussing the things they liked about the playground, the things they did not like, the feelings they had after a good playtime and those they had after a bad playtime. Children wrote and drew as individuals, and sometimes in cooperation with others, about their experiences in, and thoughts about, the playground. Huge bundles of work, writing and drawing, poured into my office. (It may be of interest that my enthusiasm for this project was only increased one Saturday evening in March when I looked at about a hundred or so contributions on 'What I don't like about the playground'. The combined impression of preventable misery and distress made on me by the contributions on these little pieces of exercise paper and bright sugar paper made me think that anything the project could do to reduce this would be worth the effort. Not, I should say, that this was in any sense the material of which video nasties are made. It was rather the opposite — an impression of the petty spitefulness and unpleasantness which can make life in the playground rather miserable for many children). The school council, composed of two representatives from each class, considered what its members reported about what children liked and did not like about the playground and what changes had been suggested. It sent its resolutions to me too.

In late March 1987, parents were told about the project at a parents' evening. Some of the children performed playlets to demonstrate common causes of conflict in the playground. Then the parents discussed the issues.

After the parents' evening John Bown and I met, after I had tried to assimilate all the children's accounts of playground experiences, the views of the school council and brief reports of the parents' discussions. We drew up a draft document *Having Fun in the Playground* (Appendix 1) which, we hoped, would go eventually to all staff, children and parents. This first attempted to give an account of our thinking so far, concentrating particularly on the children's accounts of their experiences in the playground, good and bad, as well as their suggestions for improvements. It ended with a possible Code, again taking up points the children had made, which ran as follows:

THE LAYCOCK CODE

1. We will always be kind and considerate to everybody in the playground.
2. We will look after the playground and make sure that it is always a nice place to be in.
3. We will do our best to let everybody who wants to join in our games.
4. On Tuesdays and Thursdays each week we will not play football at all and share the space so that other games, such as volleyball, netball or handball, can also be played.
5. Even if we are in the midst of something very exciting or important, we will stop and listen to any instructions an adult may give us.

In early April 1987 we had another staff meeting after school to discuss this draft, the first fruits of our whole-school effort. Again there was no money to pay support staff but some came nevertheless. The preamble was thought to be fine but with the Code there were problems.

The major problem, which had emerged in all the small group discussions as the plenary session revealed, centred on the fourth point of the Code. This restricted football to Mondays, Wednesdays and Fridays. The playground is L-shaped and in the small part of the L there was always a football game taking place between the same fourteen–twenty fourth-year junior boys. This left approximately 180 children with only the large part of the L for their activities. Point four was intended therefore to establish a more equitable distribution of the space available for play in response to comments which had been made by children, parents and staff. But both the supposed 'problem' and its 'solution' in point four were challenged. One view held that there was no football problem. The footballers were well-organized. Their energies were creatively channelled each playtime into a well-structured game, even, it was claimed, embodying unique rules to cope with the situation of having to use a school entrance as a goal. The quality of their football skills too — ball control, etc. — was praised. It would be quite wrong, this group felt, to curtail such a, not merely harmless, but in many ways highly admirable, activity. On the equitable use of space the view was that there was no real problem here. In time those who envied the fourth-years their use of the space would be able to use it themselves. They simply had to wait their turn — a recognisably fair procedure.

Another view held that there might be a problem to do with the equitable use of the space but that it was not for us as staff to sort this out; we should not interfere in the children's private space. Playtime is their time and they do not want to be organized during it by adults. Others accepted that there was a problem but thought that there was a much better solution to it. The school is in a side road and also has the use of a playground space on the other side of the road. The footballers, it was suggested, could take over this. This solution had to be ruled out because there were not sufficient support staff to supervise the two playgrounds and crossings of the road which would be involved.

This left a group which felt that there was a football problem and point four was a reasonable way of solving it. This group drew attention to the unfairness to girls whose use of the playground space would always be restricted since they would never be fourth-year boys! Doubts were also expressed about the desirability of the school's underlining the importance of hierarchy in the distribution of goods, if the use of the space was seen as a fourth year-(male) privilege. The meeting finished with the agreement that perhaps a football-free/football-less day (depending on your point of view!) might be tried for an experimental period.

A further staff meeting was held and devoted to sanctions — what to do if someone broke the Code. In the plenary session it seemed that most groups favoured some kind of special book in which names would be written after a suitable number of warnings. All staff would use the book. Repeated entries of the same name in the book would lead to parents being invited into school to talk matters over. At this meeting too the football issues were discussed again but without the differences between the goups being resolved.

It was agreed that John Bown and I would meet and attempt to tidy up *Having Fun in the Playground* into a document to be presented to a final staff meeting, before it was sent home to parents. Support staff would be paid for their attendance at this meeting. So, on 2 June 1987, John Bown and I produced another document (Appendix 2). Point three was dropped as it was clearly covered by the first point. Following discussions with the children in class and by the school council, the notorious football item no longer specified football-free days. This was largely because it was felt that now the fairness problem had really been brought home to the children it would be best (e.g., for the development of their autonomy and self-confidence) if they were able to have at least a first shot at the details of the arrangements for the sharing of the space themselves. The Code therefore now read:

THE LAYCOCK CODE

1. We will always be kind and considerate to everybody in the playground.
2. We will look after the playground and make sure that it is always a nice place to be in.

3   We will share the playground space so that other games, besides football, can be played.
4   Even if we are in the midst of something very exciting or important, we will stop and listen to any instructions an adult may give us.

At this point, because of the teachers' dispute, it was not possible to hold the final meeting in the summer term. Comments were collected on the document in the hope that a final version could be agreed so that the whole venture could be launched at the start of the next school year.

In early September 1987, using the morning of one of the new staff in-service training days, we set ourselves a strictly-timed agenda and prepared for the launch of the Code. We were encouraged by the usual start of the new year feelings when things that looked impossible in the tired days of July suddenly seem both possible and highly worthwhile and also by the very positive response I had got when I talked about the project in June in Cambridge to a conference of philosophers, sociologists and teachers interested in democracy in education. Invigorated by the congratulations we had received on our pioneering efforts, we tackled our four-part agenda in small groups.

The plenary session revealed a heartening measure of agreement on the first item on our agenda, the implementation of the Code. We would concentrate on the positive aspects, on making the playground a pleasanter place to be. As a last resort names of those breaking the Code would be entered in a book, which would be reviewed weekly by the head or deputy head. After three offences a letter would be sent to parents inviting them to come into school to discuss their child's behaviour. As far as possible the entry would be written in the book with the child present.

Item two was concerned with how we would emphasise the united approach to the Code by all staff and how we would encourage the children to be reflective about their behaviour. An impressive way of underlining the united approach of the whole school to the Code would be, it was agreed, to have an assembly to launch the project with everybody present — cook, teachers, support staff, caretaker.... Reflection on playground behaviour would be encouraged by all classes having awareness sessions on particular aspects of the Code. This was thought to be very important as several people felt that children sometimes got themselves into trouble because they were not sure how to handle certain situations and, for instance, resorted to name-calling, swearing at teachers or violence as the 'best' way of coping with a problem. Discussions of alternative methods of coping could be helpful.

In answer to item three, which concerned how we might assess our efforts, it was thought that a crude form of assessment would be the monitoring of entries in the book. More important, though, would be to get the children themselves to consider and write about their perceptions of the way life in the playground had changed since the introduction of the Code. And finally, in response to the last item, the date of the launch, we decided to make it 10th September 1987, the first day that a whole-school assembly could be arranged. We would dither on the side of the pool no longer. It was time to jump in. On 9th September 1987 a letter went home to parents setting out the revised four-point Code and how it would be implemented. The following day at 14.00 we had the whole school assembly. Everyone — all staff and every child in the school — packed into the hall. It was a memorable occasion. For thirty minutes the Deputy Head had the rapt attention of the gathering as she described the work everybody present had put into the making of the Code and how it was now to be implemented.

As I write now in mid-October 1987 the Code is in place. The book contains nine names, there has been a mixed game of cricket and the general impression is that the playground is a calmer, happier place in which children and staff feel more secure.

Some Comments

I should say, first, that the foregoing account of the project should not be taken as the definitive account. It is clearly written from one perspective and that of an outsider. Insiders would undoubtedly give a different account at least in details and emphasis and no doubt no two insiders' accounts would be identical. In this connection it was pointed out to me that an earlier draft of this paper gave the impression that the children's contribution to the formulation, revision and implementation of the Code was a rather small one.[2] I think this was perhaps because my personal participation in the project has been largely, though not totally, confined to staff meetings and this has tended to give me a staff-weighted perspective on the project. I hope that the present version gives a more accurate picture of the children's role in the project, although I still claim no definitive status for it. With that proviso, let me offer a few necessarily brief remarks on democratic practice in schools, the role of philosophers of education in projects like this one and the assessment of such projects.

First, what this project has brought home to me is the difficulty of implementing anything like a workplace democracy approach in a school in a society which is indifferent, if not hostile, to such an extension of democratic practices. Perhaps I should just make clear, in parenthesis as it were, what I understand by a 'workplace democracy approach'. This is the application to the workplace of the view that the whole rationale for democratic arrangements is that they reflect institutionally the fact that we are persons with ethical concerns. This involves, *inter alia*, devising structures which support members' self-respect and allow them to act as people with ethical responsibilities. In an educational institution the realization of this conception of people has a further significance in providing a powerful framework in which potential citizens learn from the ethos to take on the caring, responsible attitudes they experience all around them. (For a further development of this view, see White, 1983).

The extension of democratic practices, just indicated, would be likely, one would think, to have a prominent place on the agenda of any society which was intent on encouraging its young members to develop deeply-rooted democratic dispositions. Furthermore it is hard to imagine anyone having ideological or other objections to this particular project centred on making the playground a nicer place to be in. Indeed no one has raised any such objections. The aims of our project have been supported by all staff, parents, governers and indeed anyone who has heard about it. Nevertheless we have been working against the odds. All our meetings, but one, have had to be after school and we have only had sufficient money to pay support staff to come on two occasions. It could be argued that what we are doing — helping children to live cooperatively together and resolve problems of competing claims to resourses and so on — is at the heart of any democratic education but the staff of the school has had to fit these matters into the periphery of their day, always at a time when they are exhausted. The support staff, pivotal figures in this project, have shown an impressive commitment to democracy in being so often prepared to attend meetings in their own time. In a society in which the fostering of democratic practices was a priority it seems to me that our meetings would have been seen as part of everyone's professional duties.

So many important things need to be carefully thought through, not least because, as we came to realize, we had over time implicitly come to put considerable weight on the aim of encouraging the children to be more reflective about their behaviour. We had formulted a code, it is true, but it was a code which invited reflection. For instance, what is it to be considerate? What do you do if a younger child wants to join your game but lacks the skills to participate? What is the considerate thing to do then? If your mum has told you that you have got to stick up for yourself and somebody has just thumped you, what do you do? What is involved in looking after or protecting younger brothers and sisters? How do you share the playground space fairly? We have instituted 'awareness sessions' so that these and other similar questions can be discussed and the children helped to see just what the considerations are here. For these to be maximally successful, however, teachers and support staff need to have the time to think through these issues themselves, and not just as individuals but as a staff. But where is the time to be found to do this?

From my experience of working with the staff and children at Laycock over the past year, I would suggest that if resources could be found just to increase by a couple of hours a week the amount of time available for reflection by all staff and children in the school, this alone would greatly enhance the quality of what staff are able to do in what I would see as the heartland of education in a democratic society. Second, my involvement in

The Playground Project

this project has also caused me to think about the role of philosphers of education in practical projects like this one.

Presumably when other professional colleagues, sociologists or psychologists of education, participate in practical projects in school they usually contribute either knowledge or practical professional skills, for instance, statistical know-how. In my own judgement I would say that I have contributed only minimally, in any formal sense, from my philosophical knowledge and skills. Is the reason for this that once again there has not been enough time? Given much more time for this project, would it have been appropriate to arrange a series of lectures and seminars on relevant topics in moral philosophy and philosophical aspects of moral education following the point where we had our inconclusive discussion on moral education? What would have been the aim of such a series? The achievement of consensus on an approach to moral education? But is this a sensible aim? At how many philosophy seminars, or even whole courses of lectures and seiminars, is consensus ever achieved? Is there then no role for philosophy of education? I am inclined to think that there is but that the aim should be not the chimera of the achievement of consensus but the illumination of the issues to further and deepen the process of reflection which is at the heart of the project. This would be to continue in a slightly more structured way a process which we have already begun. Concretely, it would mean a series of workshops/seminars with the agenda determined by the staff's desire to probe further philosophical issues currently arising from the implementation of the code.[3]

Finally, how should a project like this be evaluated? I see the process of evaluation as having two aspects. First, there is the evaluation of the effects of our code and more particularly the effects of the reflective process which has gone into it. But how to do this? As I have said, we intend asking the children during this school year to talk and write and draw about their experiences in the playground again, asking them if indeed it is now a nicer place to be; what difference, if any, the code makes; if the code should be changed in any way and so on. Are there any other ways of seeing, to put it crudely, what difference the project is making to the life of the school? Children and staff already say that the playground feels a nicer, calmer, more secure place. How far should we be content with such subjective impressions as a measure of the success of our efforts? Any school which, as a result of learning about the Laycock project, attempts to improve life in its playground will of course have an advantage here because it will be able to undertake 'before and after' observations and impressions of a rather more rigorous kind based on our experience.

There is also the evaluation of another aspect of this project, namely the democratic procedures we are evolving. Here, too, other schools can build on our experience and focus at the start on the questions which are just becoming salient for us. For instance, have we, both adults and children, acquired knowledge, skills and/or attitudes relevant to democratic practice which we did not have before? Are there some knowledge, skills, attitudes we still need? Insofar as we feel the project might have been more successful as an exercise in democratic whole-school policy-making, what has held it back? How far has it been impeded by factors to some degree under our control? How far by factors over which we have no control? We need to find ways of getting answers to these questions. We are now however a strong community prepared to face these challenges and to take our project further because we have seen what it is possible to do, even in a climate less than favourable to the extension of democratic practices.

Acknowledgement

I would like to thank all the staff, children and parents of Laycock school without whom there would not have been the project. I would also like to thank Peter Blatchford, John Bown, Graham Haydon, Hugh Lauder, Nita McCrossan, Christina Miles, Barbara Ryan and John White for helpful comments on earlier drafts of this paper.

Notes

1. The staff involved were myself and John White, Reader in Education, University of London Institute of Education.
2. I am indebted to Graham Haydon for pointing this out and putting a number of questions to me about the children's role in the project which identified certain important gaps in the account which I have tried to fill in this version.
3. The necessary role for philosophy of education here raises questions about the wisdom of present government policies in the UK which are causing philosophy of education rapidly to disappear from in-service teacher training. After the last philosopher working in education has retired or been redeployed, who will work with teachers to pursue the philosophical issues arising from their work?

References

WHITE, (1983) *Beyond Domination: An Essay in Political Philosophy of Education*, London: Routledge and Kegan Paul.

Appendix I

Draft for discussion on 7 April 1987

This is a *draft* intended eventually for all teachers, parents and children. Please come on Tuesday 7 April 1987 with any suggestions for improving it. Could you please think particularly about how we should develop the section on sanctions.

The Playground Project

Having Fun in the Playground

The story so far...

All of us at Laycock school have been thinking about the playground. It all began when somebody had the idea — nobody remembers who it was any more - that the funny thing about playgrounds is that they are supposed to be fun places but sometimes really horrible things happen in them. You rush out all set to enjoy yourself with your friends and then... you fall off the stage, somebody pulls your hair, a football hits you, and, worst of all, your so-called friends don't want to play with you any more.

So we had a question: How can we make our playground more of a fun place? Who might give us the answer to that question? Should we look in the library? (But even in the University library there were only two books on playgrounds. Both of them described the nice and nasty things that happened in playgrounds but they didn't tell you how you could have the nice things without the nasty ones). Then somebody had a really good idea. It's *our* playground we *all* use it — children, teachers, helpers, parents — and so *we all* put our heads together and really think about how to make it a nicer place. If we all think really hard who knows what we might come up with? Just imagine all that brainpower (660 brains) all those imaginations (660 imaginations) all concentrating on the question: how can everybody have more fun in our playground?

So we all started thinking really carefully about the playground. We remembered (yes, we used our memories too!) nice things that we like doing, like playing in the ghost train, playing football, playing with the tyres. We thought of nice things we are pleased are in the playground like the flowers and the log. We thought of things we like happening in the playground like people sharing sweets, people being happy and people playing with their friends. Then we thought of things we didn't like. There were several things: the toilets without locks and lights, fighting, being rude and cheeky and generally acting silly.

Let's take the toilets first. Perhaps our school council should write down for Mr Buttle all the things that are wrong with them and invite him to a meeting to talk about what can be done.

Now what about the fighting? Here we saw something very important. We can actually do something ourselves at once about that.

NOBODY IN OUR SCHOOL LIKES FIGHTING OR BULLYING. EVERYBODY THINKS THAT THE PLAYGROUND WOULD BE A HAPPIER PLACE IF THERE WAS NO FIGHTING.

So let's stop the fighting. It is not quite that easy of course. Because sometimes things happen that really make you cross and then... So we shall all have to help one another.

Last, but not least, there's a very funny problem. It's *football*. But why should football be a *problem*? Football is a really good game. It's great when

Patricia White

your team is winning, when you score a goal... That's true but the thing about football is that it takes up a lot of the playground and not absolutely everybody wants to play football all the time. So it's a bit hard if you don't want to play football and you can't do what you want because football is taking up all the space. What to do?

So we decided to have a special Laycock code.

THE LAYCOCK CODE

1. We will always be kind and considerate to everybody in the playground.
2. We will look after the playground and make sure that it is always a nice place to be in.
3. We will do our best to let everybody who wants to join in our games.
4. On Tuesdays and Thursdays each week we will not play football at all and share the space so that other games, such as volleyball, netball or handball, can also be played.
5. Even if we are in the midst of something very exciting or important, we will stop and listen to any instructions an adult may give us.

The Laycock code will make the playground a really FUN place to be. We will need to help each other to remember it and keep to it. (Perhaps we can use a finger for each of the 5 parts.) If anyone breaks the code...

Suggestions, please!

1. Time-out?
2. Name written in special book and then...?
3. Comment on report to parents about playground behaviour?
4. ?
5. ?

Appendix II

Draft for Comments

Having Fun in the Playground

The story so far...

All of us at Laycock school have been thinking about the playground. It all began when somebody had the idea — nobody remembers who it was any more — that the funny thing about playgrounds is that they are

The Playground Project

supposed to be fun places but sometimes really horrible things happen in them. You rush out all set to enjoy yourself with your friends and then . . . you fall off the stage, somebody pulls your hair, a football hits you, and, worst of all, your so called friends don't want to play with you any more.

So we had a question: How can we make our playground more of a fun place? Who might give us the answer to that question? Should we look in the library? (But even in the University library there were only two books on playgrounds. Both of them described the nice and nasty things that happened in playgrounds but they didn't tell you how you could have the nice things without the nasty ones). Then somebody had a really good idea. It's *our* playground we *all* use it — children, teachers, helpers, parents — and so *we all* put our heads together to really think about how to make it a nicer place; all concentrating on the question: how can everybody have more fun in our playground?

We thought carefully about the playground. We remembered nice things that we like doing, like playing in the ghost train, playing football, playing with the tyres. We thought of nice things we are pleased are in the playground like the flowers and the log. We thought of things we like happening in the playground like people sharing sweets, people being happy and people playing with their friends. Then we thought of things we didn't like. There were several things: the toilets without locks and lights, fighting, being rude and cheeky and generally acting silly.

Let's take the toilets first. They could be nicer places with lights, locks and soft toilet paper but we would all need to show that we can be more careful about how we use them.

Now what about the fighting? Here we saw something very important. We can actually do something ourselves at once about that.

NOBODY IN OUR SCHOOL LIKES FIGHTING OR BULLYING. EVERYBODY THINKS THAT THE PLAYGROUND WOULD BE A HAPPIER PLACE IF THERE WAS NO FIGHTING.

So we decided to have a special Laycock code.

The Laycock code will make the playground a really FUN place to be. We will need to help each other to remember it and keep to it.

Anyone who breaks the code, will have their name recorded in a special book. This book will be reviewed weekly, which may result in children missing playtimes or parents being invited into school for their comments etc, etc.

THE LAYCOCK CODE

1. We will always be kind and considerate to everybody in the playground.

2   We will look after the playground and make sure that it is always a nice place to be in.
3   We will share the playground space so the other games, besides football, can be played.
4   Even if we are in the midst of something very exciting or important, we will stop and listen to any instructions an adult may give us.

Chapter 11

Democratic Renewal in Schools: A Place for Socio-technical Change

Martin Lawn

Introduction

In broad terms, the 1980s have seen a massive effort by government to forge closer links between the education service and industry. A welter of diverse schemes and contracts have been encouraged which are steadily moving the public service of education into an educational market and into a statutory, centralized system of 'education/industry' links. Either way, educators are under some pressure to discuss the efficiency of a new structure of 'delivery' of educational product rather than, as was once the case, the nature of the 'product' itself. Truly, 'ends' are no longer seen as the prerogative of the educators and in this situation, they may turn to industrial discourses to find ways to operate the 'means' efficiently. The old self-referential discourse of an education service which had built some consensus over the nature of its problems had been side-stepped. This means that the language of reform and practice, once common to many sections of the service, no longer serves its purpose. Now it is becoming a language used only by the dissidents in the market-place, the traders use a new language in education, that of productivity, of division of labour, of supervision, of line management and so on (see for instance, DES, 1985).

The flaw in this effort to 'industrialize' the education service, a flaw that may be used to advantage, is evident in the crude model of innovation and dissemination that is being used. In the process of negotiation it is possible to recognize opportunities to extend educational practice under the flag of education/industry links or to selectively use an 'industrial' language to justify educational practices. There is no one 'industrial' language to justify educational practices. There is no one 'industrial model' waiting to be adopted by the education service though there may be in the minds of certain politicians. Although there is an obvious concern with accounting, efficiency, markets and sales, there is some disagreement on how best to manage. This disagreement is not so fundamental as to deny the need to manage but the debate about how to do it and the consequences for different kinds of work organization includes arguments not usually heard in educational circles. In some industrial management circles there is a concern with collegial working, individual creativity and the responsibility of the industry to society which would not be unfamiliar to educators addressing problems in the education service. There is, therefore some value in showing how these management ideas link with ideas in education. In particular, there is value in this new 'linkage' if teachers felt their good practices, in say self- or school-evaluation, could now be legitimated by reference to an industrial language and practice, especially a successful one. This paper tries to make those links; it does so however not in a naïve way, suggesting that apparently similar projects in industry, to education, can be taken at face value but they may be used to extend or deepen existing good practice in schools.

Implicit in this paper is a perspective on teachers which assumes that they are active in the daily construction of the education service and that heirarchical models of management or centralized prescriptions on their work do not take account of the way in which teachers see themselves in teaching. So, although the management of teachers is moving back in time, to testing, appraisal, market wages, etc., and back to a centralized control of education after a period of indirect rule and partnership, there are two reasons why the past cannot be recreated easily by the current policy documents from the DES and as part of Baker's Education Reform Bill.

Firstly, many teachers have been trained and apprenticed in a period of educational innovation (only later a period of recession and decline). It seems reasonable to assume that their ideologies of education, their life histories and projects and their visions, created in another period, will not so easily adopt new demands and roles and that they will search out weaknesses, contradictions and progressive possibilities of the new direction. Secondly, though managers of teachers may feel that teaching can be reduced to that of operating certain tested pedagogic skills and a laid-down national curriculum, this is a simplistic error. Public service and personal design seem to overlap in teaching and many teachers, in one degree or another, see teaching as involving a choice about educational values and practices and relate them to societal change or stasis. Professionalism, the means by which teachers may express this side of teaching, is not reducible to single propositions yet neither is it realistically contained in the new proposals for teachers.

In previous papers I have argued that teaching involves the social construction of skill, that is, while the employer might try and determine the pace, content, quality and price of teacher's work, teachers find ways to try to counter these pressures. They may do this through resistance to headteacher management (Lawn, 1987) or by trying to control particular changes in schools or by exerting associational power at local or national level. The social construction of skill in teaching, a move toward operational independence and autonomy (or rather freedom from irritating constraint),

Democratic Renewal in Schools

is a consequence of working, as employees, in a system they do not control and barely influence. It manifests itself as a resistance yet it may reflect not conservatism against change but a progressive ideology seeking to exist in schooling.

This paper is written on the assumption that policy initiatives and legislative control may seek to control the nature of teaching and even affect its quality and price but teachers themselves are not inactive. For example, the recent Technical and Vocational Education Initiative which was intended to push a sponsored version of vocational training back into secondary education, has been used by humanities and social science teachers to further their own educational, rather than vocational, projects. If we assume that teachers may use aspects of policy for purposes other than those intended, then what possibilities exist within the industry/education linkage movement (which includes many current initiatives, in teacher training, teacher secondments to industry, mini-enterprises in schools, etc.) for the development of progressive education? One possibility is that the ideas of management and industry could be used to counter the selective ideas contained within the government's policy documents. Instead of ignoring or resisting these arguments on line management, on teaching contracts, leadership and supervisory roles, productivity and so on, teachers should use contrasting arguments but from the same source. Arguments about the best way to manage, to develop innovations or to train personnel are present in industry as they are in education. If the educational debates and experience of the last fifteen to twenty years is to be washed aside, as it has been, then finding parallel experiences and arguments in industry and training and using them to continue the education agenda would be wise.

This chapter suggests one possible example of a practice seen as 'good practice' in industry, itself part of a movement variously described as 'democratic socio-technical theory' or the 'quality of working life movement', which is that of 'quality circles' (QCs). This practice is discussed at some length, both to explain the idea and also some of the pitfalls and divergencies it contains. However, while it may be useful to use the idea of QCs in education, as a rhetorical device anyway, it might be possible to see if it would fit the teachers' purposes, that is, to increase their area of discretionary decision-making or professional autonomy at a time when it is being reduced.

Quality of Working Life

Industry, and to a degree, education have been influenced since the 1920s by a management model sometimes described as technocratic or systems-based. The emphasis within this model was on maximizing the quantitative production of the person and the machine, and that this was possible through a cost-efficiency testing of worker productivity and a concern for rationalizing worker input by means of close job specification, detailed supervision and regular inspection. Hierarchy, bureaucracy, specialization and fragmentation (of the work process as a whole) are the hallmarks of this approach. It is a model designed to increase output and reduce production problems by controlling the worker.

This approach has been increasingly criticized by managers and not just by workers. Most damningly from the manager's viewpoint is the tendency of the model to be anti-efficient. Quantity may be increased but often the quality suffers for it is easier to define output levels or track speeds than it is to improve quality. Gyllenhammer, the Swedish President of Volvo Cars, has argued that this model creates disruption at work, as a highly-educated work force reacts to restrictions and lack of involvement in work by absenteeism, poor work and worker discontent. In Volvo's case they had a choice, either to change the way work was organized or to employ less well-educated migrant workers and retain the system. Volvo went for increased worker autonomy, worker initiatives and collegial collaboration with each other. The system they constructed was based on the idea of the public good (and their contribution to it) and the value of the individual, both of which were seen as compatible with 'good work' and a growing industry.

Socio-technical change tries to avoid regarding work problems as being solvable by technical solutions, either by machine changes or changes to the work process produced by outside experts. Wirth (1983), in a review of the aspects of socio-technical change, argues that it depends on the commitment and enthusiasm of 'whole human beings' and their capacities for learning:

> the reality of human work is 'socio', as well as technical, and 'socio' refers to the inner purposive, intentional, evaluative, idea-generating, communicative-collaborative aspects of human beings (p. 15).

The argument then is that paid labour has to match in involvement and the potential for initiatives and creativity, other aspects of life; it can no longer be differentiated according to its lack of involvement, its de-humanization or its demand for non-participation. Industrial arguments, like Gyllenhammer's and Wirth's, were created to help reorganization in the face of strong Japanese competition. At General Motors ways had to be found to raise the quality of the goods produced in the face of better quality Japanese goods and attention was focused on the involvement of the Japanese worker in the process of production, a factor often taken as the key factor in the quality of their goods. However, when Western agencies have promoted the idea of socio-technical change, under titles like the Quality of Working Life (QWL), they have emphasized responsibility and autonomy in work and their relation to productivity and change. Sometimes this is seen as just better management practice, a more rational development of human resources, but sometimes the argument goes far deeper. Wirth reviews industrial and educational conditions in parallel to ascertain whether: 'the values of our democratic traditions can be made operative in our economic institutions as a means of renewal' (Wirth, 1983, p. 23).

A socio-technical model of work entails empowered participation, the promotion of open or recurrent learning and defining productivity as inclusive of human creativity. Therefore, Wirth's argument, which is similar to the one in this chapter, is that teachers have much to learn from new developments in industry in their fight against bureaucratic management systems, with their concomitant need to test and appraise. The quality of working life movement uses ideas which range from commonsense ideas about involvement at work to those about democratic renewal. Each of these arguments can be useful in schools to combat limited definitions of teaching and education. The base-line here is about creativity, involvement and autonomy at work as a means to increase the quality of work, as a process and as a commodity.

The reorganization of the work-place which this approach entails, obviously varies from place to place, but it would usually involve the following: group autonomy, teamwork skills training, new supervisory roles, and the redesigning of work and work settings. The fragmentation of work and the mental/manual divide are both ended by work groups, as at Volvo's Kalmar plant, where the separate functions of planning, acting and evaluating are integrated in the group, to the extent of group involvement in policy decisions. Wirth (1983) describes the move as:

> towards concepts of production which would capitalise on distinctive human capacities to see the relation of parts to the whole, to communicate effectively in generating hypotheses to cope with problems, and to tap personal, subjective dimensions of learning... (p. 216).

A QWL Unit at McGill University, described in a bulletin of the Canadian Quality of Working Life Forum, worked with three primary schools on redesigning their work and communications systems. The point of the process was to:

> enable teachers to take a fresh look at their own school and work to change it in ways that fit their students and their own needs (QWL Forum, 1981, p. 3)

One of the initiators of QWL practice at General Motors, Howard Carlson, is quoted by Wirth as saying that he could not advise other companies as:

> ... the principle that we use is to start with the organisation, where it is, not where we are. So I would want them to start where they are, understanding their own organisation and listening to it and becoming aware of it... you first need to become aware that you're hurting... (Wirth, 1983, p. 57).

Of course, the observations of McGill or General Motors do not sound unfamiliar by comparison with developments in the post-curriculum innovation period in British schools. School-accountability projects, teacher-as-researcher networks, schools as self-evaluating institutions and so on have been a response by teachers, under their own or external pressure, to improve schooling. As Rodger and Richardson (1984) point out the, 'collegial organisation of self-evaluating schools', is very much like the idea of quality circles in industry, 'both notions have as their basis the intention to improve the quality of the product'. In a review of the effective schooling literature, Reid *et al.* (1987) describe effective schools as possessing 'a culture that values reflection'; teachers-as-researchers as those 'who had extended their role to include critical reflection upon their craft with the aim of improving it', and the problem-solving school (an effective school) as 'liberating itself from a bureaucratic and control-oriented educational system'. This idea of a shift in the culture of the school, in the culture of work in the school, has much in common with the ideas of socio-technical theory. They are, in the main, educational ideas generated within a democratic pluralism, and with support from many teachers, which owe no allegiance to any industrial reorganization movement. These ideas are often a rejection of a technical/bureaucratic approach to educational management, yet the English curriculum innovation movement, of which they are a part, is threatened by a future dominated by a technical, centralized control. The good practice of building change from within the organization or by a teacher wishing to improve his/her practice are therefore being threatened by the introduction of crude measures of technical efficiency. The parallel rise in schools/industry links, vocationalism and an economic awareness curriculum appear to have been constructed, in part, to prevent teachers from self-evaluatory curriculum and organizational changes, given their association with the humanities and child-centred education. However, if teachers substitute their traditional school and child-centred discourse for the technical language associated with QWL or a socio-technical change perspective, they may be able to maintain far more control over the direction of change. The recourse to a reforming past will cut no ice with policy-makers intent on removing those very reforms. The possibility that those reforms or the processes which gave rise to them can be continued by recourse to the dominant language and modelling of industry in education will be further explored in the next section on quality circles.

Quality Circles

Quality circles are small groups of employees, usually eight to twelve in number, who meet regularly (perhaps once a week) to solve problems and search for improvements in their work. Although it is often thought of as a Japanese idea, and they exist in large numbers in Japan, quality circles were the invention of an American called Deming who was a management consultant. He advised Japanese firms on the use of QCs in the 1950s and 1960s. In a comprehensive guide to QCs, Mohr and Mohr (1983) describe them as:

> ... set up with the guidance of a steering committee and/or coordinator drawn from, or including representatives from upper management. A facilitator from outside the department monitors meetings, which are guided by a leader who is typically a first-time supervisor of the work group from which members are drawn (p. 23).

They meet to identify and solve problems in their work area, they might have had training in problem-solving, and they present recommendations for action to management. It has been suggested that circles need to be able to carry out an evaluation of their work to help prevent them from blaming other sections for failures (Dale and Lees, 1986, p. 6). Successful implementation of QCs depends on a number of factors, the most important being a long-term commitment from managers at every level. Other factors include the voluntary nature of their membership, the support of the unions, a clear definition of role and purpose in the organization, training for circle members, and whether leadership should arise naturally from the group or whether it should be designated by management. QCs can be a natural part of an existing participation management approach, they can even exist in less favourable environments but on their own they cannot transform an authoritarian bureaucratic organization.

They can be defined in a number of ways, each congruent with the premises of the socio-technical approach. They can be seen as a form of participative management, as a development of human resources and as a problem-solving forum (Mohr and Mohr, 1983, p. 28). Phrases which occur in describing QCs are also consonant with the new management approaches, for instance, 'building trust' between workers and management or 'fostering creativity' or 'developing group identity and teamwork' which are used by outside consultants and employees alike. Because of the difficulty in monitoring this approach over time, as with any innovation, and the fact that the failure of a QC is likely to lead to reaction against them, it is vital to have the continuing support of management. So a participative management style is needed to create and support the Circles, because they cannot solve problems within a management structure which is non-supportive.

QCs: The Case of Jaguar Cars

An example of QCs in British industry are those at Jaguar Cars. When Jaguar was pulled back from the brink of closure one of the ways in which it did this was through the institution of Circles. They might have borrowed the idea from Japan but they have stressed the different cultural milieu which exists in the car industry. In their Training Programme, familiar aspects of QCs are stressed: philosophy, the need to take responsibility for quality and not blame others, the necessity to have unequivocal support from top management and so on. The Circles are part of a radical change in the way Jaguar Cars are managed. These changes included a much more open philosophy. The state of the company was fully explained to employees, as well as the need for changes and employees were encouraged to 'demand answers to questions not excuses'. Prior to the introduction of QCs a similar situation appears to have existed at Jaguar as in the strongly unionized firm described in an ASTMs (1981) case study; the employees had a high regard for the company, organized collectively and they had skills which led to job satisfaction, but they had a low regard for management. In Jaguar's case, management were seen by employees as having to play second fiddle to the broader concerns of the parent group, British Leyland. In this situation, Quality Circles, with the support of the unions (in the main), were seen by employees as a chance to influence management in the revival of the company; this was particularly important for the skilled workers who saw their knowledge and capability being put to full use again. Moreover, at Jaguar, a reliance on employees in the Circles has developed; they are all treated equally within the group, they select their own problems and they refuse to allow themselves to be by-passed. Management cannot walk away from the problems raised by the Circles and Circle members can ask for further information or explanations from individual managers. If this is not forthcoming, complaints can be made to higher management levels; at Level One (the plant managers' meeting) they can attend to see how circle problems are being met.

However, though the Quality Circle idea may be associated with the progressive management practice of socio-technical theory, there are critics (ASTMS Report, 1987) who see it as a way of winning the confidence and trust of employees without altering the workers' subordinate position on decision-making and as a way of changing work practices without conflict. Collective bargaining may then be by-passed using groups of people (in QCs) who are not elected by the staff, and whose deliberations might produce staff cuts; or it may be superseded by the new 'trust' in the plant which broadens out from discussions about quality. Solidarity among workers is replaced by solidarity within companies; not against management but against other companies. This is a possibility in a weakly-organized firm but in a well-organized one, with a closed-shop agreement, the QCs may have beneficial results from the union viewpoint:

> ... local union officials argued that circles improved information flows, increasing employees' knowledge of management behaviour and action (ASTMS, 1987, p. 19).

This is, however, within a context where positive feelings about the company and job satisfaction led to a demand for increased participation in decision-making because of a distrust of management. In other words, a well-organized union membership wanted more say in the running of a company, something the QCs provided.

Greater resistance to QCs within a firm may, however, come from middle management, not just unions. Their right to manage is placed in question and their ability to 'solve' problems may be threatened. Quality controllers, supervisors and middle managers might feel their roles are being undermined. The ASTMS Report quotes the case of Wedgewood, the pottery firm, where operatives and first-line management worked together in QCs — the main problem was:

> among junior managers whose inadequacies were being shown up by supervisors and others who were obviously better at leading and commanding respect amongst the rest of the work force (p. 22).

In such cases managers may actually try to thwart or take control of QCs so as to reduce the risk to themselves.

In the British and American experience, it appears to be the effect of Japanese imports, particularly on home markets, and the necessity to compete more effectively, especially on quality, in a period of crisis which has encourged new methods of management. Quality circles seem to have arrived, at least initially, on the basis of their reputation as Japan's secret weapon. They are unlikely to succeed without real changes in management approaches and particularly without a radical revision of the drift toward more and more hierarchical and authoritarian management. Although QCs are bound within the ideas of socio-technical change, the reason for their adoption is less likely to be a concern for democratic renewal than industrial survival. There are important lessons here for the development of QCs in schools.

QCs: The Case of Education

Albert Shankar (1985), in an editorial in the American Teacher, discussed the paradox of the Japanese use of an American idea (QCs), and the conservatism of American industry and American education management still tightening up line management, supervision and testing at work. While education was lining up behind industry, industry was desperately searching for alternative methods in the bid to stave off collapse under Japanese imports! However, one or two examples of QCs in American education have been published. Kogut (1983), a professor of chemistry at Penn State University, developed a QC to improve classroom education. Groups of undergraduates were introduced to the idea of a QC and then acted as course review groups. They gave feedback as to the quality of the instruction, made suggestions to improve the course (in terms of transmission), discussed classroom situations, and how to act as catalysts in larger group discussions. His QCs led to the conclusion that tutors could improve the 'product' continually and could build a rapport with the group more easily. It is not clear what benefits the students obtained; certainly they could offer 'constructive criticism', a role denied them elsewhere perhaps. Kogut has suggested that, in addition, students could get to know a tutor better and it heightened their 'sense of responsibility' to the coursework. Yet they did not discuss course content and a suggestion to introduce a subject in the news was dismissed as needing 'additional time' and 'more advanced students'. This is not to say it was not a useful course review group nor that the 'product' was not improved, yet it seems a limited operational version of QCs.

There are a number of questions crucial to an understanding of the potential QCs which were not raised, such as 'wouldn't an external facilitator have helped the group decide what its problem was'? 'How did the group work in its second or third year, given the processes it was still learning in the first undergraduate year'? 'What benefits did students feel they had gained from the course, given the extra time they had put into it?' 'How did other faculties deal with the fact of QC operations in their vicinity'? 'Could a similar QC deal with the issue of course content, often loosely prescribed in a validated syullabus, or is this a management prerogative'

Bonner (1981), a director of special education in a Michigan public school system, discussed the institution of QCs into the special education sector. The middle management QC includes supervisors and directors, the 'staff level' QC includes classroom teachers, support and itinerant professionals, aides and members of the clerical staff (their meetings occur in school time and are voluntary). Bonner does not tell the reader what the QCs actually worked on, only that without clear interaction guidelines there was a danger the QCs could waste energy on 'arguing among themselves, struggling for power or griping aimlessly'. However, Bonner makes two points about their 'success' — 'trained members', that is, those who completed a programme in using 'selected modes of affective communication and behavioural strategies for motivation' have fewer problems with the QC process than others and seem more receptive to the video feedback on their group dynamics. Bonner also argues that these staff circles may improve upward and lateral communication, creating alternatives to adversarial relationships between staff and management.

It has been argued that management approaches reflect not just company cultures but national cultures. Bonner, in an earlier article on applying Japanese management strategies to education, argued that using another culture's approaches can help to illuminate one's own taken-for-granted management practices. But Bonner's own use of QCs in education seems to lack a rationale, and hence appears faddish or, worse, to have simply been used as a device to manipulate teachers. The QCs are grafted onto a fairly centralized bureaucracy which, arguably, simply wants a

Democratic Renewal in Schools

better information flow and 'non-adversarial' relations with its staff.

The difficulty with introducing QCs in the British context is that schools are in a state of flux, moving towards a new management system applied to a changed work process. Compliance or resistance are two choices which are likely to be made by teachers; continuing to evaluate themselves and their school may no longer be something they would choose to do in a system of reduced autonomy and increased supervision. In this context, QCs may just be seen as a device for gaining the teachers' compliance. However, teachers need to be alive to the fact that QCs could flourish in a more limited context. For example, one possibility is the development of team-based work in middle and secondary schools in an integrated project, such as health education. Another would be in the primary school, where a form of shared responsibility, such as a reading policy or a new science scheme, could involve the specialist coordinator and several class teachers. Of course, unless this was now to be seen as part of 'directed time' (given the new management of teachers' time), it would be most unlikely to flourish.

Conclusion

Socio-technical change, including QCs, are a response to a technical efficiency school of management which dominated management practice in industry for several decades. The response appears to be generated by the relative lack of usefulness in defining productivity and the nature of work in terms of quantity rather than quality. Indeed, in terms of industry as a whole, the individuals concerned in it and even the society in which it is contained, the technical efficiency school can be seen as promoting an inefficient definition of production and work; inefficient in terms of economic competition and in terms of human relations.

In Britain, though not in the USA, hierarchical line management, supervisory posts and productivity grading are new to the management of the educational system. That is not to say there was no educational management nor that it lacked supervision or concern for return on investment, but that education was not organized into a formal, hierarchical management of a narrowly regulated 'means of production'. For all its caveats about parents or school-financial autonomy and so forth, conservative policies for the last four years culminating in the proposed Education Act of 1988 have aimed at creating the sort of technical efficiency-based system foreshadowed in Better Schools (DES, 1985). There the emphasis is clear:

> The Government welcomes the sustained efforts made by many parties to negotiate a new salary structure for primary and secondary teachers, embracing new pay scales, a new contractual definition of teachers' duties and responsibilities and the

introduction of systematic performance appraisal, designed to bring about a better relationship between pay, responsibilities and performance, especially teaching performance in the classroom (pp. 55–56).

This will be seen by many teachers as an invitation to lower their involvement in education, reducing their creativity and commitment. It is based on crude ideas of performance and productivity, it combines incentives to improve with pay awards and it will reduce professionalism to a job description. This proposal owes as great deal to a model of management which is being eroded in industry, eroded often through necessity because it is inefficient and stultifies creativity. Indeed some descriptions of professionalism in respect of initiatives, responsibility, autonomy and involvement seem to have much in common with the behaviour, or the potential to generate the behaviour, associated with the ideas of socio-technical theorizing. Certainly the trend toward teamwork, collaboration, shared management responsibilities, self-assessment and school review, which have all been developing in a system of shared responsibility in education (or at least one with a degree of autonomy or 'loose coupling'), have a lot in common with the quality of working life movement in industry.

The characteristics of school self-evaluation and QCs are congruent with each other, based as they are on encouragement, exercising judgement, grounded problem-solving, agreed action and so forth. The impetus for school-evaluation might have been a move towards greater accountability but its success lay within the system of shared responsibility, autonomy and partnership in the system. The move toward school-evaluation suffered badly during the teachers' pay campaign and it would be unlikely to re-emerge in its past form in schoolwork defined by contracts, appraisal and merit pay.

Of course there were also other forms of teacher-based research that probably will survive the permafrost of Thatcherism; they were based on teacher support groups for coping with and changing work. In the absence of a management concern for teacher initiatives and autonomy, Boston (USA) teachers developed a project based on a large number of interviews with teachers over time in which the effect of the technical/cost-efficiency style of management on teachers was explored. In particular the rise of teacher stress or burnout was placed firmly within the authoritarian, institutional structure of schools and the effect this had on teachers. Competition between teachers, isolation and lack of confidence seem to be almost encouraged by a system designed to increase their productivity and management control over them. It is this removal from aspects of decision-making which a study of Alberta (Canada) teachers shows is the reason why they volunteer to get involved with province-wide curriculum committees (Young, 1985, p. 406). In a less authoritarian model of management, teachers are still isolated from management decisions (in the curriculum area, say) and from each other; they need a situation where their isolation

Democratic Renewal in Schools

and relative powerlessness is overcome and where their self-esteem and professional development is encouraged (Young, 1985, p. 409). Again, there are parallels here between education and industry. For example, the situation described at Jaguar, where the employees distrusted management and felt their skills were being under-used, is similar to that, described above, for teachers. Just as QCs helped Jaguar employees, so they could help teachers. This could only be possible, however, if a participative management approach were in operation.

There are two main arguments in this chapter centering on the sociotechnical theorizing associated with the Quality of Working Life Movement and in turn with QCs. Firstly, can the use of the terminology and practices of this approach be used by teachers and others to continue the home-grown school-evaluation and a school-networked version of teacher-as-researcher given that the current legislation and the thinking it represents would be likely to eliminate these voluntaristic, school-grounded, fairly autonomous processes? In which case a psychological advantage is retained by teachers able to justify their good practice by reference to elements of alternative industrial models. However, whether teachers will want to adopt such a discourse to retain some form of professional autonomy remains to be seen. Certainly some teachers will be spending their energies on mobilizing resistance to new managerial practices while others may be aiming to be line-managers.

The second argument is that there are real advantages to teachers in working within QCs although it is acknowledged that meaningful QCs will be difficult to work given the new emphasis on non-participative management in schools. The advantages are fairly clear. It is a way of using craft skills, intellect and tacit knowledge about schoolwork which will benefit the individual and the school collective. Problems would be chosen by the teachers, any training given in problem-solving or group work would be beneficial in the wider school context and isolation would be eased. Management could be called to account and, particularly in primary schools, it would help to retain the rudimentary collegiality it presently contains. Of course, while it would not be liberated from the wider bureaucratic frame of schoolwork, as defined nationally, it would be trying to nurture reflection and action compatible with the aims of school self-evaluation. A new national emphasis on 'good schools', given its emphasis on teacher accountability and managerial control will only inhibit the opportunities which QCs could provide to improve standards and productivity. Moreover, given the political context of the new managerialism in education, QCs are likely to be seen by teachers as a means of managerial control rather than emancipation.

The major problem faced by teachers in continuing to find ways to democratize schooling (responsibly and professionally) is that, paradoxically, the experience of renewing schools is taking place in the narrow and shrinking forum of 'education'. If it had taken place within a wider framework of, say, the Quality of Work Movement or a theoretical shift as in the socio-technical perspective, then it would have allies elsewhere already in place. The resistance of teachers to being seen as employees, which in itself is admirable and has an honourable past, means that a limited definition of 'education' is being imposed upon them. The very language and ideology they use to describe themselves and their work has been nullified and they have no natural allies elsewhere because of the 'special' way they described their public service. The arguments of this chapter may appear to be avoiding the central educational issue, which is the redirection of education toward a democratic and comprehensive education system. However, if we make the realistic assumption that the language and techniques of industrial management are going to be present in education for some time to come then QCs provide an opportunity for teachers to use the progressive elements of human relations theorizing and a beneficial practice in other kinds of work as a weapon in their continuing fight for autonomy, quality and service.

References

ASTMS Report(1987) *Quality Circles*, London: ASTMS.
BONNER, J. S. (1981) 'Applying Japanese management strategies to educational management', *Michigan School Board Journal*, December.
BONNER, J. S. (1982) 'Japanese quality circles — Can they work in education?' *Phi Delta Kappan*, June.
DALE, B. G. and LEES, J. (1986) *Quality Circle Programme Development — Some Key Issues*, Sheffield: MSC.
DEPARTMENT OF EDUCATION AND SCIENCE (1985) *Better Schools*, London: HMSO.
KNIGHTS, D. *et al.* (1985) (Eds), *Job Redesign — Critical Perspectives on the Labour Process*, Aldershot: Gower.
KOGUT, L. S. (1983) 'Quality circles — A Japanese management technique for the classroom', *Improved College and University Teaching*, 32, 3.
LAWN, M. (1987) 'Skill in schoolwork: Work relations in the primary school', in Ozga, J. (Ed.) *Schoolwork: Aproaches to the Labour Process in Teaching*, Milton Keynes: Open University Press.
MOHR, W. C. and MOHR, H. (1983) *Quality Circles — Changing Images of People at Work*, Wokingham: Addison-Wesley.
QUALITY OF WORKING LIFE FORUM (1983) *Canadian Scene*, 6, 1.
REID, K., HOPKINS, D. and HOLLY, P. (1987) *Towards the Effective School*, Oxford: Blackwell.
ROBSON, M. (1983) *Introduction to Quality Cirlces: A Practical Guide*, Aldershot: Gower.
RODGER, I. A. and RICHARDSON, J. A. S. (1984) 'The organizational implications of school self-evaluation', *School Organization*, 4, 4.
SHANKAR, A. (1985) 'How should we manage schools?', *The American Teacher*, 69, 8.
WIRTH, A. (1983) *Productive Work in Industry and Schools: Becoming Persons Again*, New York: University Press of America.
YOUNG, J. H. (1985) 'Participation in curriculum development: An inquiry into the responses of teachers', *Curriculum Record*, 15, 4.

Chapter 12

Youth Training and the Manpower Services Commission: Possibilities and Limitations[1]

Shane J. Blackman

Introduction

Today, amongst Black youth, a popular phrase is 'Know your history, know your destiny'. This chapter examines the socio-historical context of working-class youth training. The account is not meant to be exhaustive but to highlight certain issues and factors which have been neglected. I shall examine the present YTS to see what are the potentialities and limitations of the new training initiative. It is looked at in a historical perspective in order to discover continuities between current and older forms of youth training and work.

The data are drawn from the Girls and Occupational Choice labour market study (University of London, Institute of Education, Sociological Research Unit).[2] This research included formal and informal interviews with TVEI unit coordinators, TVEI evaluators, careers officers and advisers, senior and junior careers teachers in school, classroom teachers, trade unionists, YTS specialists, evaluators, programme managers and policy makers at the MSC (London), YTS managing agents, employers and training board advisers.

One of the aims of the study was to gain information on how state employees, such as members of the careers' service and MSC officials, interpret and assess their role in the guidance of young people. The concern was not to examine directly the consumers of the YTS but to investigate how state employees experience and understand the limitations and possibilities of the new training initiative in the labour market.

The 'New Pauper Apprentices'?

A missing factor in some accounts in the literature on new vocationalism is the socio-historical context of working-class youth training, although I am not suggesting that today's YTS trainees suffer the same fate of exploitation, as did the Nineteenth Century 'pauper apprentices'. But we do need to address the question, in what way is the present purchase of substantial youth labour power from the MSC by employers different from the Nineteenth Century practice of the wholesale purchase by employers of youth labour from the workhouse?

In the mid-1930s it was apparent that the provisions of youth training and work preparation was a problem for school and industry. In his survey of labour conditions, Gollan states (1937):

> The need for a new system of trade and commercial training and apprenticeship is now widely recognised. So far no new scheme in its entirety has been elaborated. Any new scheme should, we feel, combine workshop and the schools training and cover all youth in industry until the age of 20 (p. 303–4).

More recently a senior MSC official has stated:

> It has taken so long to change, it's taken political pressures because of the number of young people and unemployed to actually set up a system which probably should have been set up 40 years ago. It has got a political ill taste about it that you are managing unemployment figures.

Both quotations show that the relationship between industry and youth training is a problem largely inherited from the past.[3] To go back further, from the Sixteenth Century onwards employers made successful attempts to break the regulation governing the apprenticeship laws, to dismantle the old forms of youth training via the journeymen, to make training dependent on employers (Bailey, 1978; Dickens, 1838; Yeo and Yeo, 1981). In the Seventeenth Century 'pauper apprentices' began to be used as substitutes for proper apprentices organized under the journeyman system. The rather unhappy 'pauper apprentices' were in fact children of poverty from the workhouses, for whom the manufacturers were actually paid a premium by the workhouse master. Hammond *et al.* (1917) state:

> Instances (and not very few) have occurred in our tribunals, of wretches who have murdered their pauper apprentices, that they might get fresh premiums with new apprentices (p. 155).

At this time the formation of worker combinations or unions was illegal; as a consequence the skilled craftsmen were hit by the pauper labour in terms of wages and conditions of work. The craftsmen tried to invoke the appreticeship laws, with little success, to prevent masters from dismantling the old apprenticeship system. A result of the skilled worker being deprived of independence and status was that the independent craftsmen's young trainee became the subject of straight exploitation. Instead of an apprenticeship system to provide training it became a system of ill-treatment and direct abuse. Gollan (1937, p. 13) maintains 'In trade after trade the employers successfully petitioned Parliament for the repeal of the apprenticeship restrictions'.

The powerful guilds of the journeymen were able for a time to protect young trainees but the continued growth in manufacturers' strength and power to change the hierarchical order of skilled workers meant that the position of journeymen and apprentices steadily declined. (Thompson, 1963). In the Eighteenth and Nineteenth Century there were considerable parliamentary battles between employers and skilled workers but gradually, a new type of apprenticeship was built up through the strength of unions and skilled workers. During the second half of the Nineteenth Century, on the basis of the new machine skills the craft trade unions were able to create a new system of apprenticeship. Throughout this period one factor remains constant : the employers' spurious 'right' to exploit youth as the least protected and most gullible section of society (Garside, 1977; Rees and Rees, 1982).

Youth Training Scheme: A Good Practice?

The approach in this section is to question which aspects of training make up good or bad YTS practice. Here, I wish to concentrate upon data which reveal YTS in a good light. I shall look at how YTS has broken down a number of barriers in terms of qualifications and sexual discrimination. A Senior Careers Officer suggests:

> The Government says the Careers Service should promote the Youth Training Scheme, but we do not promote it without question, we look at the opportunities and put them over to the kids in what we think is the proper professional light.

There was consensus of opinion amongst both careers officers and teachers that the 'idea that everybody knows what a bad YTS placement looks like is a bit of an oversimplification'. Most careers teachers in school who knew of bad YTS schemes in terms of health and safety, job substitution, cheap labour, sexual harrassment, poor wages or bad working conditions, were clear that they would not on any grounds send a female or male youth to such a place. But as a consequence, this meant the careers teachers' knowledge of such work experience was limited; information on bad schemes arrived indirectly from secondary sources. A careers teacher explains 'So many times, the kids do not come to us first to see the range of YTS, they end up just going straight to it and they are unprepared'. To determine what is good or bad YTS practice is not as easy as perhaps first understood in terms of receiving an adequate training. Careers advisers, officers and teachers maintained that it was not possible to assess good or bad YTS provision in terms of a simple division such as public sector or private sector, even unionized or non-unionized. Unfortunately, owing to the structure and content of YTS, the conclusion reached was that each scheme had to be evaluated in terms of its own merit. The format of YTS allowed extensive differences to occur within and between schemes, with the result that an interpretation of YTS as a whole was practically an impossible exercise (Keep, 1986).

A Senior Careers Officer describes one example of how difficult it is to assess good from bad YTS practice:

> There are some organizations which have set themselves up to train and make a profit out of YTS. You think they will be exploiting the kids. There is a local one it has been working on such tight margins and he is doing it from the best of motives. He is trying to make a living out of it as well, and he knows about kids. He gets £27.50 for the kids and he only gives the kids £20 but negotiates with every placement that he puts his kid on that for the whole time the youngster is on the scheme that the placement will top up the kids wages by £15. So it is not simple cut and dried.

This comment could be used to support arguments for or against the YTS as either indirectly exploiting youth or showing that certain individuals can balance social responsibility with self interest.

In discussion with state employees who offer guidance to young people, the most quoted example of YTS as a good practice was in terms of breaking down barriers of qualifications to enter certain occupations. A careers officer points out:

> Something like the stock exchange scheme, I know it's small or the Bank of England scheme which unfortunately may stop under the 2 year YTS, or quite a few others like that have been really brilliant in breaking down some of those qualification barriers.
>
> With the Prudential in the past they had vacancies started at five O levels normally they recruit from the Home Counties people who come in and get a nice career. The Pru-YTS were one of the better ones, they did not set their normal entrance exam for unqualified kids, they just accepted the first 25, which was what YTS was all about, took them on, realised during the year they could do those jobs just as well as any kids who had five O levels, and they have been taking loads more.

It is well documented that employers continue to overestimate the requirement of qualifications (Ashton and McGuire, 1983; Griffin, 1985; Roberts *et al*, 1987; Watts, 1983) in an attempt to select the right type of employee who is manageable, not too bright and will not later leave. The careers officer was far from uncritical of the YTS provision; problems still exist where trainees are working alongside others who do similar work but the difference in income between trainees and non-trainees is considerable. In addition, he states 'You must not exaggerate the breakdown of qualification barriers concerning YTS but we do know of specific cases where it has happened and it has been very useful'.

Exclusion from training opportunities is an everyday experience for young women, often perpetuated by male working-class trade unions (and employers) who have not encouraged either the attitude of fellow employees to change or women to enter the trade. Has YTS made any difference in overcoming the established and entrenched barriers of sexual discrimination concerning females gaining training provisions? Cockburn (1987) has gathered a considerable amount of data which reveals that little has changed as a consequence of YTS. However, there are a number of small positive statements from the careers service. An ILEA Careers Liaison Officer notes there are some changes, but not major ones:

> The girls are opting for maybe the choice areas, particularly I am thinking of the 'taster courses'. I think one of the advantages of YTS is that they know that if they don't like a particular thing they can change it. Having said that, we still get the girls going into the office areas and boys doing building or engineering.

A more thorough assessment in relation to girls entering the 'masculine trades' is made by a Senior Careers Officer:

> YTS has helped to a very limited extent with sexual equality because CITB are a bit off — you could hardly call them progressive but I think it has probably been easier for a girl to get on CITB/YTS first year than it would have been for a girl to get into a building company's direct apprenticeship scheme. Once they are in they can prove they can do it, it is a whole new ball game to try to convince somebody interviewing them that they can do it. So what girls there are in the building industry, a lot of that is down to YTS as well as the pressure from interested groups.

YTS cannot be understood as a vehicle for challenging sexual or ethnic discrimination. A number of writers (Beechey, 1986; Marsh, 1986; Wickham, 1985), have pointed out that the structure and power of the MSC intervention into the sexually divided labour market does not directly encourage equality or have the potential to challenge structured and ascribed forms of discrimination. Some possible consequences of YTS being market-led, geared to the needs of the private employer are that firstly, the private sector does not have a good record concerning the dismantling of sexist practices or inequality in the workplace. Secondly, young women who do not have role models of women in the local environment doing other than traditional feminine jobs are not likely to challenge sexual discrimination for fear of not conforming to a sex stereotype. Finally, the history of training has been of a male structured opportunity, the new structures of training have an equal opportunities policy but are not invested with programmes of action, so traditional sexist practices remain.[4]

Most careers teachers in school felt that there was a clear division between working-class pupils who were aiming at the YTS, and middle-class pupils who were aiming at the sixth form. This division became apparent to me when interviewing third- and fourth-year pupils, prior to and after option choice. Parents were playing a dominant role in the guidance of their children, whether or not it was understood by the pupil as being a direct or indirect influence: pupils would voice parental judgements and opinions on their future.

In general, the range and variety of employment assessed by working-class pupils (in the context of YTS) were particularly stereotypical and narrow especially for girls, whilst the middle-class and the more able working-class pupils looked down on YTS as remedial. The able pupils could also maintain a variation of options both within and between different potential occupational sectors (Blackman, 1987a; Chisholm and Holland, 1986; Varlaam, 1984).

'Unhappy Bedfellows': Employers, Careers Service and the Manpower Services Commission

In this section I shall examine how both the Manpower Services Commission officials and the Careers Service staff assess their relations with employers. In the literature on new vocationalism, employers are seen in general as co-operating with the MSC to secure the domination of market forces. Here, I begin by challenging the assumptions that the MSC and employers have mutual interests and rarely experience conflict. The data reveals that the MSC is an institution where employees use bureaucratic resources as a barrier — a defence mechanism — for two inter-related reasons. First, against government intervention which controls and shapes the MSC in order to give an appearance of flexible and immediate resolution of youth labour market problems. Second, in response to criticism from outside agencies. The problem for the MSC in this situation is that it must maintain and promote its self-image in the face of potential loss of credibility due to rapid changes in training schemes. In the light of these bureaucratic responses there are a number of questions we need to ask: Is it possible to understand the role of the MSC as a supporter of the government ideology of free market forces? Is the MSC working directly for the private employers in the interest of private profit?

Can it be assumed that the MSC is simply an ideological state apparatus possessing substantial powers of persuasion? A policy-maker at the MSC assesses the relationship between private employers, the MSC and training the workforce:

My dealings with employers has been at the level of encouraging them to re-train their own staff and to look to the future and to look to the skills of their workforce to remain competitive. I find it very frustrating because that message does not seem to get very far. It works with large companies that are fairly training orientated anyway but with many small companies they are not interested in training, all they are interested in is keeping their business and ticking over for as long as they can, they are not really interested in investing in the work force. It's very difficult to get employers interested in training unless you're giving them money to pay for it all. They are not willing to invest any of their own resources in it.

The comment above requires little explanation, except that the MSC and employers do not appear to share a cosy relationship as both Left- and Right-wing advocates have claimed. The MSC is having concrete difficulties encouraging employers to train the workforce. The tradition of an *ad hoc* system of youth training continues; on the one hand the MSC asserts that it has little control over employers, and on the other hand, the employers are unwilling to finance training for their workforce unless the State pays. A South London MSC local programme manager asserts:

It is a real problem, we are trying, through YTS and through an adult training awareness campaign to persuade employers that training is an investment. But we are not succeeding in getting that message across.

The importance of the comments by different MSC officials above is that they describe how the MSC has difficult relations with employers.

MSC officials are suggesting that they have a relationship which is 'toothless' in influencing employers. In this sense the MSC is only a broker of schemes, ideology and financial allocation, without regulatory power or intervening strategies in relation to employers. Emphasis upon the MSC as a dominant institution becomes uncertain in the light of its limited power which operates at the level of advisory or consultative functions.

The MSC new training initiative is dependent upon the good will of employers. There exists a baffling range of schemes which change their name frequently, confusing not only the trainee but also the trainer.[5] These shifting features cannot be understood as a precise stategy to maintain social class inequalities by employers, MSC and the government. This may be an outcome of such disarray but it is not the organized aim. If this confusion represents any single aim it appears to be an inconsistent attempt to stabilize a tradition of *ad hoc* training. An important flaw in the analysis of YTS is that researchers appear to have taken an ahistorical look at employment; the long years of youth exploitation by employers prior to the inception of YTS seem to be forgotten.

The apprenticeship system has been dramatically romanticized to the extent that not a stain of criticism sullies it in comparison with the predefined deficiency of YTS. The apprenticeship system, in fact was only a golden age of training for the white upper working classes or the labour aristocracy, to the exclusion of most working-class males, females and ethnic groupings. Current preoccupation with exposing YTS inadequacies in a historical vacuum serves to direct attention away from the continuities of inadequate training provison throughout the century. A senior officer at the MSC reflects:

> When I started in the Department of Employment there were only around 250,000 unemployed in the country, and you still got BAD EMPLOYERS, didn't pay enough, wanted people to work exorbitant hours. With YTS we have tried to shake out the bad work experience providers.

Good or bad employers are not solely the result of YTS. The MSC officer acknowledges that bad employers exist whether past or present. He does not argue that YTS will stop bad employers but suggests that YTS has tried to reduce some of the chances a trainee faces of being exploited. A Senior Careers Officer states:

> Most of the firms in this area, would have less than satisfactory working conditions, are small clothing firms, occasionally the middling ones between 10 and 20 staff, are crowded and there is flammable material stored on wood — very dangerous and the factory inspectorate don't even know about half the firms. But I would be very surprised if it wasn't true that YTS placements and schemes are monitored much more heavily than most of the firms where young people go and work.

Obviously, YTS requires more monitoring for improvement; however, the central issue here is whether the site of youth labour is work or training; both or either have the potential to be equally exploitative. A careers teacher in the East End of London states 'YTSs are merely cosmetic measures. Employment itself is more exploitative than many Youth Training Schemes'.

An MSC official dealing with Non-Advanced Further Education (NAFE) asserted that 'Employers have this very narrow view of what teachers do in school and they have a lot of prejudices which they repeat ad nauseam to people like me'. In addition, he notes, 'Small employers, what they really expect is for the schools, the education system to provide people who have skills that they can build upon fairly easily and quickly and I hear them criticize all the time, the education system for not producing that'. There exists a subtle contradiction here: the MSC officials reveal that employers want employees they can manage and shape; school is criticized for low standards but at the same time employers demand high qualifications. MSC and Careers Service employees argue that not only did employers frequently overstate the job but the advertisement was not the 'plain truth'.

For Michels (1911) large organizations, for example the MSC, have a necessity to create bureaucracy to run an efficient service, resulting in the establishment of a specialized division of labour. The hierarchical administrative duties are incomprehensible without a coherent knowledge of, and training in, the bureaucratic logic. Can this organizational criticism apply to the MSC? There is considerable evidence to support the claim that the bureaucratic structure is worked for those who run it rather than for the people it is supposed to serve. However, it could be argued that MSC bureaucracy is a defence mechanism against political policy which continually changes, i.e., scheme alteration. The MSC is without direct accountability but has to jump to the Government's political or ideological demands. The bureaucratic structure of the MSC may create confusion for outside agencies but may meet internal aims in terms of stability for MSC employees.

The skill of MSC officers appeared to reside in efficiency of bureaucratic duties rather than dealing with the content of the training provision. An official from the Greater London Training Board (GLTB) specified this problem with a concrete example, the Occupational Training Families (OTF), which are:

> supposed to relate to local labour markets. I worked in Leicestershire, the OTF there didn't relate to the local labour market at all. They were training kids in things like graphics and there was no graphics industry in the area at all.

This experience of lack of familiarity with conceptions of training and local labour market by the MSC is borne out by a Senior Careers Officer who suggests:

> They come into it as raw civil servants that would be sorting documents up in Whitehall or passing DHSS claims so you can't expect them to know anything in particular, they are not selected because they are interested in doing that sort of thing, they just get bunged into it. They are pretty well informed eventually; I don't think they know particularly much about local labour markets, or employers in an area, they are not that good at knowing if a scheme is proposed, whether there will be loads of jobs going or no jobs at all — they tend to come to us for that sort of information. It would be better if they knew a bit more but they can be officious.

In attempts to answer these problems of bureaucratic malfunctioning the two most frequent explanations by members of the MSC staff in London were 'It needs coordinating much more' and 'It does get a bit confusing working in the department at times'. A YTS research project director reinforces this interpretation of the MSC as a bureaucratic body:

> Our experience has been that our local MSC office is only interested in the functions and the numbers.

> They are there for things like meeting minimum criteria, maintenance of occupancy levels, sufficient training places in each occupational family, in a given geographical area.

The functioning of an organization is not only determined by its internal structure and goals but by how it has to manage its public image. The working relations within the MSC in London were described by a number of employees as not providing a great deal of work satisfaction. All staff regarded themselves as under 'great strain' especially in relation to the way in which the government just announces a change and requires them to move to the command while at the same time trying to manage some form of credibility with critical and interested outside organizations such as the TUC and the local councils. MSC officials differed with respect to how much they thought that the work was political. Some staff were in fact politically naive, 'We do seem to be as a department politically prominent for some reason'. Other staff dissociated themselves from the official MSC line by stating something like, 'I'm going to state a personal opinion now' or 'This is a political issue I think'. One MSC official understands that a major criticism of the organization is the haphazard nature of changing scheme titles:

> It is difficult enough for us to understand, it's taken me several months to understand what Pick-up is, NAFE, TVEI, CPVE and REPLAN, RESTART and how they match in with the schemes we have and people outside must think we are lunatics. We have just closed down the training opportunites scheme, which had been running for 10 years. A lot of people know about TOPS. It's now the job training scheme, it's basically the same scheme but nobody knows it's the same scheme and people who want to go on it are totally confused. It's been brought within the adult training strategy, now called Job Training Scheme, but with minor differences it is the same as TOPS. Changing the name all the time just totally confused people.

The MSC is facing fundamental problems but there is no public and little internal acknowledgement of these difficulties. The staff are having 'serious worries' about coping with change, implementing change, ironing out problems, maintaining the level of information and coping with change again.

More of the Same: ad hoc Youth Training

In Britain there has been a tradition of *ad hoc* youth training which requires that training for the job should be the responsibility of the employer, and should be conducted on the job, namely in the workplace. Williams' (1957;

1963) points to the inability of Britain when compared with other European countries to produce an adequate supply of skilled labour. However, there were some good practices during the 1950s and 1960s, such as training schemes within the iron and steel industry and the National Coal Board. In some cases the effort of an individual firm was backed up by the industry as a whole, for example the National Foundry Craft Centre established in 1948 to encourage the development of training in the industry (Carter, 1966). Also in some areas of the country local authorities played an important role in setting up different types of training schemes (Cotgrove, 1958).

The Carr Report (Ministry of Labour, 1958) was concerned with issues of training an adequate quantity and quality of young workers for industry. The introduction of new technology was seen by some trade unions as undermining not merely the apprenticeship system but displacing the older skilled workers. (There had been a pretence by both employers and trade unions, where the 'so called' apprentices, had been trained to 'non-existent' skills). On one side, employers gained an opportunity for cheap labour, with only small demand for training. On the other side, trade unions sought to protect older skilled workers through limiting apprentices by insistence on rigid quotas: older workers feared that young skilled workers would swamp and disadvantage the trade (see Leipmann, 1960).

The Industrial Training Act of 1964 provided an entirely new initiative by shifting the responsibility for training from employers to the state. The act set up twenty-four Industrial Training Boards (ITBs) with the responsibility for training in each industry and for financing certain industries' training needs through a levy on the firms within the industry.

There was rapid dissatisfaction with the ITBs since they failed to increase the proportion of young people entering apprenticeships. Roberts (1984) argues:

> Before long the training boards were under attack for burdening industry with their own costly bureaucracies and a flood of paperwork. Firms complained that training was being tailored to meet bureaucratic criteria rather than genuine needs (p. 33).

The result of the criticism of the ITBs (Farley, 1985, p. 76) was the Employment and Training Act of 1973 which set out to change the structure of youth training through the creation in 1974 of the Manpower Services Commission. Finn (1987) has documented considerable evidence of MSC's inadequacies, largely with reference to the YTS, in the provision of low standards of training, lack of integration with real work processes, poor forms of training assessment and virtually no accountability of the sites in which trainees receive work experience. Some of Finn's claims are supported by Youthaid (1985) which:

> Found that half of the schemes that subcontracted some or all of their work experience gave no information at all to the AMB on the individual employers or where it would take place. Only a third of

> Mode A schemes gave a complete list of the work experience providers. This overall picture for the four boards was seen at its worst in the case of the Southeast board whose officials said that it was too difficult to supply information on work experience providers and no list was provided for any scheme (p. 288).

This criticism of MSC policy and practice parallels previous accusations made against the bureaucratic behaviour of the ITBs for inadequate progress, assessment and coordination of training in occupations and skills. Many of the schemes which subcontracted their work experience were approved by the Boards without information about the locations at which the trainee would be working. Work experience is the major element of YTS, and the most vital part of it; as a consequence the fundamental lack of accountability reinforces problems associated with the previous schemes such as YOP which the MSC themselves regarded as inadequate (Holt, 1987). Finn (1985) argues:

> In Cheshire, sixteen managing agents who were given approval to provide 2,500 places are subcontracting the trainee's work experience to over 1,300 placements; all but a few dozen of which are the same small shops and businesses that were involved in YOP (p.122).

Finn is not alone in arriving at this description of inadequate provision on YTS — see also Cockburn, 1987; Lee *et al*, 1987; Raffe, 1983; Roberts, *et al*, 1987.

A Critical Assessment of Training

In an attempt to move beyond the descriptive pluralist models and interpretations of the labour market, Marxist sociologists and educationalists have occasionally exhibited an uncritical acceptance of Marxist social theory in two of its inputs, first the deskilling thesis (see Jordan, 1986) and second, the thesis of social control through ideology. An important issue concerning the debate on the concept of skill in new vocationalism is the duplication of terms which describe and interpret how skill operates or is operated. Ainley (1986) asserts the urgent necessity of having precise definitions for the purpose of clarity and movement within the discussion. Here I point to some problems with reference to how the two terms 'deskill' and 'reskill' have been applied. I introduce the term 'taskill' to refer only to how the MSC defines and operates skill, in isolation from its knowledge base and practice of the social relations of work.

Finn (1987) has two approaches to the analysis of MSC training initiatives, first, a direct list of MSC inefficiencies and inadequacies in the provision of youth training, which is not linked to theory, and second, a Marxist determinist perspective which assumes the MSC programmes are designed to deskill working-class craftspersons and to ideologically restructure the working class to reinforce their subordinate class location. Finn has a tendency to present a functionalist analysis of his material from within a Marxist framework, without clear theoretical elaboration of the way in which data supports or confirms his original thesis. Jordan (1986) makes a constructive criticism of Finn's approach, in suggesting that he misses a crucial part, that of 'Reskilling within MSC training schemes, and the new social divisions this creates within the working classes, the quasi-employed on training schemes and the unemployed' (p. 6).

Finn accepts the Braverman thesis (1974) of deskilling and reinforces this with the argument that a major role of the MSC is to ideologically remodel the working class through new forms of curriculum and assessment. It is perhaps Finn's concentration upon the effects of deskilling within the skilled trades which overshadows his more underdeveloped themes of remaking working-class youth within the sites of pre- and post-16 schooling of labour.

If we accept that one of the ideological functions of the MSC is to restratify working-class youth, we can ask: how is this achieved? Currently, trades are being forced to deskill owing to new technology, but reskilling appears to be based not upon a trade, but in a strategy of individual task performance (Cohen, 1984). As a result, workers' autonomy is no longer invested in a trade skill but in the individual person. Consequently, an individual's independence resides in adaptability, and the capacity to demonstrate a task or 'so called' transferable skill. Nevertheless, despite the new definition of skill, there also exists a new hierarchy of skill within YTS which reflects a previous hierarchical order within and between working-class trade skills. An important question, then, is whether transferability actually counts as being reskilled, because the trainee is still positioned within a hierarchy from skilled to unskilled. In my view, the MSC training initiatives serve to recreate previous status divisions within the working class based upon the hierarchy of skill possession. To reskill is an inaccurate assessment, trainees receive a 'taskilled' strategy which restratifies the working class, as the previous old skill divisions decay.

Jordan's (1986) emphasis is on analyzing the learning or internalizing processes through which profiling creates new forms of control based upon behaviourist models of pedagogy. He undertakes an internal assessment of how these new learning procedures create the potential to reskill trainees so that they actively take part in their own surveillance to reinforce their location in the class structure. Jordan presents an interpretation of the way in which trainees receive 'new schooling' as a substitute form of work ethic; the discipline of profiling prepares the trainees to accept inequalities and hierarchy within the labour market.[6]

In contrast, Lee et al. (1987) are not primarily concerned with educational processes but internal hierarchies and barriers inside the labour market. They specify the supply and demand of a substitute youth labour market created by YTS — what they call the surrogate labour market. Inside the substitute labour market there are internal labour markets, in which quasi-apprenticeships largely accessible through family contacts in large or more well established firms exist. YTS increases existing inequalities of gender and ethnic discrimination based upon socially ascribed values and a hierarchy of training. The trainees at the top skill levels are part of the remains of the old apprenticeships whilst trainees lower down the occupational hierarchy receive not a skill but an application of transferability and its ideology. Lee *et al.* argue that YTS has created a substitute labour market alongside the real labour market on the basis of managing agents subcontracting out work experience to private employers (Finn, 1987; GLTB, 1983, 1985; Youthaid, 1985).

Unfortunately, in the Marxist analysis of new vocationalism not only is there a tendency towards an ahistorical interpretation but also the apprenticeship system is romanticized as a jewel in the crown of the past golden days of trade union strength. However, the historical record shows skilled craft apprenticeships supported a training hierarchy, with the labour aristocracy at the top and the reserve army of labour at the bottom. Working-class strength arose from the solidarity and struggles of skilled craft workers, which preserved a status hierarchy within the working class to the disadvantage of working-class women, ethnic groupings, youth and adult males lower down the skill hierarchy. The training initiatives of YTS continues, if not reinforces, the acceptance of training hierarchies within the labour market. This takes place through new forms of assessment in YTS such as profiling, and legitimates restrictions of access within occupational sectors of the labour market by placing the trainee on a non-movable scale of skill acquisition. Trainees at the lower end receive the ideology of transferability, that is, a set of procedures which are *task* oriented not skill based.[7]

Alternatives: Inside and Outside the MSC Framework

What is or is not an alternative, is itself a highly controversial matter of debate in the field of new vocationalism. Radical critics of the MSC assert that to consider an alternative to the MSC framework gives it credit which it does not deserve. Here the focus will be upon first, alternative policy within the MSC framework and second, upon those schemes operating outside the MSC framework. At the outset it is important to be aware that the concept of an alternative presents problems and so does the division between what is inside or outside the MSC guidelines, (Eversley, 1986). A trade unionist states:

> There are examples of practices within the existing system which are considerably better than the achievement of the MSC but by the MSC rules. There are examples of operating under different rules

but using the MSC framework and delivering something different. There are examples of alternative institutions, of alternative content of training schemes and of different ways of actually creating jobs instead of not creating jobs, which is the MSC's principal problem.

This statement is complex and reveals a number of issues; first, that the site of training allows immense variability — there exists little coherence or uniformity of scheme training owing to the structural nature of the YTS; second, at a concrete level there are different inputs of skill training, resulting in different outputs of trained individuals; finally, these differences within and between training at the level of course structure, content, institutional site and employment opportunities allows the framing of skills in YTS to be arbitrary and isolated from 'real work' (Bernstein, 1977). Such a policy serves to retain youth training within an ambiguous position of being employer-led without sustained and rigorous State public accountability (Mace, 1986; Marsden, 1986). To place the onus of training on employers puts pressure on employers, who have historically served up a variable quality of skill provision.

Working within the guidelines of the MSC a GLTB training adviser describes two examples of YTS with an alternative structure and content, to challenge the male domination within manual skilled trades,
First scheme:

> We tried to create an all girl painting and decorating training group, and a construction trade area of work and we managed to recruit the girls, and that was not easy; when the girls had done their training we had a lot of problems with them getting jobs. Those girls had no difficulties; they knew what they wanted they'd had a year's good quality training on YTS. At the end of the day, I think 3 of them got what they wanted and they've been taken on and they are black girls too.

Second scheme:

> We have got a policy now that women do not go into construction industry placements as part of their training on their own. We found it in our first year apprenticeship in transport, the girls cannot survive in the garages, it is just too bloody difficult for an individual young woman or an older women even, to survive. We did monitoring on that, and the only ones that survived were in one particular garage where there was an older motherly woman in the office who took the girls under her wing, supported them through it. She would say, 'It's all right, you stick at it, you are going to be a mechanic'.

Both schemes point to various problems in establishing equal opportunities of training within the segregated sexual division of the world of work. In the first scheme, the GLTB demand YTS to be single sex with reference to particular courses due to problems of female/male contact within a traditionally defined male skill. The training provision had difficulties at a number of different levels; first, prior to the scheme the strength of sexual stereotypes influences the girls to turn away from such employment, also the girls carry the stereotype throughout the course in how they identify themselves and are identified by others; second, the site of training had to be one where the work environment was not directly sexist for the girls to learn the skills, with respect to behaviour from fellow trainees, older workers and supervisors.

For the girls on the second scheme there exist difficulties of a similar type as with the first scheme, but the adviser gives emphasis to the more hostile environment which women encounter at such workplaces. Ironically, she states how the sexual stereotype of the 'older motherly' woman protected the young women from discrimination by men.

Both schemes within the YTS framework have been adopted by the GLTB but show limitations in how far it is possible to advocate an alternative strategy inside the MSC guidelines where there are not women supervisors or female workplaces (Fawcett Society, 1985).

In terms of an alternative framework for training outside MSC guidelines a GLTB training adviser argues:

> There's quite an active programme that goes on at Denham in terms of work that they do, not just training, that's another level but in terms of discussion and in terms of the way the trainees participate in the scheme. Trainees are active at all levels, we have a big trade union education push — this is another area of our critique of YTS that it has not got. There is trade union education, the kids belong to a trade union, they have got shop stewards, so they have channels. They have got a structure through the participatory democratic way a scheme is run, they go to staff meetings, they have all their own council meetings, and with the manager. When you have all that you can deal with issues like sexism and racism.

Education and participation within training are the two major facets of the GLTB's alternative YTS. Discussion of the nature of work processes, with a high level of general education in combination with responsibility to other workers, ensures that individuals have equality of rights and an opportunity to take part in raising the standards of training. The priority is to educate the trainees and provide them with competence to continually develop their abilities and skill. The over-concentration of specific vocational relevance within TVEI and YTS is at the expense of broad and general education, and this narrow vocational preparation does not coincide with the changing demands of the labour market (Carter, 1966; Brown and Ashton, 1987).

Schooling and training for the young trainee needs to challenge social assumptions about the rigid allocation of work roles and how sexual stereotypes affect occupational choice (Lees, 1986). In discussion with different members of the careers service there was sustained criticism that the MSC intervention into the labour market does not have the capacity to change existing inequalities. The GLC and other Metropolitan Boroughs were good examples of an alternative strategy for training upon the institution of local authorities, trade unions and industrial training boards, both inside and outside the MSC framework. However, with the abolition of such bodies any formation of alternative strategies of training on this basis is strictly ruled out. A trade union educational researcher notes the important features of an alternative training strategy to the MSC:

> You could have a decentralized programme not based on market forces and that in practice means not working through the MSC in any major sense but through local elected authorities and through institutions that are accountable to people who work in the industries in which the trainees are placed for work experience. Crudely, Industrial Training Boards, local authorities and local education authorities. Broadly speaking I think it is possible to have a much more sector-based system in which trade unions, employers and young people play a much bigger role in shaping the kind of training. In order to make it work you do need a more regional level at which industries integrate.

In this sector I have tried to pull together some of the disparate suggestions concerning alternative training strategies held by educational practitioners. Out of them, four central issues arise which would help to structure an alternative democratic-socialist programme: first, the necessity for equal opportunities to acquire and practice skills; second, youth trainees require education in the nature of work processes and to be able to participate in decisions and discussions which affect training; third, increased accountability and monitoring of training needs to be combined with local co-ordination between commerce, industry, employers, schools, teachers, unions, colleges and the careers service; and fourth, state intervention into the labour market requires long term aims and adaptability with financial assistance to support both private and public employers upon a sustained and planned, rather than *ad hoc* basis for training.

Conclusion

If we date the factory system as beginning in 1775 (Cunningham, 1903) when mills and factories in towns began to employ child and youth labour rather than imported apprentices, we see that it was over forty years before any effective controls were imposed on the wholesale cruelty of employers. It is now over forty years since Gollan (1937) elaborated 'A charter of youth rights — an immediate programme' (p. 299–307). Both the factory reforms of the early Nineteenth Century and the youth training reforms of the Twentieth Century show that, whether the site is employment or training, working-class youth have been exploited. The history of youth training in Britain has been marked by class struggle and aspirations of social mobility. Employers petitioned Parliament to alter the terms of apprenticeships to suit their short-term aim of profit, trade unions and employers have fought through the courts the battle for power and control over access to youth training. The importance of examining the distant and recent past is that it shows us that the problems of training and the demand for more training are not new (Abbott, 1933; Banks, 1955; Board of Education, 1931; Leipman, 1960). The continuity of training in Britain has been marked by its discontinuity and inadequate provisions. We have tried to explain this in terms of the power enshrined in a private employer *ad hoc* tradition, which has been able to resist or accommodate change.

A central issue of youth training is its political nature; in the 1980s it has been tied to the private sector of industry by a government ideologically committed to a market-led training scheme. The Right argue that market forces can determine the scale, type and range of training. Where is the evidence for such an argument? It is questionable whether the strategy of allowing the free play of market forces will be constructive or even encourage long-term investment in British industry and commerce. Moreover, because market forces are unpredictable they undermine planning of the future and subject to extreme hardship those people without economic or cultural capital. The unrestrained operations of these forces is therefore incompatible with the concept of 'freedom' which is fundamental to democracy.

Historically, employers have been reluctant to train the workforce and this is, and has been, fatal to market-led strategies for training. At present, MSC officials are speaking out about the difficulties they face at ground level in getting employers in the private sector to invest in training. Further, we identified difficulties within the MSC such as scheme title alteration, erratic planning and inconsistent contact with relevant bodies, which are a result of the Government demands that the MSC should be flexible in adapting to its latest political ideology. The major factors in the development of the MSC have been the combination of political intervention at a policy level by central Government, voluntarism in terms of employer-led training and the limited consultative powers belonging to the MSC, all of which foster the preservation of the complex British class hierarchy of traditional *ad hoc* youth training.

At the level of practice, careers officers and teachers have taken an objective and critical look at YTS in terms of whether it still contains the bad kernel of YOP (Edwards, 1984), or whether there exists an opportunity to redress inequalities. In general, evidence shows that YTS continues to legitimate unequal access to training for skilled work (Cockburn, 1987; Finn, 1987; Youthaid, 1985). However, this does not mean that YTS is to be dismissed out of hand because there are some indications that under a state regulated system of training, the MSC could democratise the training process and more efficiently adjust training to the demand for skills. It is important not to dismiss too readily the partial success that the scheme has achieved, in terms of breaking down a variety of different barriers to jobs and training. The MSC has the possibility to build upon examples of alternative strategies, ideas and resources for training which were developed by the GLC and other Metropolitan Boroughs.

Acknowledgements

I would like to thank Professor Basil Bernstein, Lynne Chisholm, Dr Janet Holland, Norah Marks, Jean McNeil, Barbara Cook and my father who all played different but very valuable roles in the production of this paper.

Notes

1 This chapter is a considerably shortened and revised version of the paper, *Schooling Labour: Youth Training Schemes, Careers Service, Manpower Services Commission and the Labour Market*, Blackman, S.J. (1987b) Girls and Occupational Choice Project, Working Paper No. 11. Sociological Research Unit, Institute of Education.
2 The research team comprised Lynne Chisholm, Tuula Gordon, Janet Holland, Shane Blackman and Jean McNeil. The GAOC Research Project has been funded by the Economic and Social Research Council, with additional funding from ILEA, EOC and the Institute of Education Research Fund. The Girls and Occupational Choice Project has two interrelated strands: first, research into the processes through which girls of 11 to 16 come to decisions about their future work. Boys are included in the study but the focus is on the girls. Questionnaires and recurrent interviews are the major techniques employed in this aspect of the study; second, an action research component which involved working in close collaboration with teachers on the development of intervention strategies designed to break down sex-stereotyped occupational choice for both sexes, directed towards first- and third-year pupils in three London schools. This aspect of the study necessitated long periods of immersion in schools in interaction with teachers and pupils, developing, transmitting and evaluating tailor-made curriculum intervention programmes, and using a wide range of research techniques. These included pre- and post-intervention questionnaires for participants and control pupils, post-intervention interviews for participants, observation, participant observation, feedback from teachers involved in the programme and others in the school via formal and informal discussion and interview. The entire process has been documented in detail by the members of the research team. For further details see GAOC Working Paper Series, University of London Institute of Education, Sociological Research Unit.
   I also conducted numerous interviews with pupils in secondary school and some with ex-YTS trainees, and employed and unemployed youth.
3 As Banks (1955) pointed out in her analyses of the relation between education and production during the inter-war years, in neglecting technical courses and practical skills, education has only been reflecting industry's values.
4 Chisholm and Holland (1986).

5 I would also add that MSC officials are confused by the rapid nature of changing schemes. It had an important effect upon job satisfaction for state employees of the MSC.
6 Another significant contribution to the debate is by Raffe (1986) who develops Turner's (1961) typology of sponsored and contest mobility, to create a model of YTS sectors.
7 On the one hand transferable skills could be defined as a liberal, even radical opportunity for the skilled workers, providing them with skills, the instrumental use of which could increase worker autonomy. If it occurred at a high level of skill such transferability would be a valuable asset to a skilled worker. On the other hand, the weight of transferability at the lower end of skill, results merely in the creation of a pliable workforce without independence or autonomy and with little self respect.

References

ABBOTT, A. (1933) *Education for Industry and Commerce in England*, London: Routledge and Kegan Paul.
AINLEY, P. (1986) 'No future for the knack', *Times Higher Education Supplement*, 19.12.86.
ASHTON, D. and MAGUIRE, M.J. (1983) *The Vanishing Youth Labour Market*, London: Youthaid.
BAILEY, P. (1978) *Leisure and Class in Victorian England*, London: Routledge and Kegan Paul.
BANKS, O. (1955) *Parity and Prestige in English Secondary Schools*, London: Routledge and Kegan Paul.
BATES, I., CLARKE, J., COHEN, P., FINN, D., MOORE, R. and WILLIS, P. (1984) *Schooling for the Dole?* London: Macmillan.
BEECHEY, V. (1986) 'Women and employment in contemporary Britain', in BEECHEY, V. and WHITELEGG, E (Eds) *Women in Britain Today*, Milton Keynes: Open University Press.
BENN, C. and FAIRLEY, J. (1986) (Eds) *Challenging the MSC*, London: Pluto Press.
BERNSTEIN, B. (1977) 'Aspects of the relations between education and production', in *Class Codes and Control, Vol. 3*, (second edition), London: Routledge and Kegan Paul.
BLACKMAN, S.J. (1987a) 'The labour market in school : new vocationalism and issues of socially ascribed discrimination', in BROWN, P. and ASHTON, D. (Eds) *Education, Unemployment and Labour Markets*, Lewes: Falmer Press.
BLACKMAN, S.J. (1987b) *Schooling Labour: Youth Training Scheme, Careers Service, Manpower Services Commission and the Labour Market*. GAOC Working paper No. 11, University of London Institute of Education, Sociological Research Unit.
BOARD OF EDUCATION (1931) *Report of the Committees on Education for Engineering Industry*, London: HMSO.
BRAVERMAN, H. (1974) *Labour and Monopoly Capital*, New York: Monthly Review Press.
BRITISH YOUTH COUNCIL PROJECT, (1985) *YTS Trainee Participation Project*, Final Report, BYC.
BROWN, P. and ASHTON, D. (1987) (Eds) *Education, Unemployment and Labour Markets*, (1987) Lewes: Falmer Press.
CARR REPORT (1958) *Training for Skill*, Ministry of Labour, London: HMSO.
CARTER, M. (1966) *Into Work*, London: Penguin.
CHISHOLM, L. and HOLLAND, J. (1986) 'Girls and occupational choice: Anti-sexism in action in a curriculum development project', *British Journal of Sociology of Education*, 7, 4, pp. 353–65.

CLASH, The (1977) 'Career opportunities', on the *Clash*, London: CBS Records.
COCKBURN, C. (1987) *Two-Track Training*, London: Macmillan.
COHEN, P. (1984) 'Against the new vocationalism', in BATES, *et al. Schooling for the Dole?* London: Macmillan.
COTGROVE, S. (1958) *Technical Education and Social Change*, London: Allen and Unwin.
CUNNINGHAM, W. (1903) *The Growth of English Industry and Commerce*, Cambridge: University of Cambridge.
DALE, R. (1985) (Ed.) *Education, Training and Employment*, Oxford: Pergamon Press.
DEPARTMENT OF EDUCATION AND SCIENCE (1984) *The Youth Training Scheme in Further Education 1983—84. An HMI Survey*; London: HMSO.
DEPARTMENT OF EMPLOYMENT AND EDUCATION AND SCIENCE (1986) *Working Together — Education and Training*, cmnd. 9823, London: HMSO.
DICKENS, C. (1838) *Oliver Twist*, (Penguin Edition 1986).
EDWARDS, T. (1984) *The Youth Training Scheme: A new curriculum? Episode One*, Lewes: Falmer Press.
EVERSLEY, J. (1986) 'Trade union responses to the MSC', in BENN, C. and FAIRLEY, J. (Eds) *Challenging the MSC*, London: Pluto Press.
FARLEY, M. (1985) 'Trends and structural changes in English vocational education', in DALE, R. (Ed.) *Education, Training and Employment*, Oxford: Pergamon Press.
FAWCETT SOCIETY (1985) *The Class of 84: A Study of Girls on the First Year of the Youth Training Scheme*. London: National Joint Committee of Working Women's Organisations.
FINN, D. (1985) 'The Manpower Services Commission and the Youth Training Scheme: A permanent bridge to work?' in DALE, R. (Ed.) *Education, Training and Employment*, Oxford: Pergamon Press.
FINN, D. (1986) 'YTS: The jewel in the MSC's crown?' in BENN, C. and FAIRLEY, J. (Eds) *Challenging the MSC*, London: Pluto Press.
FINN, D. (1987) *Training Without Jobs*, London: Macmillan.
FLOUD, J. and HALSEY, A.H. (1961) 'English secondary schools and the supply of labour', in HALSEY, A.H., FLOUD, J. and ANDERSON, G.A. (Eds) *Education, Economy and Society*, New York: The Free Press.
GARSIDE, W.R. (1977) 'Juvenile unemployment and public policy between the wars', *Economic History Review*, 2nd Series, 30, 2, pp. 322–34.
GOLLAN, J. (1937) *Youth in British Industry*, London: Victor Gollanz, Camelot Press.
GLTB (1983) *The Youth Training Scheme in London*, London: GLC.
GLTB (1985) *Review of the New Training Initiative 1981–84*, London: GLC.
GRIFFIN, C. (1985) *Typical Girls?* London: Routledge and Kegan Paul.
HALSEY, A.H., FLOUD, J. and ANDERSON, C.A. (1961) (Eds) *Education, Economy and Society*, New York: The Free Press.
HAMMOND J.L. and HAMMOND, B. (1917) *The Town Labourer 1760–1832*, London: Longman, Green and Co.
HOLLAND, J. (1987) *Girls and Occupational Choice: In Search of Meaning*, GAOC Working Paper, No. 10, University of London Institute of Education, Sociological Research Unit.
HOLT, M. (1987) (Ed.) *Skills and Vocationalism: The Easy Answer*, Milton Keynes: Open University Press.
KEEP, E. (1986) 'Designing the stable door: A study of how the youth training scheme was planned'. *Warwick Papers in Industrial Relations*, School of Industrial and Business Studies, Industrial Relations Research Unit, University of Warwick, Coventry.
JORDAN, S. (1986) 'Profiling and Pedagogy in YTS: some problems in the Sociology of the New Vocationalism', *PSEC Working Paper, No 5*, University of London Institute of Education.

LEE, D. et al (1987) 'Youth Training, life chances and orientation to work', in BROWN P. and ASHTON, D. *Education, Unemployment and Labour Markets*, Lewes: Falmer Press.
LEES, S. (1986) *Losing Out*, London: Hutchinson.
LEIPMANN, K. (1960) *Apprenticeship: An Enquiry into its Adequacy Under Modern Conditions*, London: Routledge and Kegan Paul.
MACE, J. (1986) *Education, the Labour Market and Government Policy*, paper given at BEMAS National Seminar, University of Birmingham, Easter.
MARSDEN, D. (1986) *The End of Economic Man? Custom and Competition in Labour Markets*, Brighton: Wheatsheaf.
MARSH, S. (1986) 'Women and the MSC', in BENN, G. and FAIRLEY, J. (Eds) *Challenging the MSC*, London: Pluto Press.
MICHELS, R. (1911) *Political Parties*, New York: The Free Press.
MINISTRY OF LABOUR (1958) *Training for Skill* (The Carr Report), London: HMSO.
OFFE, C. (1985) *Disorganised Capitalism*, Cambridge: Polity Press.
RAFFE, D. (1983) 'Education and unemployment: Does YOP make a difference and will the Youth Training Scheme?' in GLEESON, D. (Ed.) *Youth Training and the Search for Work*, London: Routledge and Kegan Paul.
RAFFE, D. (1986) *The Context of the Youth Training Scheme: An Analysis of its Strategy and Development, CES Working Paper No. 8611*, Centre for Educational Sociology, University of Edinburgh.
REES, G. and REES, T. (1982) 'Juvenile unemployment and the state between the wars', in REES, T. and ATKINSON, P. (Eds) *Youth Unemployment and State Intervention*, London: Routledge and Kegan Paul.
REES, T. and ATKINSON, P. (1982) (Eds) *Youth Unemployment and State Intervention*, London: Routledge & Kegan Paul.
ROBERTS, K. (1984) *School Leavers and Their Prospects*, Milton Keynes: Open Universitiy Press.
ROBERTS, K., DENCH, S. and RICHARDSON, D. (1987) 'Youth rates of pay and employment', in BROWN, P. and ASHTON, D. (Eds) *Education, Unemployment and Labour Markets*, Lewes: Falmer Press.
ROSIE, A. (1986) *YTS and Ethnography*, paper given at St. Hilda's College, Oxford, September.
STYLE COUNCIL (1985) 'With everything to lose', on *Our Favourite Shop*, London: Polydor Records.
THOMPSON, E.P. (1963) *The Making of the English Working Class*, London: Penguin.
TURNER, R.H. (1961) 'Modes of social ascent through education : sponsored and contest mobility', in HALSEY, A.H., FLOUD, J. and ANDERSON, C.A. (Eds) *Education, Economy and Society*, New York: The Free Press.
VARLAAM, C. (1984) (Ed.) *Rethinking Transition*, Lewes: Falmer Press.
WALKER, D. (1982) 'Holland's finger in the dole dyke', *New Society*, 6 May, pp. 214-5.
WATTS, A.G. (1983) *Unemployment, Education and the Future of Work*, Milton Keynes: Open University Press.
WEST MIDLANDS YTS RESEARCH PROJECT (1984) *The Great Training Robbery : an Interim Report on the Role of Private Training Agencies within the YTS in Birmingham and Solihull*, West Midlands County Council: TURC.
WEST MIDLANDS YTS RESEARCH PROJECT (1985a) *The Great Training Robbery Continues*, West Midlands County Council: TURC.
WEST MIDLANDS YTS RESEARCH PROJECT (1985b) *Racial Discrimination and the Youth Training Scheme*, West Midlands County Council: TURC.
WICKHAM, A. (1985) 'Gender divisions, training and the state', in DALE, R. (Ed.) *Education, Training and Employment*, Oxford: Pergamon Press.
WILLIAMS, G. (1957) *Recruitment to Skilled Trades*, London: Routledge and Kegan Paul.

WILLIAMS, G. (1963) *Apprenticeship in Europe*, London: Chapman and Hall.
WILLIS, P. (1977) *Learning to Labour*, Farnborough: Saxon House.
YEO, E. and YEO, S. (1981) (Eds) *Popular Culture and Class Conflict 1590–1914: Explorations in the History of Labour and Leisure*, Brighton: Harvester Press.
YOUTHAID (1985) *The First Year: The Youth Training Scheme in London 1983–1984*, London: GLTB/GLC.

Notes on Contributors

Stephen J. Ball is lecturer in the Sociology of Education at the Centre for Educational Studies, King's College, London. He is author of *Beachside Comprehensive* (Cambridge University Press) and *The Micro-Politics of the School* (Methuen). He is also co-editor (with Staffan Larson) of *The Struggle for Democratic Education: Equality and Participation in Sweden* (Falmer Press). He has visited Sweden on several occasions to conduct research in schools and to interview policy-makers.

Shane Blackman is currently working as a part-time lecturer in the continuing Education Unit at Thames Polytechnic and is an honorary associate in the Department of Sociology of Education, Institute of Education, London. He has published a number of papers about the new vocationalism, the development of anti-sexist materials for use in schools, and has recently completed a Ph.D. concerned with ethnography and youth cultural styles.

Phil Brown served his craft apprenticeship with British Leyland before training to be a teacher and youth worker. He is currently a lecturer in Sociology at the University of Kent at Canterbury. His publications include *Schooling Ordinary Kids* (Tavistock, 1987) and is co-editor (with D. Ashton) of *Education, Unemployment and Labour Markets* (Falmer Press, 1987).

John Evans taught PE in a number of comprehensive schools and was involved in research on mixed-ability grouping and teaching. He is currently a lecturer in the Faculty of Educational Studies at Southampton University. He is author of *Teaching in Transition: The Challenge of Mixed Ability Grouping*, and editor of *Physical Education, Sport and Schooling: Studies in the Sociology of Physical Education* (Falmer Press).

Michael Fielding is a deputy head at Stantonbury Campus, Milton Keynes. He has taught in comprehensive schools for the past eighteen years and has published mainly in the field of applied philosophy. His forthcoming publications focus on the relation between the personal and the political and on an emancipatory, school-based staff development.

Notes on Contributors

Alison Kelly took a degree in physics and spent two years teaching maths and science in a secondary school. She then switched into educational research, and now lectures in sociology at the University of Manchester. Most of her research has been on gender differences in education, particularly in physical science. She has written extensively on this topic, and has recently edited a book, *Science for Girls?*

Colin Lacey started his teaching career as a science teacher in a London comprehensive school. After returning to Manchester University to read for a Ph.D. in sociology he has specialized on research into education. He is now a Professor at the University of Sussex. His publications include *Hightown Grammar* and *The Socialisation of Teachers*.

Hugh Lauder is senior lecturer in Education at the University of Canterbury, Christchurch, New Zealand. He taught in London schools for six years before moving to New Zealand in 1978. He has published many papers and is currently completing a book with David Hughes entitled *Social Inequality and School Outcomes: An Empirical Study*.

Martin Lawn is a senior lecturer in Teaching Studies at Westhill College, Birmingham. He has written a number of papers and among his recent publications is the edited volume (with G. Grace) *Teachers: The Culture and Politics of Work* (Falmer Press, 1987).

Robert Moore taught social education in London schools and is currently a lecturer in the sociology of education at Homerton College, Cambridge. He has written several papers and is a co-author of *Schooling for the Dole*.

Patricia White is senior lecturer in Philosophy of Education and current chairperson of the Philosophy of Education Department at the Institute of Education, University of London. She is the author of *Beyond Domination: An Essay in the Political Philosophy of Education* (RKP, 1983) and many papers, particularly on social and political issues with philosophy of education.

AnnMarie Wolpe is a lecturer in Sociology at Middlesex Polytechnic. She has written many papers, and edited a number of volumes concerning education and feminist issues. She is also the author of *Within School Walls: The Role of Discipline, Sexuality and the Curriculum* (Routledge, forthcoming).

Index

Abbott, A. 238
Abercrombie, N. 6
academic curriculum 35
accountability
  and MSC 237
  and YTS 232
ad hoc youth training 230–2, 238
adult education, in Sweden 84
Ahier, J. 4, 20
alienation, of working-class pupils, 12
Althusser, L. 7, 105
America, and quality circles 215
The American Teacher, 215
anti-racist science 160–1
Apple, M. ix, 30, 33, 184
applied science 151
apprenticeship system 222–3, 227–8, 238
Armstrong, P. 28
Arnman, G. 83
Arnot, M. ix, 134
Aronowitz, S. 7, 8, 20, 107–8, 127
ascription 1, 2
Ashford, D. 25–6
Ashton, D. 224
assessment, of training 232–4
Assisted Places Scheme 2
Association for Science Education (ASE) 150, 159, 163, 164–5, 166
ASTMS Report 214–5
atomization 65
attainment, and class 118
automony, and QWL xii, 211
awareness sessions 198, 200

Bacon, A. 132
'badges of ability' 13
Bailey, C. 126
Bailey, P. 222
Baker, Kenneth viii, 2
Ball, S.J. 31, 75–90, 178
Banks, O. 238
Barker, B. 58
Baron, S. 20
Barreu, G.V. *et al.* 183

Barrett, M. 140
Beechey, V. 225
Bell, B. 170
Bengtsson, J. 78
Bentley, D. 156, 157, 158
Bernbaum, G. 5
Berner, B. 28
Bernstein, B. 4, 33, 103, 113, 117, 125, 181, 234
Better Schools (DES) 217
Bevan, A. 183
Blackman, S.J. xiii, 14, 221–43
Black Papers 76, 109
Board of Education 238
Bonner, J.S. 216
Bonniface, M. 179
Boudon, R. 104, 113, 117, 125
Bourdieu, P. 31, 33, 113, 116–7, 118, 125, 137
Bowers, C. 38
Bowles, S. 5, 7, 28, 32–3, 75, 100, 105, 106, 109
Bown, J. 193, 194, 195, 197
Brandt, G. *et al.* 159, 161
Braverman, H. 233
Brown, Phillip x, 1–19, 35, 36
bureaucracy, and MSC 226–7
burnout, in teachers 218

Callaghan, James viii, 178
Canadian Quality of Working Life Forum 211
careers service, and MSC 226–37
Carlson, H. 21
Carnoy, M. 30, 32, 85, 105, 109
Carrington, B. 187
Carr Report (Ministry of Labour) 231
Carter, M. 231, 236
Castles, S. 136, 144
celebration 61, 63, 67–8, 87
Central Council for Physical Recreation 177
Challenge for the Comprehensive School, The (Hargreaves) 54, 56–7

246

Index

Chamberlain, P.L. 159
Chaplin, I. 132
Chemistry from Issues (Harding) 156–7
child care 135
Children's Learning in Science Project 170
Chisholm, L. 226
citizenship education 22, 24–5, 36, 78, 80–1
city technology colleges 34, 96
Clarke, J. 182
class
   and attainment 118
   and science 152–5
   and YTS 226
   inequality 111–3
classless society 27
Cobb, J. 13
Cockburn, C. 168, 225, 232, 238
Cohen, P. 233
Cohen, S. 8
Cole, G.D.H. 52, 61
collective intelligence xi, 14, 94
collectivism, and domestic work 140
Collins, R. 105
Comber, L.C. 80
commodification 114
common culture 102
common core curriculum 150, 168–9
communitarian paradigm 57, 58, 59, 60, 61, 64–8
compensatory education 5
competition xii, 96, 186
comprehensive reform 26
comprehensive schools x, 5, 50–74, 102
Comprehensive Values (Daunt) 56
Conservative Party, and education 76, 133
constructive education 94–6
contextualized science 169–70
contract compliance 124, 126
conventionalism 127
Cooksey, G. 63
core curriculum 167
corporate capitalism 30
correspondence theory xi, x, 20–1, 30, 33–4, 100, 106–8, 117, 125, 126
Cotsgrove, S. 231
counter-school culture 6–7
Countesthorpe College 56, 69
craft, design and technology (CDT) 151
credentialisation 116, 117–8
critical education 94–6
critical literacy 13, 14
critical reflection 38
critical self-understanding 38

Crompton, R. 124
Crosland, Tony 26–8, 30, 36
Crossman, H. 157
cultural capital 119, 137
cultural differentiation 6, 7
Cunningham, W. 237

Dahl, R. 50
Dahms, M. *et al.* 158
Dale, B.G. 213
Danish schools 68
Darnton, J.H. 164
Daunt, P. 56, 87
David, M. 134
Davies, B. 178
Davies L. 142
Deem, R. 134–5, 139
democracy
   and fraternity 50–74
   and science education xii, 150–73
   in British education xi–xii, 20–49, 75–84
   in Swedish education 75–90
democratic discourse 84-9
democratic renewal,
   in schools 207–20
democratic socio-technical theory 207-20
Department of Education and Science x, xii, 4, 150, 159, 165, 167
de-skilling theses 28, 137, 232–3
Dewey, J. 14, 65, 75, 127
Dickens, Charles 222
discourses of democracy 79, 84-8
discourses of derision 84-8
discovery learning 151, 152, 162
discrimination
   and YTS 225–6, 234, 235–6
   in comprehensives 66
distribution, and reform 103–5
domestic division of labour 131, 144-7
Downes, D. 15
A Dream of John Ball (Morris) 72
Driver, R. 166, 170
dual labour market theory 120-4
Durkheim, E. 67-71
Dukeries 67

Easlea, B. 158
Ebbutt, D. 156
economy, and education 102, 103, 106
economic efficiency xi
educability, of working class 4
education, in YTS 236–7
Education Act (1944) 3
educational differentiation 6, 7

Index

educational policy, and socialism 20-49
education/production relationship 110-1
Education Reform Bill viii, x, 16, 208, 217
Edwards, T. 238
effective schooling movement 16, 212
elitist democracy 50
Elster, J. 79-80
emancipatory citizenship 59
emancipatory imperative 70-1
empiricism 32
Employment and Training Act (1973) 231
employers
    and qualifications 122-3
    and MSC 226-37
empowerment 14, 211
Engels, F. 52, 71, 136, 140
engineering, and science education 151
Entwistle, H. 169
epistemology 127
equality, in Swedish schools 75-90
Equality (Tawney) 132
equality of opportunity 1, 4, 22, 50-1, 55-7, 100, 101-3, 185
    and passive revolution 22-6
    and social democratic ideals 132-8
    and YTS 237
equality of skills 40
equal value 55-7
    and PE curriculum 186-7
Essentials of Democracy (Cole) 61
ethnic discrimination 234
Evans, J. xii, 174-91
Evans, M. 187, 188
Eversley, J. 234
excellence 86-7

Fabian social democracy 26, 103
'fallacy of individualism' 57
familism 139, 141
family roles, and education xi, 131-2, 138-47, 142-7
Farley, M. 231
Fawcett Society 239
fellowship, and democracy 52-4
'feminine' science 156, 157-8
feminist leisure studies 176
'feminist' science 156, 158-9
Fielding, M. xi, 50-74, 87-8, 184, 185
Finch, J. 134-5
Finn, D. 231, 232, 233, 238
Flannery, M. 132
Fletcher, C. 76
Floud, J. 2, 4, 99
Flude, M. 4

Forbes, I. 190
'forms of knowledge' thesis 39
forum democracy 79
frames of reference (FOR) 9-11
France 25
fraternity xi, 36, 50-74
Freeden, M. 24
free market concept 2, 133
French revolution 51
Freud, S. 141
Frith, S. 105
functional sociology 92
Furlong, A. 138

Gagnon, J. 141
Garside, W.R. 223
GCSE 96, 163
General Household Survey (1982) 118
General Motors 210, 211-2
gender
    and science education 150, 155-9
    discrimination 234
    division 137-8
    identity 146-7
Genderwatch (EOC) 143
Giddens, A. 28
Gill, D. 159
Gilligan, C. 157
Greene, M. 176-7
Grieco, M. 123
Griffin, C. 224
growth, theory of 32
Guardian, The 140, 141-2

Hacker, A. 140
hall structure in comprehensive schools 65-6
Hall, S. 3, 21, 22, 23
Halsey, A.H. 2, 4, 28, 37, 53-4, 57, 58, 71, 99, 101, 103
Halsey, A.H. *et al.* 112-3, 114-5, 116
Hamilton, D. 171
Hammond, J.L. 222
Harding, J. 156-7
Hargreaves, D. 6, 12, 16, 52, 56-7, 64, 71, 168
Hargreaves, J. 175, 181, 182, 185
Harnquist, K. 78, 83
Harris, C.C. 2
Harris, K. 30
Hathersley, R. 132
Having Fun in the Playground 195-6, 197, 203-6
'health career' 182-3

Index

Health Education Council 180
Health Related Fitness (HRF) 179–81, 182, 189
hidden curriculum 64–5, 142–3
hierarchy of skill possession 233
Hine, R. J. 152–3
Hirst, P. 32, 39, 126, 127
historic blocs 34
Hjelm-Wallen, L. 78
Hogan, D. 10
holism 59, 60
Holland, J. 226
Hollings, M. 159, 160
Holt, M. 232
home economics, and gender 143–5
Hoskyns, A. 151, 154–5
human capital theory 107, 100, 118
Humberstone, B. 187
Hunt, A. 88

Ignatieff, M. 71–2
immaculate theoretical conception 15–16
independent schools 2, 167, 169, 188
individualism 57–8, 72, 86–8, 96, 182–3, 185
individualized curriculum 168
Industrial Training Boards (ITB) 231, 232
industrialization of education 207
in-service education 170
integrated curriculum 29–40
intelligence tests 3, 55, 93–4
internal labour markets 121–2
International Association for the Evaluation of Educational Achievement 85
isolation, of teachers 218–9

Jamlikhet 77
Jaguar cars, and QCs 213, 219
Japan, and QCs 212–3, 215, 216
Jencks, C. 104
job search strategies 123
Johnson, R. 135, 144
joint housework 145
joint parenting 145
Jones, G. 124
Jones, K. 59, 161
Jonsson, I. 83
Jordan, S. 232, 233
journeymen 222, 223

Kahn, A.J. 167
Karabel, J. 101, 103
Keep, E. 224

Keeves, J.P. 82
Keddie, N. 152
Keller, E.F. 158
Kelly, A. xi–xii, 150–73
Khan, G. 37
King, R. 176
Kirk, D. 176, 180, 181, 183, 186
Knight, T. 79
knowledge production 31–2
Koblitz, A.H. 158
Kogan, M. 1
Kogut, L.S. 215–6
Korpi, W. 89
Kundura, M. 57

labour market
    and credentialization 117–9
    and MSC 229
    and production 119–24
    processes xi, 125
    reform 42
Labour Party, and education policy 20–49
Labour Party Collective on the Education of Women and Girls 133
Lacey, C. xi, 6, 13, 14, 91–8
Laski, H. 55, 58
Lauder, H. x, 7, 20–49, 132
Lawn, M. xii, 207–20
Lawrence, P.A. 77
Laycock School 192–206
Laycock Code 196, 204, 25–6
Learning to Labour (Willis) 6–7
Lee, D. *et al.* 232, 233, 234
Lees, J. 213
Lees, S. 142, 237
Leipmann, K. 231, 238
Levidow, L. 159
Levin, H. 30, 32, 85, 105, 109
LGR 80 80–2
liberal democratic reform x, 2, 4, 24
liberty xi, 50–1
life skills 145–6
Lindsay, L. 159, 160
Little, A. 111–2, 114
London School of Philosophy 32
Lovux, 77

McCulloch, G. *et al.* 150
Macdonnell, D. 175
McGill University 211–2
McGuire, M.J. 224
McIntosh, M. 140
McKenzie, G. 28
McMullan, T. 55, 56

249

Index

McPherson, A. 12, 28
Mace, J. 235
Mahoney, P. 143
management in education xii, 207–8, 215–20
Manpower Services Commission (MSC) xiii, 34, 50, 96, 221–43
market place, in education viii, ix, 79, 207, 238
Marklund, S. 82
Marsden, D. 56, 235
Marx, K. 52, 71, 111, 136–7, 140
Marxist theory
   and educational change 3, 5–6, 30, 101, 135–6
   and training 232–4
Matiesen, T. 15
Matthews, M.R. 127
Michels, R. 228
Michigan school system 216
Milliband, R. 25, 103
Millar, R.H. 154
Mohr, H. 213
Mohr, W.C. 213
Moore, R, x, xi, 31–2, 99–130
moral development 192, 194
Morris, W. 52, 71, 72
multiculturalism 160–1, 168
Murphy, J. 4
Mutual Support and Observation Programme 67

National Coal Board, training scheme 231
national curriculum 167, 188
National Foundry Craft Centre 231
national testing 2
Network Project 98
network recruitment 123
new comprehensive paradigm 71–2
new liberalism 24, 26, 28
new physical education 176–8
new realism 21
new sociology of education 100, 107, 110
Newton, D.P.L. 162, 163–4
new vocationalism 16, 234
Non-Advanced Further Education (NAFE) 228
non-reformist reforms 21–2
Nott, M. 159
Nuffield Foundation 151, 168
numerical approach to happiness 24, 28, 42
Nystrom, P. 82

objective probabilities 117
Occupational Training Families (OTF) 229
150-Hours project, Italy 42
oppression of women, in family 138–9
opting out 2, 96
'ordinary kids' 9–11
Owen, R. 136, 139, 144
Oxford Mobility Study 112–3

Palme, Olof 77
parental choice 2
parentocracy x, 1
participation 115–6
   in management 213
   in YTS 236
participatory theory of democracy x, xii, 50–74
Passeron, J.C. 5, 113, 116–7, 118
passive revolution 22–35
pauper apprentices 221–3
Payne, S. 180
Pecheux, M. 75
Penn State University 215–6
personal coherence 61–4
person-centred schools 59, 60
Peters, R.S. 126, 127
philosophers of education 199, 201
physical education xii, 174–91
Piaget, J. 32
Playground Project xii, 192-206
'politicised curriculum' 80
popular politics of education 11–17
positioning 117
positivism 127
'possessive individual' 30, 32
power relations, in families 146–7
private schools
   and PE 188
   and science 167, 169
production, and education 99–130
Professional Development Partnership 67
profiling 68, 233, 234
progressive education 100
public realm 61, 68–70

qualifications, and YTS 224–5
quality circles (QC) xii, 212–3
   and education 215–20
   and Jaguar cars 213–5
Quality of Working Life Movement (QWL) 209–12, 219
Quinton Kynaston School 68, 69, 70

Index

racism
  in labour market 16
  and science education 150, 159–62
radicalism 107–8
Raffe, D. 232
Rampton Committee 159
'rational man' 32
realism 127
'really useful knowledge' 144, 146
recruitment strategies 122
recurrent learning 211
Rees, G. 223
Rees, T. 223
reflection, in school 192, 198, 200, 201, 212, 219
Reid, K. 16
Reid, K. *et al.* 212
Reith Lectures 53–4
'rems' 9–11
reproduction, and production 105–10
Rescuing the Comprehensive Experience (Barker) 58
resistance, to education 3, 7–9
Resler, H. 103, 112, 114
Reynolds, D. 16, 169
Richardson, J.A. 212
Right wing and education, viii, 12
Roberts, K. 231
Roberts, K. *et al.* 224, 232
Robinson, E. 133
Rogers, I.A. 212
ROSLA 15
Rousseau, J. 53
Rustin, M. 134

Scraton, S. 187
Scruton, R. *et al.* 80
Secondary Science Curriculum Review (SSCR) 155, 166–7, 168, 170
Seeds of History booklets 161
Sennett, R. 13
sexism
  and PE 187
  in labour market 16
  in working-class areas 8
sexuality, and family roles xi, 141, 142–7
Shankar, A. 215
Sharp, B. 30
Sherlock, J. 185
SIA Report 78
Simon, B. x, 9, 20, 52, 141
Siraj-Blatchford, J. 159–60, 162
Smail, B. 156
Social Affairs Unit 2

social construction of skills 208
social control 232
Social Democratic Party, Sweden 77, 84
socialism, and education policy 20–49
Socialism and Education (Labour Party) 132, 133
socialist education
  for girls xi, 131–49
  physical education 174–91
  policies x, 13, 91–8, 100–5
social justice ix, 16–17, 40
social mobility 112–3
social predestination x, 1
'social relations of production' 125
social reproduction 92
social wage 25
society, and science 162–4
sociology of education 4, 100–5
socio-technical theory, of management xii, 207–20
solidarity 36, 37, 214
'solidary' experience 66–7
Spybey, T. 77
standards debate viii, xi, 1, 2, 85–6, 123
Stantonbury Campus, Milton Keynes 62–70
state employees, and YTS 221
state intervention, in labour market 237
Street, J. 190
stress, in teachers 218
Sullivan, M. 169
Svenska Dagbladet 85
Sweden, and education xi, 25, 31, 75–90
'Swots' 9–11

'taskill' 232, 233
Tawney, R.H. 16–17, 131, 132
Taylor, B. 139
teacher support groups 218
Teaching Games for Understanding (TGFU) 179–81, 182, 189
technical functionalism 105, 107
technological education 136–7
technology, and gender 168–9
Thatcherism, and education ix, xiii, 16, 29, 87–8, 89
'third wave' policy x, 1–4, 17
Thomas Bennett School 55, 56
Thompson, E.P. 223
Times Educational Supplement, The 177
Today 177–8
Toffler, A. 1
Tomvall, A. 81
'traditional' family life 141

251

Index

transferable skills 233
transformation 101, 113–5
transition, school to work 182
TVEI 13, 16, 34, 96, 209, 236

underachievement, of working-class children 7
unions 96

Varlaam, C. 226
vocationalism 1, 14, 96
Volvo xii, 210, 211

Wadsworth, N. 143, 144
Walford, G. 162–3, 188
Watts, A.G. 224
Watts, M. 156, 157, 158, 159
Wedgwood 215
Welfare State viii–ix, 3, 15, 24–6, 100
West, R.W. 165, 166
Westergaard, J. 103, 111–2, 114
Whannel, G. 175, 181, 187
White, P. xii, 36, 37, 192–206
Whitty, G. ix, 7
Wickham, A. 225
William Tyndale affair 109
Williams, G. 230–1
Williams, T. 187

Willis, P. ix, 6–7, 8, 30, 31, 33, 37, 182
Willms, J.D. 12, 28
Wilson, E. 139
Wilson, H. 27
Wirth, A. 210–11
Wolpe, A. xi, 131–49
women, and YTS 225
Wood, E.M. 88
Wood, J. 142
Wood, S. 28
workforce training 226–7
working class
    schooling x, 1–19, 35
    youth training 221–43
workplace democracy 199–200
Wurstenberg, W. 136, 144

Yee, B. 34
Yeo, E. 222
Yeo, S. 222
Young J.H. 218–9
Young M.F.D. 100, 152–4, 155, 170
Youthaid 231, 234, 238
Youth Opportunities Programme (YOP) 232
Youth training xiii, 221–43
Youth Training Scheme (YTS) 221, 223–6